T0305391

EBB TIDE IN THE BRITISH
MARITIME INDUSTRIES

'This is a significant and original contribution to the field of
maritime history. There have been a welter of single industry
studies and company histories—many of excellent quality—but
there is no work which draws all of these elements together.
This is a serious, synthesised account of how and why Britain
lost its position as the world's leading maritime power.'
Lewis Johnman, University of Westminster

EBB TIDE IN THE BRITISH MARITIME INDUSTRIES

CHANGE AND ADAPTATION, 1918–1990

Alan G. Jamieson

UNIVERSITY
of
EXETER
PRESS

First published 2003 by
University of Exeter Press
Reed Hall, Streatham Drive
Exeter EX4 4QR
UK
www.ex.ac.uk/uep/

British Library Cataloguing in Publication Data
A catalogue record for this book is available from the British Library.

ISBN 978 0 859 89728 0

Typeset in 12/13pt Garamond 3
by Kestrel Data, Exeter, Devon

Printed and bound by CPI Group (UK) Ltd, Croydon, CR0 4YY

In memory of my father,
Arthur G. Jamieson (1922–1995)

Bulk carrier *Atlantic Bridge*, built in Japan in 1968 for Bibby Line of Liverpool as part of the Seabridge consortium. Withdrawn from Seabridge in 1977 and renamed *Dorsetshire*, the vessel was sold to a Greek owner in 1982.
(Photo: FotoFlite, Ashford, Kent)

Contents

Maps, Tables and Illustrations

Maps

Tables

Illustrations

Acknowledgements

First my thanks to to the Leverhulme Trust which funded the research for this book. The project was based in the Centre for Maritime Historical Studies, University of Exeter, and my thanks go to the members of the Centre's management committee, especially Dr Michael Duffy, Dr Basil Greenhill, Dr Stephen Fisher and Dr Alston Kennerley. Also my thanks go to the students I taught on the Centre's MA course in maritime history, especially David Bailey and Ivor Howcroft.

At the University of Exeter Press I wish to thank Simon Baker, Genevieve Davey, Anna Henderson and Nicola Sivills for their assistance.

I am very grateful to the following for reading drafts of this book and giving me their comments: Professor Peter Davies, Professor Gordon Jackson, Dr Adrian Jarvis, Dr Lewis Johnman and Dr David Starkey. All remaining errors in the text are the responsibility of the author.

Other valuable academic assistance was provided by Professor Lewis R. Fischer, Professor John Armstrong, Professor Richard Goss, Dr David Williams, Dr Olaf U. Janzen and Dr Richard Gorski.

Much of this book was written during my residence in Vancouver, Canada, and I must thank the staffs of the University of British Columbia Library and the Vancouver Central Public Library for their assistance, and Dr Richard Unger of the University of British Columbia for his generous hospitality.

The staffs of the following institutions are thanked for their assistance: University of Exeter Library; University of Plymouth Library; Modern Records Centre, University of Warwick; Public Records Office, Kew, London; The British Library, London; Science

Museum Library, London; Docklands Library and Archive, London; Library of Lloyd's Register of Shipping, London; Historical & Records Section, Cabinet Office, London; Admiralty Library, Ministry of Defence, London; Institute of Marine Engineers, London; Welsh Industrial & Maritime Museum (then at Cardiff, to be reopened at Swansea).

Trade associations and companies for whose assistance I am most grateful include the Chamber of Shipping of the UK; the UK Offshore Operators Association; British Petroleum; Shell; P&O; H. Clarkson; Graig Shipping; Lowline (particularly the assistance of Mr Horace G. Davy); Christian Salvesen; Harrisons (Clyde) Ltd.; Stirling Shipping; Ocean Inchcape Ltd; Suffolk Marine; Ropner; Hunting; London and Overseas Freighters; Thamesport (London) Ltd; Bristol Port Company; Felixstowe Dock & Railway Company. I also received help from the Commission of the European Communities, Brussels; the Federal Maritime Commission, Washington DC; and Shetland Islands Council.

Mr and Mrs Philip E. Bates gave me both hospitality and assistance. Philip shared his great knowledge of Brocklebank, Cunard and Atlantic Container Line with me, but unfortunately died before this book was completed. Other welcome assistance came from Mr T.L. Beagley, Mr R.C. Livesey, Mr T.E. Evans, Mr H.L. Tottenham and Captain P. Hore RN.

My thanks for illustrations go to FotoFlite, Ashford, Kent; Docklands Library and Archive, London; Tyne & Wear Archives, Newcastle-upon-Tyne; Aberdeen Maritime Museum; and Aberdeen Journals Ltd.

1

Introduction

In the spring of 1953 Britain's prime minister, Sir Winston Churchill, was a worried man. Newspaper reports pointed to the relative decline of the British shipping and shipbuilding industries which had dominated the world throughout Churchill's lifetime. Ministers hastened to reassure the premier. They pointed to the 'striking recovery' of British shipping since 1945, a recovery which was all the more remarkable because of the heavy British war losses and the vast wartime growth of the United States merchant fleet. American expansion had 'threatened at one time to swamp the world's shipping market'. However, much American tonnage had now been laid up in the US reserve fleet or sold to other countries, so that in 1953 Britain could still claim to have 'the largest fleet afloat under any single flag.'

Nevertheless, the ministers concluded by warning Churchill: 'We could not afford to lose our position as the leading shipbuilders and shipowners of the world. If there were any such threat, the government would have to take drastic steps, as they did in the thirties, to assist these industries.' In the meantime, the two industries seemed prosperous and all the government had to do was ensure that they could operate on equal terms with foreign competitors.[1]

It seemed that British domination of world shipping and shipbuilding had been restored by 1953, but this was an illusion. Only three years later Japan replaced Britain as the world's leading shipbuilding nation.[2] In 1967 Liberia replaced Britain as the nation with the world's largest merchant fleet.[3] After 1975 the decline of both British shipping and shipbuilding was to be dramatic, until by 1990 the former was much reduced and the latter was on the verge of extinction.[4]

The British maritime industries had been in relative decline since the end of the First World War, but their virtual collapse in a fifteen-year period was unprecedented. In part it was caused by a general collapse of the world shipping and shipbuilding markets after 1975, the worst such depression since the 1930s, but even so Britain's precipitate decline seemed to indicate other long-term factors at work. Had the industries failed to adapt to a changing world because of internal failings? Was unfair foreign competition just too strong? Had government failed to take the 'drastic steps' promised in 1953 to keep the industries going? Before we consider these questions it is necessary to consider the place held by the maritime industries in the political and economic history of Britain.

One eminent maritime historian has observed that in the nineteenth and twentieth centuries 'talk of a [British] government policy regarding the maritime sector is too generous'.[5] However, in the seventeenth and eighteenth centuries there had certainly been a state policy towards the maritime industries which was shaped by both defence and economic considerations. The need to encourage merchant shipping and seamen in peacetime to create the constituents of a fleet in wartime was a concern that dated back to medieval times. In the mid-seventeenth century it was joined with commercial concerns and the new economic doctrine of mercantilism to produce the Navigation Acts. These laws formed the basis of government policy towards the maritime industries for the next two hundred years.[6]

Certain trades, and especially those involving the growing number of British colonies, were to be reserved for British ships alone, with foreign vessels largely restricted to carrying the produce of their own countries to Britain. A British ship had to have been built in British territory and most of her crew had to be British seamen. This shipping protectionism, together with additional bounties to encourage the building of big ships and the growth of fishing, which was seen as a nursery of seamen, was to provide a powerful encouragement to the growth of the nation's maritime industries. In wartime those industries could then provide the seamen and the shipbuilding facilities needed to support the navy as it protected the home island and its trade and colonies overseas. As early as the beginning of the eighteenth century, Britain was perhaps the only maritime power in Europe with a large enough pool of seamen, skilled labour and maritime industries to be able to absorb significant losses of ships and men in wartime.[7]

Trade, colonies and the navy formed the bases of British maritime policy, and British commerce began to look outside Europe for its markets. In 1700–01 some 82% of British home exports went to Europe, but by 1772–73 the proportion had sunk to 40%. Similarly imports from Europe fell from 68% of all imports to 47% in the same period. In terms of Britain's total overseas trade, Europe's share fell from 74% in 1713–17 to 33% in 1803–07.[8] The protectionist maritime policy came to be seen as the basis of British power. As a contemporary observed in 1779, 'the source of our power and greatness [is] our trade and commerce, the consequent number of our seamen, and our naval superiority, which all inseparably give us riches and power'.[9]

It was the interlocking nature of the policy that seemed to provide the perfect virtuous circle: the government supported the maritime industries, the maritime industries provided the seamen and material resources needed to expand the navy in wartime, and the navy protected trade and captured new colonies for economic exploitation. However, the system received a heavy blow when the American colonies won their independence in the second half of the eighteenth century. They had come to provide a significant portion of the shipping and shipbuilding resources of the British empire.[10] Their independence as the United States of America created an increasingly formidable rival, although it also forced the British government to further stimulate its own shipping and shipbuilding industries.

With victory in the Napoleonic wars in 1815 the British maritime policy seemed finally to have achieved its goal of world domination outside Europe, but at its moment of triumph the policy began to be questioned. The free traders believed that an end to protectionism was the road to both peace and prosperity. Despite many objections from the shipping community, most of the Navigation Acts were repealed in 1849 and protection of the British coastal trade ended in 1854.[11] This big change for one side of the strategic and economic triangle of 'trade, colonies and the navy' hit the other two sides as well. Hostility to expanding the formal empire increased and the size of the navy was reduced.[12]

Many people in the maritime industries felt the government was throwing away the hard-won victory of protectionism and during the 1850s the ever-increasing challenge of American shipping and shipbuilding seemed to show they might be right. However, the American Civil War ruined the US merchant fleet and after the war was over Americans looked away from the sea towards the internal

3

development of their continental state.[13] Not only was her most powerful maritime rival removed, but Britain took advantage of her own technological lead in the production and operation of iron, later steel, steamships to raise her domination of the world's oceans to new heights in the period 1870–1914. While many British industries began to falter in the face of new foreign rivals, shipping was one of the growing service industries which kept the British balance of payments in credit, and shipbuilding was 'Britain's greatest industrial success story of the post-1850 period'.[14]

In the years immediately before the First World War the British maritime industries still appeared to dominate the world, despite the increasing challenge from Germany and other rivals. This British dominance was sustained with little government support, unlike some of the maritime industries being built up abroad. In 1910 the merchant marine of the British empire made up about 40% of total world tonnage, with its nearest rival Germany on only 8%.[15] In 1911 the 1,804,000 gross tons of new shipping produced by British shipyards amounted to 68% of world output; in the same year French shipbuilders produced barely 5% of world output.[16] According to the 1911 census Britain's shipping industry employed 119,000 men and shipbuilding 155,000. Fishing accounted for 53,000 workers and the ports 167,000. If naval personnel and naval dockyard workers were put together they came to 93,000 men. In all nearly 600,000 men worked in some maritime occupation in 1911, nearly 4% of the male population, and as a comparison it can be noted that nearly 400,000 men worked on Britain's railways at that time.[17]

If a policy of government support and trade protectionism had served the British maritime industries well between the mid-seventeenth century and the mid-nineteenth century, it seemed by 1914 that the government's decision to end the old mercantilist system after 1850 had produced even better results. Bolstered by the industrial revolution and the later worldwide spread of British services such as banking and insurance, the maritime industries had enjoyed great success in the free trade era, especially in the 1870–1914 period. Far from throwing away the mercantilist victory, the shift to free trade had built on the basis of earlier achievements to extend and consolidate British dominance of the maritime world.

It would seem to be a perfect demonstration of the theory of hegemonic stability, when one power, having achieved predominance, is ready to allow a liberal trading system.[18] When the Dutch dominated the maritime world in the seventeenth century, Grotius put forward the doctrine of the freedom of the seas. Once protectionism and war had brought Britain to maritime predominance in the first half of the nineteenth century, free traders like Cobden felt that abolition of the old mercantilist system would bring both economic and political benefits, increased trade and world peace. The result was, as a later commentator put it, that between 1870 and 1914 'the carriage of the world's seaborne trade was developed under British commercial leadership, . . . as a cosmopolitan professional undertaking' that 'tended to remove at least one potential cause of friction between nations'.[19]

This 'golden age' of free trade was not of course entirely altruistic since the British remained confident that their maritime industries would continue to outstrip any potential rivals. The period is now seen by some writers as the first attempt at 'globalisation', a time of expanding economic opportunity and ever-diminishing barriers to trade and communication around the world.[20] However, hegemonic stability can break down. The Dutch maritime hegemony gave way to an age of protectionism and war, with the most protracted struggle being the 'second Hundred Years War' between Britain and France. The British maritime hegemony ended in what might be termed the 'second Thirty Years War', with Germany in conflict with the rest of Europe. The First World War was followed by the interwar period of depression and economic nationalism, then the plunge into the Second World War. When peace returned in 1945 the new hegemonic power was not even European, but rather the United States, which was committed to a liberal world trading system. This flourished in the long boom of 1945–73 and was renewed in the 'globalisation' of the 1990s after the end of the Cold War.

The period from 1914 to 1945 was a time of trial for the British maritime industries and perhaps their greatest achievement was simply to survive both the ravages of war and the debilitating interwar depression. Although the United States revealed in both world wars a maritime power that could eclipse Britain, in peacetime its merchant ships and shipyards proved uncompetitive on the world stage. After both conflicts Britain was eventually restored to her position as the world's leading shipowner and shipbuilder. Indeed in the late 1940s and early 1950s Britain seemed to have returned to a maritime prosperity unknown since before 1914. Her shipowners had no lack of business and the order books of her shipyards overflowed. However, it all proved to be shortlived. Foreign rivals like Japan were soon equalling then surpassing the British maritime industries. Similarly, although the USA made no direct challenge to British shipping, the encouragement given by American companies to the growth of flag of convenience fleets soon gave them indirect control of world bulk shipping.

Only at the end of the 1950s, when overtonnaging led to a slump in world shipping and shipbuilding, did the British government become seriously aware of the impending crisis in the maritime industries. As the prime minister, Harold Macmillan, observed in 1961, when considering a proposed maritime board to bring under one authority shipping, shipbuilding and ports: 'These industries face a difficult future. Politically it must be seen that we have made some effort to help them.'[21] The government might, for example, intervene to oversee a planned contraction of the shipbuilding industry, but it was warned that such action 'would arouse bitter memories [of the 1930s depression] and attract considerable odium'.[22]

Unlike most of British industry shipping and shipbuilding had not received tariff or other protection after the British government gave up free trade in 1931–32. They remained exposed to the vicissitudes of international competition, the unfair aspects of which their leaders blamed as the chief cause of their decline, whereas other commentators blamed the internal failings of the industries themselves.[23] One member of the government even went so far as to propose a return to protectionism for Britain's maritime industries, a latter-day Navigation Act, but he found few supporters.[24]

Politicians felt they needed to precede any action to deal with the growing crisis in the British maritime industries by large-scale investigations. The 1960s witnessed a whole series of parliamentary and other inquiries. First came the Fleck report of 1960 on the fishing industry, then the Rochdale report of 1962 on the major British ports, followed by the Devlin report of 1965 on dock labour. The Geddes report on the shipbuilding industry appeared in 1966, the Pearson report on seamen in 1967, and finally the Rochdale report on the shipping industry in 1970.[25] No other sector of the British economy came under such intense scrutiny in these years. At a time when the British economy in general was experiencing considerable growth, the maritime industries were making slow progress, stagnating, or going into definite decline.

Reluctantly British governments during the 1960s felt compelled to give assistance to the maritime sector. Port authorities and fishing companies received support for capital investment, but the two areas which were to absorb most public money over the next twenty years were dock labour and, above all, the shipbuilding industry. Merchant shipping received less support because from the mid-1960s trading conditions began to improve. Indeed by 1975 the British merchant fleet had reached its postwar peak of thirty-three million gross tons.[26]

In 1973 Britain joined the European Economic Community (EEC), a change which was to have a considerable impact on the nation's maritime industries. Within a decade Europe featured more prominently in British trade statistics than it had done since the early eighteenth century. By 1986 58% of Britain's exports went to Western Europe (48% to the EEC) and 66% of her imports came from that area (52% from the EEC).[27] The impact on British shipping was profound. In 1971 59% of British trade tonnage operated deep-sea; by 1986 the figure was down to 28%.[28] The ships which had spread across the oceans to create a world empire were now deserting the distant trade routes. It had been obvious by the late 1950s that Britain's future international economic policy could no longer be based on the Commonwealth, to which Britain had turned with renewed emphasis during the 1930s depression, and the only alternative seemed to be closer links with Europe.[29] Now this had come about and the ships which had bound the British empire together had lost much of their importance.

This blow to one sector of Britain's maritime industries was exacerbated by another event of 1973. The rise in oil prices after the Yom Kippur war in October eventually produced a quadrupling of the price. This rise effectively killed the so-called supertanker boom that had been leading the great expansion of world shipping and shipbuilding after the closure of the Suez Canal as a consequence of the Six Day war in June 1967. By 1975 the world's shipping and shipbuilding industries were in the worst depression since the 1930s and it was to last, despite occasional moments of hope, until the early 1990s. Against such a background some decline of Britain's maritime industries was inevitable, but in a short time they went from relative to absolute decline and then on down to virtual collapse. By 1990 Britain's maritime industries had reached a level of insignificance, nationally and internationally, that they had not held since perhaps the middle of the sixteenth century.

Even in 1983 one commentator could point out that over the previous ten years in 'shipping, shipbuilding and fisheries the record has been disastrous'.[30] He called on politicians to establish 'a maritime policy to go with their defence policy', but as has been shown above any real attempt by government to run an integrated maritime policy ended with the repeal of the Navigation Acts in the middle of the nineteenth century. After that the maritime industries were largely left to fend for themselves in the global market place, even after general government economic policy swung back from free trade to protectionism in 1931–32. Despite some interventions during the 1930s and a much more sustained effort from the middle of the 1960s until the 1980s, government has generally preferred to let the maritime industries go their own way. Nobody could doubt their vital importance to the very survival of Britain in the First and Second World Wars, but after 1945 the nature of warfare changed and as early as the late 1950s there were serious doubts whether conflicts like the world wars would ever recur, largely because of the nature of nuclear weapons.[31] A defence justification for government aid to the maritime industries seemed less certain than in the years, indeed the centuries, prior to 1945.

So, appropriately perhaps, the British maritime industries were left to sink or swim. They sank. It is the purpose of this book to survey the decline of those industries from 1918 to 1990. In particular it will examine how they adapted (or failed to adapt) to the changes taking place in the national economy and the world economy during that period. Some decline was inevitable since Britain could never preserve her pre-1914 maritime predominance totally intact in the face of ever more numerous and powerful rivals. However, the pace of decline steadily increased until the final acceleration in the years after 1975. Was the decline largely due to external factors, such as subsidised and protected foreign competition? Was the decline due to internal factors, such as poor management, bad labour relations and the small size of firms? Or was government policy to blame, avoiding intervention until it was too late? All these questions will be considered.

As already noted above, a number of activities could come under the label of maritime industries, including shipping, shipbuilding, ports, fishing and naval defence, including dockyards as well as warships. In this book I will restrict myself to the first three, although mentions of fishing and naval defence will be made where appropriate. The British fishing industry went into serious decline in the 1970s when the deep-sea trawlers were finally driven out of distant fishing grounds, especially off Iceland in the so-called 'cod wars', and the middle and near water fishing vessels became subject to EEC fishing laws that eventually opened their fishing grounds to foreign exploitation.[32] The naval dockyards would clearly qualify as an industrial undertaking, but they ceased shipbuilding at the end of the 1960s and are now considerably reduced and largely in private hands. The Royal Navy might be seen as a service industry providing maritime defence, but its policies and operations belong more to the political sphere than the economic.[33]

To shipping, shipbuilding and ports is added a fourth and most recent British maritime industry, the offshore oil and gas industry. Arguably the discovery and exploitation of North Sea oil and gas was one of the most important economic events for Britain in the post-1945 period, second only in significance to joining the EEC in 1973. This new maritime industry appeared in the 1960s at a time when the older maritime industries were in increasing difficulties. North Sea oil and gas appeared to offer new opportunities not just to the British economy in general, but to the old maritime industries in particular. How they responded (or failed to respond) to this new challenge is an important subject for examination and requires a more detailed treatment than subjects in earlier chapters.

It is not the intention of this book to provide a complete history of British shipping, shipbuilding, ports and offshore energy in the chosen period. Rather the aim is to address the theme of change and adaptation in those industries in a series of linked interpretive essays. In particular, other than in the ports chapter, labour history and social history are not dealt with in detail.[34] In part this is because shipping at least had a largely untroubled labour history between the 1920s and the seamen's strike of 1966.[35] Dockers and shipyard workers were of course renowned for their militancy from the 1950s onwards, but it has recently been argued that it is 'wrong to regard trade unions as the all-encompassing cause of Britain's poor industrial performance between 1945 and 1979'.[36] The soldiers in the workplace had their failings, but so too did their superiors, the officers in management and the generals in government.

Finally, the conclusion will give an outline of events in Britain's maritime industries during the 1990s, when some rays of hope pierced the gloom, and an overview of the book's consideration of the nature of change and adaptation in those industries since 1918. For at least four hundred years the maritime industries were considered to be of vital importance to Britain. That seems to be no longer the case. A final question will be: does it matter?

2

Vanishing Fleets
Shipping 1918–1990

'At the outbreak of the war the British mercantile marine was the largest, the most up to date and the most efficient of the merchant navies of the world.'[1] So wrote a government committee while the First World War still raged in 1918. Back in 1914 the mercantile marine of the British empire had amounted to over 45% of total world tonnage, with its nearest rival, the German merchant fleet, trailing behind with only 11%.[2] (For figures of UK and world fleets, see Table 2.1.) The first two years of the Great War inflicted losses on the British merchant fleet, but until the autumn of 1916 these did not seem unbearable. Likewise, although more and more British merchant ships were taken under government control, those remaining free made handsome profits for their owners as wartime freight rates soared. By the summer of 1916 there were considerable complaints that British shipowners were making excessive profits from the war. In reply shipowners pointed out that neutral ship-owners were making even greater profits and would provide increased competition for British shipping after the war.[3] It was to consider the likely postwar position of British shipping and ship-building that the government set up in 1916 a committee under Sir Alfred Booth, chairman of the Cunard Line.[4]

While the committee went about its deliberations, the position of British shipping suffered a dramatic collapse. Unrestricted German submarine warfare from early 1917 inflicted appalling losses until the initiation and spread of the convoy system began to reduce enemy success.[5] Meanwhile almost all British shipping was taken under government control and most neutral shipping was forced into allied service, although still at better charter rates than British

Table 2.1: UK-Registered Merchant Fleet and World Merchant
Fleet, 1914–1990 (Millions of gross tons)

Year	UK Fleet	World Fleet	UK as % of World
1914	19.3	49.1	39.3
1921	19.3	58.8	32.8
1930	20.3	68.0	29.9
1939	17.9	68.5	26.1
1948	18.0	80.3	22.4
1960	21.1	129.7	16.3
1965	21.5	160.4	13.4
1970	25.8	227.5	11.4
1975	33.2	342.1	9.7
1980	27.1	419.9	6.5
1985	14.3	416.2	3.4
1990	4.1	426.0	0.9

Source: Lloyds Register of Shipping.

shipowners received.[6] The fleets of the neutral countries and allies
such as Japan and the USA still seemed to be growing at Britain's
expense. What would be the position of British shipping after the
peace?

The Booth committee reported in the first half of 1918. It noted
the growth of foreign shipping competition during the war and the
burden which government control imposed on British shipping.
Losses to enemy action were made worse by the restrictions on
merchant shipbuilding in Britain, which in turn had led to a
considerable rise in the price of second-hand tonnage. Unable to
obtain many new ships, the largest British liner companies had
obtained additional tonnage by buying up tramp fleets at inflated
prices. The committee made it clear that once the war ended the
immediate priorities for British shipping should be to end government control and to obtain additional tonnage through seizure of
enemy shipping, purchase of war-built standard ships, and new
construction.[7]

A successful outcome to the war would crush Germany, Britain's
principal merchant shipping rival in 1914, but the Booth committee concluded that the rise of other foreign competitors during
the war would reduce Britain's domination of the world carrying
trade in the postwar period. Nevertheless certain factors were

expected to keep British shipping ahead of its rivals: the strong industrial position of the UK; continued free access to world markets; Britain's worldwide empire; and a large coal export trade that gave an outward cargo to British ships.[8] However, these sanguine views were soon to be undermined by postwar realities.

Depression and War 1918–1945

Immediate postwar problems led to a strong shipping boom in 1919–20, with speculators rushing into the market.[9] The boom had collapsed into a deep depression by 1921 and for most of the remainder of the interwar period world shipping faced difficult conditions, which became a global depression in the 1930s.[10] Shipping is a service industry deriving its demand from international trade. The fundamental fact of the interwar period was the collapse of trade. Using an index of world seaborne trade in which the level in 1913 equals 100, that level was not regained until 1924 (106) and the peak was reached in 1929 (135). The onset of the great depression brought seaborne trade back down to the 1913 level in 1932 (101) and the 1929 peak was not regained until the late 1930s.[11] While world seaborne trade struggled to reach prewar levels, the world merchant fleet continued to expand. A world fleet of forty-nine million gross tons in 1914 had become sixty-one million tons by 1922 and reached almost sixty-nine million tons in 1931. It slipped back during the 1930s, but it had almost regained the 1931 figure by the outbreak of the Second World War. Too many ships chasing too little cargo led to ever lower freight rates and this was the crippling reality for world shipping in the 1920s and 1930s.[12]

As the world's leading shipping nation, Britain was bound to be hit hard by this chronic imbalance between demand and supply, but special aspects made her position worse. Britain's huge prewar coal export trade had given her ships a valuable outward cargo, but in the interwar period exports slumped. In 1929, the peak year of the later twenties, British coal exports were only 84% of the 1913 exports, and by 1937, the best year of the thirties, they were down to 57%.[13] The slump was caused by the rise of new coal-exporting nations and the increasing use of new energy sources such as oil, and it did serious damage to the tramp sector of British shipping. The transatlantic passenger trade had depended on the steady flow of European emigrants to the USA, but in 1924 the Americans imposed new restrictions on immigration, greatly reducing the flow. This move hit all transatlantic passenger lines, but since Britain dominated that trade, she suffered most. Efforts to encourage tourist passengers and to foster cruising only partly made up for the reduction in the emigrant trade.[14]

How did British shipowners react to the new conditions in world shipping? At first many took the view that the conditions were only temporary, part of the normal shipping cycle, and that better times would soon return. However, as bad year followed bad year, hopes of a return to the prosperous days before the Great War began to fade. Abroad economic nationalism was increasingly seen as the only solution. Nations would support their merchant fleets and reserve cargo for them through flag discrimination and other protectionist measures. In the 1920s the USA was considered by many to be Britain's chief maritime rival and the Americans openly provided government support and subsidies for their merchant fleet.[15] Even within the British empire both Canada and Australia had government-owned shipping lines in the 1920s, and Australia also reserved her coastal trade exclusively for local vessels.[16] The authoritarian states such as the USSR, Germany, Italy and Japan naturally supported their merchant fleets, especially in the 1930s.[17]

British shipowners were traditionally committed to free trade and hence it was a shock to many when in 1931–32 Britain also embraced economic nationalism as a way to cope with the collapse of world trade.[18] Tariffs were imposed on imports and preference given to goods, especially food, from within the British empire. The change appeared beneficial to some British shipowners, such as the liner companies which ran the so-called 'Empire food ships' from Australia and New Zealand in the 1930s.[19] However, most shipowners were unhappy with the turn away from free trade. British shipping was not among the industries receiving protection under the new policy and the shipowners felt increasingly exposed, facing rivals who were often directly supported by their governments. In late 1933 the tramp shipowners, the most vulnerable sector of British shipping, were forced to ask government for a subsidy.[20]

If the shipowners had been reluctant in applying for a subsidy, the government was initially reluctant to grant it. However, once it was decided to combine the subsidy with a scrap and build scheme to assist the ailing British shipbuilding industry the plan became more acceptable. The result was the British Shipping (Assistance)

14

Act of 1935. Tramp shipowners would receive a subsidy if freight rates dropped below a certain level, but they were also asked to set up their own minimum freight rate scheme, including foreign tonnage, for the grain trade from Argentina, Canada and Australia. However, by 1937 trading conditions had improved, so the subsidy lapsed, but in the following year world trade went into recession again. In 1939 the government put forward a new British Shipping (Assistance) bill which would renew the tramp subsidy; extend it to liner shipping; support the building of new ships; and create a merchant ship reserve. However, the outbreak of the Second World War prevented the bill becoming law.[21]

If world trade collapse and overtonnaging of the world merchant fleet were the external realities that British shipowners could not change and whose dire results their government could only partly offset with subsidies, was it not possible for British shipowners to exploit new technologies and new trading opportunities that might allow British shipping to preserve its lead over its foreign rivals? It has been argued that through conservatism and complacency British shipowners did not seize such opportunities, with slow adoption of the motorship and reluctance to set up independent tanker companies being pointed out as the chief failures.[22]

The marine diesel engine was first pioneered on the continent before the Great War and the first diesel-engined ship (or motorship) to put to sea was the *Vulcanus*, a Dutch-built tanker, in 1910. This vessel was in fact built for Anglo-Saxon Petroleum (now Shell), a British company, whose chairman, Marcus Samuel, was an enthusiast for the potential of marine diesel engines. Such enthusiasm was not widely shared in Britain at the time, and it was left to the Europeans, and especially the Scandinavians, to forward the development of the motorship.[23]

The Scandinavians lacked both coal and oil of their own so they could view the two fuels more objectively than the British with their great existing commitment to coal. Oil seemed to offer important advantages. Diesel engines were more fuel efficient than steam engines; they required a smaller engine room staff; and oil bunkers took up less room than coal, thus freeing more space for cargo. Although oil fuel was more expensive than coal and diesel engines more costly than steam engines, over time diesels were reckoned to be more efficient than steam engines, especially on longer trade routes.[24] The Scandinavians moved into motorships in a big way, so that by 1939 such vessels made up 62% of

15

the Norwegian merchant fleet, 52% of the Danish fleet, and 46% of the Swedish fleet. In the same year motorships made up only 25% of the British merchant fleet.[25]

Yet despite the percentages the fact remains that in 1939 it was Britain which had the world's largest motorship fleet: 1,500 vessels totalling five million gt compared with Norway's 600 vessels totalling three million gt in second place.[26] So British shipowners cannot have been entirely left behind in the move to motorships. Lord Kylsant, arguably the most dynamic British shipowner of the 1920s, ordered many motorships for the fleets of the Royal Mail shipping group.[27] The collapse of that group in 1930 was due to Kylsant's finances not his technological choices. Other British shipping firms, such as Furness Withy and Bank Line, were keen to obtain motorships, but one should not be too swift to condemn those shipowners who did not rush to adopt marine diesels. T. & J. Harrison evaluated them and decided they did not have a comprehensive advantage, while Lyle Shipping continued to achieve good results with mainly coal-fired tramps.[28] Early marine diesels were expensive to buy and often unreliable in service. Shipping companies had to decide whether motorships were suitable for some or all of their trades, and hence they might have a variety of ships in their fleets: coal-fired steamships; oil-fired steamships; and motorships.[29]

That the choice was not clear cut is shown by the debates in the British Tanker Company (the shipping arm of the Anglo-Persian Oil Company (now BP)) about propulsion units for its tankers during the 1920s. It might be thought an oil company would automatically choose oil engines, but during the decade new tankers appeared with steam engines, steam turbines or diesel engines. The operating results of each type of engine were analysed and although diesels were chosen as the preferred power unit in 1929 it was by no means an easy choice.[30] Geared steam turbines were becoming more widely used by merchant ships at the time and in some countries, notably the USA, they were preferred to diesels.[31] Even the Scandinavians did not choose diesels for all trades. They were favoured for tankers, refrigerated cargo carriers and tramps suitable for charter to liner companies, but in the North Sea coal trade and the Baltic timber trade steamships were still common.[32]

Thus British shipowners cannot be so clearly condemned for not rushing into motorships since the choice was more complex than some commentators have previously appreciated. It is in not

16

building up a large independent tanker sector that British ship-owners may have been more at fault. Before 1914 most tankers were owned by oil companies, but after the Great War conditions changed. As the world petroleum trade grew rapidly so did oil companies' tanker fleets. However, trade cycles might leave the companies with excess tonnage in a downturn, so it suited them to encourage the growth of independent tanker companies. The ships belonging to such firms could be chartered when business was good to carry extra cargoes, but in a depression it would be those vessels, not company tankers, that went first to lay-up.[33]

Such was the motivation behind the decision by Anglo-Saxon Petroleum in 1926 to sell off some of its old tankers to independent owners with a ten-year charter back. Some twenty-two tankers were sold to Norwegians, but only two each went to German and British shipowners. One of the British vessels was later sold on to Norway, leaving one tanker in the possession of Hadley, a British company specially set up to take advantage of the scheme.[34] The late 1920s was a buoyant period for the tanker trade and the Norwegians used skills acquired operating their Anglo-Saxon purchases to move on to bigger things. With further charters promised by oil companies the Norwegians persuaded shipyards to build new motor tankers for them, and Swedish shipyards found it worthwhile to produce a series of standard motor tankers for their Scandinavian customers.[35] By 1932 Norway owned 18% of the world tanker fleet, a big increase from her 3% share in 1920.[36]

Why were there so few British shipowners willing to go into tanker ownership? In part it was due to the close links between British shipping and the coal industry, the rival of oil, but perhaps more important was the continued dominance of oil company ownership in the British tanker fleet. In 1939 of the total tonnage of the top ten British tanker companies 66% was owned by the three main oil companies (Anglo-Iranian, Royal Dutch Shell and Esso), 15% by companies associated with them, and only 19% by independent tanker owners.[37] Anglo-Saxon Petroleum (Shell) was certainly willing to give charters to independent tankers, but the Anglo-Iranian Oil Company (formerly Anglo-Persian) tried to transport all its oil in its own British Tanker Company ships. Chartering independents was avoided if at all possible, although the company did charter more outside tankers in the late 1930s.[38] Faced by such oil company dominance it is not entirely surprising that British shipowners did not rush into the tanker business. Apart from a few small operators like Hadley (whose owners did have links to the Houlder Line, part of the Furness Withy shipping group), the principal new British tanker operator in the interwar period was Athel Line, set up in 1926, but this was a subsidiary of the United Molasses Company. The carrying of liquid molasses had priority over oil cargoes. The few old-established British independent tanker operators, such as Hunting & Sons, active in the oil trade since the 1890s, continued their operations, but few new firms joined them.[39]

After 1930 the tanker market collapsed and by 1933 15% of the world tanker fleet was laid up (and of the world independent tanker fleet 40% was laid up). In 1934 the Schierwater scheme set up a world tanker pool that stabilised the market and by the late 1930s the world tanker trade was improving.[40] With a new war looming the British now became conscious of the strategic danger of not expanding their tanker fleet. It was reckoned that to meet the wartime oil transport needs of the British empire some 200 extra tankers would be required and they could only come from the Norwegians, who had the world's largest independent tanker fleet by 1939. It was more by luck than judgement that those tankers came under British control in the early years of the Second World War.[41]

In shipbuilding and other industries the strains of the difficult interwar economic conditions led to rationalisation in the hope of producing more efficient businesses.[42] In shipping, however, any restructuring that took place was largely unplanned and only grudgingly accepted as a consequence of the apparently endless bad economic conditions. In the view of some scholars British shipping was by the 1920s a mature industry.[43] By the end of the Great War 25% of UK tonnage was controlled by the 'big five' liner shipping groups—Peninsular & Oriental (P&O), Royal Mail, Cunard, Ellerman and Furness Withy; and by 1939 the 'big five'—with Ocean Steamship (Alfred Holt) replacing Royal Mail—controlled over a third of UK tonnage.[44] (see Table 2.2.) By 1930 the greatest liner group, Royal Mail, controlled 15% of UK tonnage and was the largest shipping company in the world.[45] New entrants to the liner trades were few because of the high costs involved, and the principal new liner companies that prospered in the interwar period were both progeny of wealthy parents: Blue Star, backed by the Vestey meat interests, and United Africa Company (later Palm Line), a subsidiary of Unilever.[46]

The great liner companies seemed secure, but during the 1920s

18

Table 2.2: Principal British Shipping Groups/Companies with over 500,000 gross tons of Shipping, 1919–1968

	Gross Tons
1919	
Royal Mail	1,899,273
P&O	1,762,428
Ellerman	793,772
Furness Withy	781,451
Cunard	558,380
1939	
P&O	2,113,100
Furness Withy	1,099,000
Cunard	821,674
A. Holt {Ocean}	744,200
Ellerman	671,200
British Tanker Co. [BP]	635,838
Anglo-Saxon Petroleum Co. {Shell}	596,970
1960	
P&O	2,369,000
Shell	1,506,000
Furness Withy	1,420.000
British Petroleum	1,383,000
A. Holt [Ocean]	971,000
Cunard	947,000
British & Commonwealth	872,000
Ellerman	631,000
1968	
British Petroleum	2,296,000
P&O	2,130,000
Shell	1,602,000
Furness Withy	1,139,000
Esso	839,000
A. Holt [Ocean]	816,000
Cunard	692,000
British & Commonwealth	628,000

Sources: 1919—Boyce, *Information, Mediation and Institutional Development*, p. 128; 1939—Talbot-Booth, *His Majesty's Navy*, pp. 423–425, 427–428; 1960—Sturmey, *British Shipping and World Competition*, pp. 360–361; 1968—Rochdale Report, p. 429.

the finances of several became strained. P&O made large profits in the Great War, and used those that had been put away as secret reserves to cover up its worsening financial position in the 1920s. The chairman of P&O, Lord Inchcape, aimed to hang on until good trading conditions returned, but by the time he died in 1932 they seemed as far away as ever.[47] The Royal Mail group under Lord Kylsant used up its wartime profits buying tonnage at inflated prices in the immediate postwar boom, then borrowed heavily against government guarantees under the Trade Facilities Acts to build new ships during the 1920s. Finally in 1930 the whole edifice collapsed with the loss of £50 million, perhaps the largest British business failure up to that time.[48] Kylsant's collapse would be long remembered. Shipowners became reluctant to borrow, while investors viewed shipping investments with scepticism; an unfortunate legacy for the post-1945 period when British shipping would need new investment.[49] In the short term the structure of British liner shipping seemed to change very little. The Royal Mail companies were sold off, usually to rival groups, and Ocean Steamship replaced Kylsant's group in the 'big five'.

It was the tramp sector that suffered most in the interwar period. In 1914 the balance within British shipping was said to be 60% tramp tonnage and 40% liner tonnage, but the Booth committee was worrying about the disappearance of tramp companies even during the Great War. Tramp fleets were sold, often to liner companies, and there was no certainty that the sellers would reinvest their money in shipping.[50] The boom of 1919–20 led to much speculation in tramp tonnage and its collapse led to the disappearance of further tramp firms as well as discouraging investors from any further investment in tramp shipping.[51] The decline in Britain's coal export trade deprived many tramps of an outward cargo and so gave an advantage to low cost rivals such as the Greeks. In 1933 the Chamber of Shipping noted that since 1913 the number and tonnage of British tramps had declined by over 50%, while foreign tramps had increased in number and tonnage by about 33%.[52] (For principal British tramp companies in 1934 see Table 2.3.)

While many tramp firms disappeared, very few new ones arose to replace them, a notable exception being J.A. Billmeir, who set up the Stanhope Steamship Company in 1934 and had a fleet of sixteen ships by the time war broke out in 1939.[53] This lack of new entrants was particularly damaging for the future of the British

Table 2.3: The Twenty Largest British Tramp
Shipping Companies, 1934
(Thousands of gross tons)

Company	Based	Ships	Tonnage
Sir R. Ropner & Co.	W. Hartlepool	50	240.0
Hain Steamship Co.*	London	31	149.8
Haldin & Phillips	London	26	145.5
Dodd, Thomson & Co.	London	20	102.2
W. Runciman & Co.	Newcastle	21	99.1
J. & C. Harrison	London	19	97.0
Evan Thomas Radcliffe	Cardiff	16	84.2
Sir William Reardon			
Smith & Sons	Cardiff	16	83.1
R.S. Dalgliesh	Newcastle	18	80.9
Common Bros.	Newcastle	15	78.5
H. Hogarth & Sons	Glasgow	21	74.9
Carlton S.S. Co.	Newcastle	13	70.8
Larrinaga S.S. Co.	Liverpool	12	65.6
Glen & Co.	Glasgow	20	62.5
W.J. Tatem	Cardiff	13	58.8
Watts, Watts & Co.	London	14	56.9
Turnbull Scott	London	12	54.1
F.C. Strick*	London	12	53.6
Capper, Alexander			
& Co.	London	12	50.4
Headlam & Sons	Whitby	13	49.8

*Company owned by P&O.
Source: Volume 'Tramp Shipping 1933–34', Chamber of Shipping Archives,
University of Warwick.

shipping industry because tramp shipowning was traditionally the entry level for the industry. Given the continuing decline of the sector it is not surprising that the tramp shipowners were the first to go to the government asking for a subsidy, which they received under the 1935 Act. In return the government required the notoriously individualistic tramp shipowners to co-operate in administration of the subsidy and to work out minimum freight agreements in the grain trades, including foreign rivals such as the Greeks in their collaboration.[54]

British shipowners had greeted peace in 1918 with hopes of a return to normalcy. Instead they soon faced the most depressed conditions in their industry's history. The depression went on for almost two decades and the shipowners struggled to adapt to the new conditions. Eventually they had to put their strong individualism and free trade principles aside and ask for government support in the mid-1930s. With regard to seizing new opportunities, British shipowners were readier to accept motorships than some commentators have suggested, but the failure to develop more British independent tanker companies was to have serious consequences during the Second World War and after. At one level the structure of British shipping did not seem to change greatly during the interwar period, but depressed conditions did show the vulnerability of even the biggest liner group and led to a significant reduction in tramp companies, thus discouraging new entrants from joining the industry. The internal failings of British shipping were not insignificant in the interwar period, but the basic external realities of depressed world trade and a surplus of ships circumscribed what British shipowners could do to adapt to the changed conditions. External factors were again to predominate during the Second World War. (For principal British shipping companies in 1939 see Table 2.4.)

The new conflict inflicted more severe losses on British shipping than the Great War. Tonnage lost was 62% of the 1939 figure for the British merchant fleet, while in the previous war losses were only 41% of the 1914 figure. Among the crews more than twice as many men died in the Second World War than in the previous conflict.[55] No other British industry lost so much of its capital equipment and labour force between 1939 and 1945 as did British shipping. British shipyards were permitted to build some replacement ships during the war, but most new tonnage came from American and Canadian shipyards where standard ships, such as the Liberty, Fort and Park types, were in series production. Despite replacements, British merchant tonnage in 1945 was still five million tons below the 1939 figure and the British share of world tonnage had fallen from 27% to 18% by the end of the war.[56]

British shipowners did not make up for their lost ships with windfall profits in this war. The government took control of shipping early in the conflict and did not permit freight rates to rise dramatically. Similarly, although the government was ready to provide compensation for lost ships, this did not necessarily cover the full replacement cost. Financially British shipping companies,

Table 2.4: The Twenty Largest UK Flag
Shipping Groups/Companies, 1939
(Thousands of gross tons)

Company	Sectors	Ships	Tonnage
P&O	L, TP	371	2,133.0
Furness Withy	L	129	1,099.0
Cunard	L	64	821.6
A. Holt {Ocean]	L	115	744.2
Ellerman	L	135	678.9
British Tanker Co. [BP]	TK	94	635.8
Anglo-Saxon Petroleum Co. {Shell}	TK	93	596.9
Union Castle Line	L	28	380.8
Clan Line	L	56	368.8
Blue Star Line	L	37	368.5
Canadian Pacific	L	18	324.7
Andrew Weir	L, TK	54	306.6
T. & J. Harrison	L	43	261.9
Anglo-American Oil Co. {Esso]*	TK	51	244.4
Eagle Oil Co.	TK	29	236.5
Elder Dempster	L	41	214.6
Sir R. Ropner & Co.	TP	42	206.0
United Molasses	TK	24	183.4
H. Hogarth & Sons	TP	39	152.3
Donaldson Line	L	21	138.3

*Subsidiary of a foreign company.
L—Liner
TP—tramp
TK—tanker
Source: Talbot-Booth, *His Majesty's Merchant Navy*, pp. 423–425, 427–428.

who ran not only their own ships but also others on behalf of the government, made only modest profits and were unable to build up large reserves to fund new ships after the war.[57]

Nevertheless, if British shipowners had a hard time during the war, they could take some comfort from the fact that neutrals did not enjoy rising freight rates in the free market for long. By 1942 nearly all the principal maritime nations of the world had been drawn into the war on one side or the other. Altogether all countries other than Britain lost twenty-one million gross tons of shipping, as against six million tons in the First World War, and these losses were divided equally between the enemy countries and the neutral and allied countries other than Britain.[58] Only a few countries, such as Canada and the USA, expanded their merchant fleets, but American expansion was on a massive scale.[59] In 1939 the USA had only 14% of the world fleet, but by 1945 that share had soared to 56%. Although the Second World War was a time of trial for British shipping, it was at least in a much better condition than most of its foreign rivals in 1945. The great exception was the USA, and the future of British shipping after 1945 would depend on what the Americans chose to do with their maritime predominance and on how British shipowners adapted to the challenges of the postwar world.

Prosperity without Change, and a Return to Depression, 1945–1965

'The world shipping position is dominated by the enormous American fleet . . .', wrote a British commentator in 1946, 'and the future of world shipping must depend on the use the Americans make of that fleet.'[60] The Americans faced a dilemma. On the one hand they wanted to keep a big US-flag merchant fleet for national security reasons. On the other hand, 'the existence of a large ocean-going fleet in commercial service under the American flag is incompatible with the natural flow of economic forces'.[61] This was because the costs of American shipping were so much higher than those of rival fleets in the international shipping market.

In fact the Americans soon decided to dispose of much of their huge merchant fleet. The 1946 Merchant Marine Sales Act made surplus ships readily available to both American and Allied owners. Almost 2,000 ships were sold: 800 to Americans and over 1,000 to foreigners, including 200 ships to British owners. In addition the US government laid up thirteen million tons of merchant shipping as a reserve fleet which would be activated only in a future war or emergency. Because of these disposals the American share of world merchant shipping fell from 60% in 1945 to 36% in 1948. The USA still had a major fleet, but its actions had permitted the revival of the British and other Allied merchant fleets, such as the Norwegians and the Dutch.[62]

However, these reductions did not imply any lessening of US

24

government support for its merchant fleet. American liner shipping companies continued to receive subsidies, while cargo reservation became an established policy. Under the 1948 Foreign Assistance Act it was laid down that at least half of all US foreign aid cargoes had to be carried by American flag ships, and in 1954 the Cargo Preference Act mandated that half of all government-generated cargoes were to be carried in 'privately-owned United States flag commercial vessels'.[63] Such flag discrimination was anathema to states like Britain that believed in free trade in shipping services, but other countries around the world began to follow the American example.

Traditionally the US government did not provide assistance to American ocean-going tramp shipping in the bulk trades, largely because the USA seemed to be self-sufficient in raw materials such as oil and iron ore. After 1945 the world trade in such bulk items expanded and the USA began to be an importer of raw materials. There now appeared to be a need to maintain a major US presence in world bulk shipping, but high costs and no government aid seemed to rule out the prospect of using US flag vessels. The solution was a great expansion of flags of convenience, or flags of necessity as some American shipowners called them. Flags of convenience were foreign countries under whose flags US-owned shipping could be registered and operated at low cost, including little taxation and cheap crews. Panama had been used in this way to a small extent in the interwar period, but its fleet grew rapidly in the immediate postwar years. However, concerns about political stability and other aspects of Panamanian registration led American business interests, supported by the US government, to establish Liberia as a new flag of convenience in 1949. The Liberian flag fleet expanded rapidly and exceeded that of Panama by 1956.[64]

The reduction in the US flag merchant fleet helped other nations to re-establish their merchant fleets, but the greatest boost to world shipping after 1945 was the steady growth in world seaborne trade. By 1948 it exceeded its 1938 figure (490 million tons over 470 million tons) and by 1959 had doubled the 1948 figure (to 985 million tons). The greatest increase was in the oil trade. In 1938 it made up 27% of world seaborne trade; in 1948 43%; and in 1959 almost 50%.[65] By the end of the 1950s world shipping tonnage had grown to exceed the requirements of rising world trade, leading to a serious shipping depression, but in general the period 1945 to 1958 was a good time for shipping. For British shipowners it was

1. Tanker *London Enterprise*, built by Furness Shipbuilding Co. Ltd., Haverton Hill-on-Tees in 1950 for London & Overseas Freighters Ltd. LOF, perhaps the most dynamic British independent tanker company of the 1950s, sold the vessel to a Liberian company in 1956.
(Photo: FotoFlite, Ashford, Kent)

the best time since before the First World War. Yet during those good years their industry steadily lost ground to foreign rivals.[66] Why was this?

As the seaborne trade figures showed, the greatest postwar boom was in the oil trade, but as in the interwar period British shipowners seemed unable to seize the opportunity. The British tanker fleet continued to be dominated by vessels owned by the oil companies, chiefly British Petroleum and Shell. The oil companies expanded their building programmes and constructed bigger tankers, Shell's *Velutina* of 1950 being regarded as the first 'supertanker', although only 28,000 dwt. Yet demand continued to rise and independent tanker tonnage had to be chartered to meet it. British Petroleum, which in the 1930s had tried to carry at least 90% of its cargoes in its own ships, was by 1951 carrying only 57%.[67] Charters went mainly to foreign independent tanker owners because there were so few British independent tankers available.

26

Norwegians took many charters, but the expansion of their tanker fleet was hampered by foreign exchange problems which led to a ban on building ships abroad between 1948 and 1951. The big gainers postwar were the Greeks, who had traditionally concentrated on dry cargo tramps and had little previous experience of tanker operation. Some Greek shipowners spent the war in New York and became acquainted with American oil companies and banks. Postwar they obtained bank finance on the basis of oil company charters and began construction of new tankers. These ships were largely registered in Liberia and they were ordered in batches, with their size increasing with every new order. By 1960 58% of the world tanker fleet was owned by independents and only 37% by oil companies (governments owned the other 3%), and the Greeks now rivalled the Norwegians as the owners of the principal independent tanker fleet.[68]

Given the great international success of the Greeks in starting independent tanker companies, it is perhaps no surprise that the newest and most dynamic British independent tanker company after 1945 should be set up by Greek shipowners based in London. The Kulukundis and Mavroleon interests had run dry cargo tramps since the interwar period, but when they set up London & Overseas Freighters (LOF) in 1948 their aim was to establish an independent tanker company. By 1960 LOF was the largest British independent tanker company with 190,000 gross tons of tankers. Its nearest rival was Hunting, with 172,000 gross tons, a firm which had operated tankers since the 1890s.[69]

Other older independent tanker owners such as John I. Jacobs and C.T. Bowring still had small fleets, and a few old-established tramp companies made limited forays into tanker ownership. Ropner, for example, acquired two tankers in the 1950s, one chartered to British Petroleum and the other to Shell.[70] The latter oil company tried to stimulate the interest of British shipowners by offering to sell them tankers under construction with a charter attached, but found only a few takers, including Hadley (two tankers), Turnbull Scott (two), Evan Thomas Radcliffe (two) and Pacific Steam Navigation Company (one).[71] The latter firm was a liner company and what expansion there was in British independent tanker ownership during the 1950s owed as much to liner interest as to tramps. Clan Line set up Scottish Tankers in 1951, and from 1955 the companies of the P&O group moved into tankers in a substantial way (with a total of 157,000 gross tons of tankers by

1960), being eventually brought together in Trident Tankers.[72] The tramp firm Common Brothers built up one of the widest spreads of tanker interests: the company's own tanker fleet was expanded; it managed the Lowland Tanker Company for British Petroleum; and it managed and helped develop Kuwait's national tanker company.[73]

These various endeavours showed British shipowners were taking a somewhat greater interest in tanker ownership in the 1945-60 period, but the total impact was not great. LOF was the only new company and it seemed more an offshoot of the worldwide growth of tanker owning by Greek shipowners than a uniquely British effort. Most British tankers outside oil company ownership were small by ever-growing world standards and comparatively few in number. In 1960 over 75% of British flag tankers were owned by oil companies at a time when such companies owned only 37% of the world tanker fleet.[74]

Greeks like Aristotle Onassis and Stavros Niarchos had achieved phenomenal postwar success in developing independent tanker companies, but the majority of Greek shipowners still concentrated on dry bulk trades, their tramp fleet boosted by large purchases of war-built Liberty ships.[75] Most of the vessels were registered under flags of convenience, helping to reduce costs, and increased world seaborne trade brought good profits. Since the dry bulk trades were also the traditional staple of the British tramp companies, could they not thrive as well? Despite the conditions, the British tramp sector continued the decline which had begun back in the 1920s. The British deep-sea tramp fleet declined by 20% between 1938 and 1960, while the world tramp fleet doubled in size in that period.[76]

If British tramp owners had been unduly optimistic after the First World War, leading to the short-lived boom of 1919-20, they were more pessimistic after 1945. High shipbuilding prices discouraged early replacement of war losses with new ships, while some owners sold off their fleets at the time of the Korean War boom. Others held on, waiting for the slump that would reduce new building prices. It failed to appear, so when tramp companies finally ordered new ships in the 1950s the cost was even greater. Also the companies often ordered only slightly improved versions of the old small, slow tramps.[77]

The tramp sector was being squeezed from two sides. On one side liner companies were taking more of the smaller tramp cargoes. One answer to this challenge was for the tramp companies to build fast, modern vessels which could be chartered to the liner companies. A few British companies did this, but foreign competitors such as the Norwegians did it more widely.[78] The other pressure was the increased demand by bulk charterers for larger vessels that would bring economies of scale. This led to the creation of the bulk carrier market from the 1950s, made up of large, single-deck vessels with easy unloading access to their holds.[79] Bulk carriers represented the future for dry bulk carriage worldwide, but British shipowners moved into them only slowly.

Just as Shell had tried to stimulate the interest of British shipowners in tankers, so the British Iron and Steel Corporation (Ore) Ltd. (BISCO), the company responsible for importing ore for Britain's steel industry, tried to get British tramp firms to take up bulk carriers. The ore carriers were built to BISCO designs and offered for sale to shipowners with a time charter. The Glasgow firm Denholm had set up Scottish Ore Carriers as early as 1949 to seize this opportunity; Lyle Shipping took up the BISCO offer in 1956; and Common Brothers bought ore carriers for their own fleet in that year and set up, with BISCO, a separate ore-carrying fleet called Vallum Shipping.[80] The ore trade became even more attractive after the shipping depression began in 1958. The downturn initially hit tankers harder than the dry bulk trades, and some tanker companies, such as LOF and Hunting, converted several of their tankers into bulk ore carriers.[81] Yet while BISCO's initiative led to the addition of ore carriers to the fleets of a number of British tramp shipowners, these vessels were comparatively small by world standards (the biggest were 16,000 dwt) and less likely to be successful in the international market.

Thus, viewing the British tramp sector overall in the twenty years after 1945, it can be said that at a time of ever-increasing world seaborne trade shipowners missed important opportunities or only took them up on a small scale. British independent tanker companies made no major expansion, except for LOF, and even the growing use of bulk carriers, partly stimulated by BISCO, was perhaps too closely linked to the British market and missed wider international opportunities for bigger ships. Nevertheless the move into bulk carriers was by the 1960s vital if British dry cargo tramps were to survive at all.

What few new British flag tramp companies there were after 1945 were largely linked to foreign interests.[82] There was no significant British new blood, while many older British tramp firms, such as Morel and Billmeir, got out of shipping altogether.[83] In theory world tramp shipping was open to all, but British entrepreneurs had more attractive economic prospects on which to risk their capital in the postwar period.

Entry into the liner trades had always been more difficult and expensive. A few British tramp companies, such as Ropner and Common Brothers, had short-lived liner ventures immediately after the war, but most of the few new entrants into British liner shipping after 1945 were linked to existing businesses, such as Tate & Lyle's Sugar Line.[84]

With the American decision not to impose a new maritime regime on world shipping after 1945 (at least outside the bulk sector and flags of convenience), the old prewar liner system seemed to have been safely re-established. Controlled by the shipping conferences in each trade and closely linked to the European colonial empires, the world liner trades seemed restored to British domination.[85] With the rising level of world trade, the outlook for liner shipping seemed good. However, it soon became clear that liner shipping faced major challenges.

One sector the British particularly dominated was ocean passenger carrying, particularly on the North Atlantic, and in the ten years or so immediately after the war this traffic continued to grow. However, by 1960 more passengers were crossing the North Atlantic by air than by sea, and this trend was likely to spread to other passenger routes around the world as time went on.[86] British shipowners had been interested in getting into passenger aviation since the 1930s, but both the British and the American governments had discouraged them on the North Atlantic route for fear of monopoly. There was a short-lived link between Cunard and the British Overseas Airways Corporation during the 1960s, but it brought little benefit to either company.[87] British passenger liners were losing out to air travel and the new trend could not be defeated. One way to adapt was a new emphasis on cruising, but initial British efforts were hampered by a reluctance to accept that specialist cruise ships would have to be built rather than just cruising redundant 'ocean greyhounds'.[88]

The decline of ocean passenger traffic was one blow to British liner companies, and another was the rise of national shipping lines and flag discrimination. Other nations were not slow to notice that the world's most powerful state, the United States of America, followed protectionist shipping policies in relation to the US flag merchant fleet. From the 1950s Latin American countries began to build up their national shipping lines by laying down cargo preference rules on the American model.[89] As the European empires began to break up, the new states of Africa and Asia also began to establish national shipping lines, reserve cargo for them, and demand access to the shipping conferences that served their areas.[90]

India, Pakistan and Burma (now Myanmar) followed nationalist shipping policies almost from independence and the British liner companies, such as P&O, British India, Bibby, Clan and Brocklebank, that had for so long controlled their seaborne trade were forced to make concessions or face restrictions on their access to local cargo. The lines complained to the British government and it made protests against such shipping protectionism, but there were clear limits to how much pressure could be exerted.[91] Some liner companies sought to 'guide' new national shipping lines, as Elder Dempster and Palm Line did with the Nigerian national line, but this could only be a short-term measure.[92]

Pressure from comparatively weak nations was one thing, but renewed hostility to liner shipping conferences from the USA was another. In the late 1950s and early 1960s American anti-trust officials sought to attack shipping conferences in the trades to the USA. This was a major challenge to Britain and the other 'traditional maritime nations' (European nations such as Norway, Greece, the Netherlands and West Germany, plus Japan), who formed both shipowner and government groupings, largely to negotiate with the USA on shipping questions.[93]

Under pressure from emergent nations on one side and the USA on the other, British liner companies saw their traditional trades being reduced. One reaction was to move into other shipping sectors, particularly the tramp trades. P&O took up tanker ownership in a big way from the late 1950s and in the 1960s set up a bulk carrier operation as well.[94] Furness Withy went into the bulk carriage of iron ore for BISCO in the 1950s by setting up Ore Carriers Ltd. Furness Withy also made a big effort in developing new Great Lakes trade with its Manchester Liners subsidiary after the St Lawrence Seaway was opened in 1959.[95]

Another reaction to outside pressures was to continue the consolidation of British liner companies that had begun before 1914. Among the regroupings were Blue Star's purchase of Lamport & Holt in 1944 and of Booth Steamship Company in 1946; the merger of Clan Line and Union Castle in 1956 to form British & Commonwealth Shipping Ltd.; and Ocean Steamship's securing complete control of Elder Dempster in 1965.[96] By 1960 the eight largest liner groups—P&O, Furness Withy, Cunard, Ellerman, Ocean Steamship, British & Commonwealth, Vestey (Blue Star) and Andrew Weir (Bank Line)—owned together over 80% of British liner tonnage. P&O, with 2.4 million gross tons, was the largest shipping group in the world and had interests in tankers and bulk carriers as well as liner shipping.[97] P&O was also the only purely shipping company which in 1964 featured among the top twenty-six British companies with assets over £100 million. It was at number seven in the listing, but three of the companies above it, Shell, British Petroleum and Unilever, also had large shipping interests.[98]

P&O was one of the publicly quoted liner shipping firms and from the mid-1950s such companies were under increasing pressure from investors because of the low returns they were generating in comparison with companies in other British industries and at a time when world shipping in general was prospering. For the period 1950 to 1957 estimates of the profits of all (not just liner) shipping companies gave an average return of 10.3% on capital employed, little more than half the return achieved by all British companies included in the calculations. For the period from 1958 to 1969 the average return of all shipping companies was 3.5%, well below the all-companies average of 13.6%. When shipping profits are considered by sector for the 1958–69 period it is clear liner services were not yielding high profits, with passenger liner services as definite lossmakers after 1960. General purpose tramp shipping also brought poor returns, but bulk carriers, especially ore carriers, and tankers did better in most years.[99]

Thus although British tramp and liner companies did quite well in the 1945–57 period, they might have done better, especially in the tramp sector. The liner companies were largely content to defend their old dominance, with a few forays into new areas like tankers and bulk carriers. Some tramp companies did move into those areas as well, but they did so only slowly and on a small scale. World seaborne trade continued to expand, but after 1957 (and until the mid-1960s) the expansion of the world merchant fleet exceeded it, leading to a serious shipping depression. With the return of difficult conditions British tramp shipowners singled out low-cost flag of convenience ships as being particularly damaging to their interests. British liner companies blamed the rise of national lines and flag discrimination for their troubles. Both tramp and liner owners looked to the British government to do something to help them, as it had done in the 1930s.

Even by the end of 1958 it was clear to the British government that the world shipping depression might be as bad as in the interwar period. Fearing that it might be compelled to intervene in shipping and shipbuilding as in the 1930s, the government ordered civil servants to report on conditions in those industries. Among other things, the reports noted the steady growth of shipping protectionism around the world, while British shipping still clung to the ideal of free trade in international shipping services. One report, in 1962, thought a decline in the British merchant fleet was inevitable and concluded 'there can be little hope that the trend away from free competition in world shipping will be reversed in our lifetime'.[100]

Yet blaming British decline chiefly on foreign shipping protectionism gave a distorted picture of the world shipping industry. Such restrictive measures were largely confined to the liner trades and were severe on only a few routes. As the Minister of Transport told the House of Commons in February 1962: 'the greater part of world shipping is still open to free competition. It is not all dominated by flag discrimination. The prize goes to the most efficient.' It was pointed out that Scandinavian shipowners, who received no greater state aid than their British counterparts, had achieved greater success by investing in new types of ship. Many British shipowners seemed all too ready to blame their difficulties on foreign restrictions rather than seizing new opportunities.[101]

Nevertheless the government came under increasing criticism for doing little to help British shipping except send diplomatic protests to countries guilty of protectionist shipping policies. In 1961 it was proposed to set up a new maritime board to supervise the shipping, shipbuilding and ports industries, but this plan was dropped in the following year.[102] Instead the government decided to establish the Shipping Advisory Panel to encourage greater competitiveness in the British shipping industry. Sadly the panel directed its first efforts to yet another study of foreign shipping protectionism rather than any consideration of the internal problems of British shipping.[103] In 1964 it was suggested to the panel that since shipping protectionism was spreading across the world it might be time that Britain made plans for a return to shipping protectionism as well. This heretical proposal was swiftly rejected by the panel.[104] When a new Labour government came to power later in 1964 it abolished the Shipping Advisory Panel.

Although the shipping industry had been a source of concern to the government from 1958 onwards, the government's greatest worry in the maritime sector of the economy was about the future of British shipbuilding. However, the two areas were intimately related. By 1960 the majority of orders for British shipyards came from British shipowners and they were cutting back on new orders because of the shipping depression. By 1962 British shipowners were reluctant to build replacement tonnage let alone expand their fleets. Finally, in 1963, the government decided as a temporary, one year, measure to offer loans to British shipowners if they would order new ships in British shipyards. Given statutory approval by the Shipbuilding Credit Act of 1964, the scheme led to the ordering of almost one million gross tons of shipping from British builders in return for government loans totalling £75 million. However, once the scheme ended domestic orders for British shipyards slumped back to their previous low level.[105]

During the shipping depression the government had done very little to help the British shipping industry adapt to changing international realities. Its one gesture, the Shipbuilding Credit Act, was aimed more to help shipbuilding than shipping. The Japanese shipping industry was also in a difficult position because of the depression after 1958, but its government was more willing to provide assistance. Legislation was passed in 1963 which led in the following year to the reorganisation of the industry, especially through the merger of shipping companies.[106] The British government was not ready for such an interventionist approach and preferred to restrict itself to advice and encouragement for British shipowners.

Change and Modernisation, 1965–1973

By the mid-1960s there were signs that the shipping depression was coming to an end, but now British shipowners had to face a major new challenge as the technological changes in shipping that had been growing since 1945 culminated in the age of the supertanker and the container ship.

Containerisation promised to alter completely the world of liner shipping. The traditional break-bulk cargoes in liner shipping had been slow to load and unload even without the additional problem of increasingly militant dockworkers. After 1945 such problems increased and long turn-round times in port meant that liner vessels often spent more of their time at the dockside than at sea.[107] Ports became not a link in a logistical chain but a bottleneck which increasingly held up the transport process. The solution to this problem was to put break-bulk goods in unit loads which would not require slow, individual handling by dockers, but could be moved swiftly from ship to shore (and vice versa) and sent on by land transport (rail or road). This would be an integrated transport system permitting rapid transit through the port.

Although the unit load could take a number of forms, the most common became the metal container. These units could be moved to and from ships via lift on, lift off (lo-lo), using a gantry crane, or roll on, roll off (ro-ro), using a towing motor vehicle. The former method was to become predominant for deep-sea shipping and the latter method for short sea crossings, although hybrids were developed in both sectors.[108] The efficiency gains from containerising liner shipping were to be considerable. In 1968 more than fifty British break-bulk cargo liners worked in the UK–Australia trade. Nine container ships were to take over 80% of their trade, carrying it faster at sea and loading and discharging it faster in port.[109]

The idea of containerisation was not new, but its full potential began to be realised after 1945. Although largely an American invention, there were already some lo-lo and ro-ro container services across the Irish Sea in the 1950s, as well as a ro-ro service from Tilbury to the continent.[110] In time British liner shipowners might have applied these methods to deep-sea cargo-carrying, but there was little sign of it before the American challenge forced change upon them in the mid-1960s.

The father of modern container shipping is usually given as Malcolm McLean, the owner of various trucking companies, who in the mid-1950s began to send trailer units from Texas to New Jersey by sea rather than land. This service began in 1956 and was later extended to Puerto Rico. McLean's shipping company was renamed Sea-Land Services Inc. in 1960. If the newcomer McLean led the way in containerisation on the east coast of the USA, it was the old-established Matson Line which had that role on the west coast. In 1958 Matson started a container service from San Francisco to Hawaii. The Grace Line was the first American operator to attempt an international container service, from the USA to Venezuela, but

2. Container ship *Encounter Bay*, built by Howaldswerke, Hamburg, in 1969 for Overseas Containers Ltd. This vessel made the first OCL voyage from Europe to Australia in 1969. After thirty years' service for OCL and P&O, the vessel was scrapped in China in 1999.
(Photo: FotoFlite, Ashford, Kent)

it was unsuccessful. Sea-Land was more successful, establishing a USA to Europe container service on the North Atlantic in 1966, while Matson was planning a transpacific service to Japan.[111]

Some writers have seen the American leadership in containerisation on the world's trade routes as an attempt to achieve a dominance in the liner trade to match that achieved by the use of flag of convenience shipping in the bulk trades.[112] Labour costs were one of the reasons American liner shipping was so uneconomic, but containerisation marked a major substitution of capital for labour. Fewer ships with smaller crews could carry more cargo more efficiently, while mechanised cargo handling at ports cut out most dock labour. However, the capital costs of new ships, new containers, and new port terminals were huge. The American liner companies, hampered by anti-trust laws, had to containerise without collaborating, but British and other European liner operators felt the capital costs of containerisation demanded the setting up of consortia to meet the American challenge.[113]

In April 1965 four of the leading British liner shipping companies announced the formation of Overseas Containers Ltd. (OCL). It was a product of the initiative of the so-called 'four knights', Sir Donald Anderson, Sir John Nicholson, Sir Nicholas Cayzer and Sir Errington Keville, chairmen respectively of P&O, Ocean Steamship, British & Commonwealth and Furness Withy. The initial plan was to containerise their operations on the UK–Australia route, with a joint investment of £45 million in six cellular container ships, terminal equipment and containers. Trial shipments involved carrying containers on the partners' existing conventional cargo liners, but in March 1969 the first OCL container ship, *Encounter Bay*, sailed from Europe bound for Australia. This ship departed from Rotterdam because industrial action prevented the use of the intended terminal at Tilbury until May 1970. OCL next started container services to the Far East and then on to other routes.[114]

Some of the other main British liner companies with interests in the UK–Australia route set up another container consortium, Associated Container Transportation Ltd. (ACT). Its members were Ben Line, Blue Star, Port Line (owned by Cunard), Ellerman and T. and J. Harrison. Between them the members of OCL and ACT owned more than 80% of UK deep-sea cargo liners. Membership of the consortia did not necessarily preclude members from setting up their own container operations on other routes, for example, Blue Star container services to the west coast of North America.[115]

British container operations on the North Atlantic route began with a single firm rather than a consortium, although the firm, Manchester Liners, was part of the Furness Withy shipping group. In November 1968 the *Manchester Challenge* inaugurated the first British deep-sea fully cellular container vessel service with a voyage from Manchester to Montreal.[116] A larger North Atlantic container operation was Atlantic Container Line (ACL), set up by a consortium of British, Dutch, Swedish and French lines. The British participant was Cunard and it was Philip Bates of that company who ran day-to-day management of ACL from Southampton. ACL specialised in hybrid container/ro-ro vessels, allowing flexibility in the type of cargo carried.[117] Another multinational container consortium on the North Atlantic was Dart Container Line Company, formed by British (Bristol City Line), Canadian (Clarke Traffic Services) and Belgian (Compagnie Maritime Belge) firms. The

Bristol City Line interests were later taken over by Bibby, the Liverpool shipping company.[118]

By beginning the container revolution the Americans seized a lead in world liner shipping which they were to sustain for a decade and more. However, the British liner companies were not far behind them. In 1971 the USA owned seventy-five container ships (out of a world total of 231), aggregating 1,067,468 gt (world total 2,780,681 gt), while Britain was in second place with fifty-one container ships, totalling 627,448 gt.[119] Containerisation was one challenge to which British shipowners adapted quickly and successfully, adopting the latest technology whatever the cost.

Containerisation was to divide further liner shipping from tramp shipping. Any cargo that could be containerised would be eventually, and many of the small parcels of bulk cargo that had been the preserve of the smaller general purpose cargo ship were now taken by container ships. To survive the dry cargo tramp companies had to move into bulk carriers, which grew in size to achieve economies of scale. However, the bigger the vessel the greater the capital cost, so dry bulk tramp companies also began to form consortia.

The most important British one was Seabridge, set up in 1965. It came to include six firms: Bibby, Bowring, H. Clarkson (shipbrokers), Houlder Brothers (part of Furness Withy), Hunting and Silver Line. Hunting and Bowring were significant independent tanker companies, but the tanker depression of the early 1960s had encouraged them to move into the dry bulk trades where there were better freight rates. This need for flexibility between sectors of world shipping was one reason the ships built for the consortium included not only pure bulk carriers but also OBO carriers. These latter vessels could be switched between oil, bulk (e.g. grain) and ore cargoes as the market dictated. In all the consortium aimed to deploy twenty-six bulk and OBO carriers, totalling 2.5 million dwt, and forming one of the largest single bulk fleets in the world.[120]

If British shipowners had made a swift and successful adaptation to container shipping, and finally moved into bigger-scale operations with bulk carriers, they still remained reluctant to develop independent tanker ownership on a large scale. In doing so they largely missed out on the biggest tanker boom in history between 1967 and 1973. As a result of the Six Day War in June 1967 the Suez Canal was blocked and most oil supplies from the Gulf to Europe and North America had to make the long journey round the

Cape of Good Hope. To make such voyages profitable ever larger tankers were to be constructed to obtain economies of scale.[121] Back in the early 1950s the first so-called 'supertanker' had been only 28,000 dwt. The true supertankers of the late 1960s were in a different class and received new labels: when they went over 200,000 dwt they were called Very Large Crude Carriers (VLCC) and once 300,000 dwt was passed they became Ultra Large Crude Carriers (ULCC). At the start of the 1970s the 400,000 dwt mark was passed.[122] Such vessels inspired awe and, after the *Torrey Canyon* disaster of 1967, fear.[123]

As in the past most of the British flag tanker fleet was owned by oil companies and they joined the rush to build ever larger tankers. Between 1958 and 1973 the largest of Shell's individual British tankers grew in size from 38,000 to 205,000 dwt.[124] Most of the British independent tanker companies were reluctant to move into the big league, and even London & Overseas Freighters, so dynamic in the 1950s, would only order a single 255,000 dwt VLCC as a joint venture with partners.[125]

It was the liner companies, who had diversified into tanker (and dry bulk) operations, who were ready for bigger tankers. P&O's Trident Tankers, the largest British independent tanker company by the late 1960s, ordered a number of vessels over 200,000 dwt, some tankers and some OBO carriers.[126] When the traditional liner company Ocean Steamship finally moved into tankers (and bulkers) at the start of the 1970s its first tanker was the aptly named *Titan* of 230,000 dwt.[127] Yet these vessels were exceptional and the fact that several of the world's largest ships—477,000 dwt Globtik tankers—were intended for the British merchant fleet in the early 1970s owed less to British enterprise and more to foreign entrepreneurs finding the financial benefits of British registry attractive for a time.[128]

Back in the mid-1960s when British shipping had been in a difficult position and confidence in the industry had been further shaken by the seamen's strike of 1966, the government set up a committee under Lord Rochdale to examine the state of British shipping.[129] At the start of the 1960s Rochdale had overseen an inquiry into British ports which led to important changes in that industry.[130] When his committee on British shipping reported in 1970 it provided much information about the industry, but made few major recommendations for change.[131] This may have been because in the years between the committee's inception (1967) and

Table 2.5: The Twenty Largest UK Flag
Shipping Groups/Companies, 1968
(Thousands of gross tons)

Company	Sectors	Ships	Tonnage
British Petroleum	TK	121	2,296
P&O	L, B, TK	178	2,130
Shell	TK	65	1,602
Furness Withy	L, B, TK	111	1,139
Esso*	TK	34	839
A. Holt {Ocean]	L	97	816
Cunard	L, TK	60	692
British & Commonwealth	L, B	58	628
Texaco*	TK	25	498
Andrew Weir	L, B	56	478
Vestey Group	L	52	398
Ellerman	L	66	383
E.G. Thomson	L	33	319
Tate & Lyle	B, TK	24	287
Bibby Bros.	L, B	18	266
London & Overseas Freighters	B, TK	19	256
Fred. Olsen & Co.*	TK	4	239
T. & J. Harrison	L	30	234
Mobil*	TK	7	234
Dene Shipping	B	10	164

*Subsidiaries of foreign companies.
L—liner
B—bulk
TK—tanker
Source: Report of Rochdale Committee on Shipping, 1970, p. 429.

its report (1970) the British shipping industry seemed to make great progress and was at last adapting to changes in the international shipping industry that had been steadily increasing since 1945. (For principal British shipping companies in 1968 see Table 2.5.)

Indeed, although in 1967 Britain finally lost her position of having the world's largest active merchant fleet under one flag to Liberia (and was soon overtaken by Japan as well), the country still possessed the world's third largest merchant fleet in 1973. Britain also had the world's third largest oil tanker fleet (dominated by the ships of the Shell, Esso and British Petroleum oil companies); the fourth largest ore and bulk carrier fleet; the second largest fleet of cellular container ships; the largest fleet of refrigerated cargo vessels in the world; and the largest fleet of liquefied gas carriers in the world. Also it was an increasingly modern fleet, the average age of its ships falling from over nine years in 1968 to under 6.5 years in 1974, and over 55% of the tonnage was less than five years old.[132] Foreign rivals were beginning to overtake it, but the British merchant fleet remained a major force in world shipping in the early 1970s and would reach its postwar peak in 1975 at 33.2 million gross tons.[133] (For top ten merchant fleets see Table 2.6.)

Most of the modernisation and expansion of the British merchant fleet took place between 1966 and 1973, when nearly ten million gross tons was added to the fleet. Why did British shipowners change and adapt so successfully in this period when progress had been largely sluggish from 1945? World trade was certainly increasing, especially in the oil trade, but such conditions had also existed in the good years of 1945-57 when British shipowners were criticised for their complacency. The Rochdale committee claimed that a 'new spirit of enterprise' in shipping management was the cause.[134] It was certainly true that British shipowners could no longer avoid reacting to change. Liner companies had to get container ships or disappear; tramp firms had to adopt bulk carriers or go out of business. In both cases the increased cost of new vessels led to consortia and other collaboration between shipping firms. However, if British shipowners now had the will to change it was only possible because in the late 1960s and early 1970s they had finance available to make it possible.

After interwar debacles such as the tramp ship boom and bust of 1919–21 and the collapse of the Royal Mail liner shipping group in 1930, British shipowners became reluctant to borrow money. Compensation for wartime losses had barely covered increased postwar building costs, but the government had given some tax concessions from the 1950s onwards to assist the traditional method of financing new building out of retained profits. Although the conservative finance of British shipowners was criticised by some commentators, it was not unusual. The Rochdale committee pointed out that in the period 1958–69 less than 20% of expenditure on new ships by British shipowners was derived from borrowing.[135] Yet during the period 1946–73 the supposedly more

Table 2.6: The Top Ten Merchant Fleets in the World,
1930–1983

	Millions of gross tons
1930	
United Kingdom	20.4
USA*	14.0
Japan	4.3
Germany	4.2
Norway	3.6
France	3.5
Italy	3.3
Netherlands	3.1
Sweden	1.6
Greece	1.4
1947	
USA*	27.5
United Kingdom	18.7
Norway	6.2
Panama	3.9
France	3.8
Italy	3.4
Netherlands	3.3
Japan	3.2
Sweden	2.5
USSR	2.2
1963	
USA*	23.1
United Kingdom	21.5
Norway	13.6
Liberia	11.3
Japan	9.9
Greece	7.0
Italy	5.6
USSR	5.4
Netherlands	5.2
France	5.2

	Millions of gross tons
1973	
Liberia	49.9
Japan	36.7
United Kingdom	30.1
Norway	23.6
Greece	19.2
USSR	17.3
USA*	14.9
Panama	9.5
Italy	8.8
France	8.2
1983	
Liberia	67.5
Japan	40.7
Greece	37.4
Panama	34.6
USSR	24.5
USA*	19.3
Norway	19.2
United Kingdom	19.1
China	11.5
Italy	10.0

*USA figures include in some years Great Lakes shipping and (post-1945) the US reserve fleet.
Source: Lloyd's Register of Shipping.

progressive Norwegian shipowners derived only 11% of their money for new ships from borrowing.[136]

The great change in world ship financing after 1945 was the tremendous expansion of charter-backed financing. This was what allowed the so-called 'golden Greeks' like Onassis and Niarchos to build up their tanker fleets on the basis of bank loans with oil company charters as collateral. As the world tanker boom grew after 1967 some bankers were prepared to lend against a mortgage on the ship itself, with little additional security. This change removed the link between supply and demand. During the period of charter-backed finance new building was restricted by the availability of charters. If the ship itself was the collateral, there was no limit to the number of ships that could be ordered. By 1973 this ever-expanding credit allowed 105 million dwt of tankers, representing 55% of the world fleet, to be ordered in a single year.[137]

Thus by the early 1970s shipowners the world over did not lack for finance, leading to an overexpansion of tonnage that was to have unhappy consequences. Most British shipowners found their financial assistance close to home and were assisted by government action. In 1966 the 40% investment allowance for new ships (given in 1957) was ended. Instead a 20% cash investment grant was made available for new ships built anywhere in the world. Grants were only available to UK companies and a new ship had to remain on the UK register for at least five years after completion. In answer to criticisms that this measure did not help British shipbuilders, the government stated that was not its purpose. The aim was to help British shipowners acquire first-class modern ships and the owners must be free to get the best ships at the best price, delivered on time and with the right credit arrangements, regardless of where the shipyard was in the world.[138]

Between 1966 and 1970 nearly one thousand grant-assisted ships were built for the UK register, with the total government subsidy amounting to £620 million. Many of these ships were built in Japan, especially VLCCs and bulk carriers, and over half the new tonnage, some five million tons, was beneficially owned by foreigners who had set up UK companies to obtain the grant. This foreign exploitation of British government generosity led to the abolition of the grant in 1970. Nevertheless it remained a fact that since the 1950s an increasingly large proportion of the UK fleet was beneficially owned abroad—about 26% in 1970.[139]

In addition to the cash investment grant scheme, a new shipbuilding credit scheme was started in 1967 to encourage British shipowners to place orders with British shipyards. The scheme was originally proposed as a temporary measure during the reorganisation of the British shipbuilding industry as recommended by the 1966 Geddes report.[140] The scheme was included in the 1967 Shipbuilding Industry Act, but it was now to be open-ended, and in fact lasted, in one form or another, until the early 1980s.[141] Altogether, with a subsidy to build anywhere in the world between 1966 and 1970 and loans available to build in Britain from 1967 onwards, the late 1960s was a time when British shipowners were almost overwhelmed by government assistance in building new ships. For a country supposedly committed to a free market regime in world shipping, Britain was at this time providing some of the most generous state aid to shipping in the world.

Sinking Fast, 1973–1990

The year 1973 was to have profound consequences for both British and world shipping. At the start of the year the United Kingdom finally joined the European Economic Community (EEC) and a reorientation of British trade towards Western Europe, already begun during the 1960s, soon became explicit. In 1970 37.7% of British imports by value came from Western Europe and 41.1% of exports by value went to that area. By 1980 the figures were 55.9% for imports and 57.6% for exports.[142] This shift in trade patterns did not necessarily imply major changes in the development of British shipping since that industry was not solely dependent on carrying British trade. Nevertheless there was a clear shift away from ocean-going shipping in the years after joining the EEC. In 1971 59% of British trade tonnage operated deep-sea. By 1986 the figure had declined to 28%.[143] In any case some old imperial partners like Australia had been turning away from Britain even before she joined the EEC. In 1966–67 Japan had replaced Britain as Australia's most important market.[144] Short sea routes to Western Europe came to seem more important than old imperial liner routes to South Africa or India. Indeed the container lines came increasingly to concentrate on services between the world economic hubs of North America, Western Europe and Japan rather than those between developed and developing nations.[145]

The second major event of 1973 was a consequence of the Yom Kippur war in October. The Organisation of Petroleum Exporting Countries (OPEC) imposed oil sanctions on western nations supporting Israel and drove up the price of oil.[146] The rise continued into 1974 and it soon became clear that the oil trade boom that had begun in 1967 was over. By 1975 a severe depression had engulfed the oil tanker trade (more than half of world shipping), with new supertankers being completed every month just as demand was falling.[147] The depression soon began to affect other sectors of shipping. Higher fuel costs hit all ships, while a worldwide recession had by the second half of the 1970s cut demand in the dry bulk and the liner trades as well.[148] Although its impact varied from sector to sector and signs of revival appeared from time to time, the depression in world shipping was to last until the early 1990s.

The supertankers suffered worst in the collapse of the oil trade. Since few old-established British shipping companies had gone into supertanker ownership, except the oil companies, they might hope to avoid the worst consequences of the market downturn. Certainly British shipowners did better than those Norwegian shipowners who had rushed into supertankers in the early 1970s using borrowed money and were crippled by the collapse of the tanker market.[149] The main British oil companies like British Petroleum and Shell could survive the downturn, partly because much of their oil was carried in independent tankers that could be dispensed with as their charters ended.[150] However, Burmah, one of the smaller British oil companies, came to grief. The company had set up an oil terminal in the Bahamas with the intention of shipping in oil via VLCCs then sending it on to US ports in smaller tankers. Burmah secured a large fleet of tankers for the operation, but then the collapse of the tanker trade made it economical to ship oil direct from the Middle East to the USA in small tankers. Burmah was left with an unwanted fleet of tankers and huge losses. Only British government intervention in 1975 stopped the total collapse of the company.[151]

The collapse of a similar project in 1976 damaged two British independent tanker operators who had invested in new ships during the boom. The Newfoundland Refining Company was to import crude oil in VLCCs, refine it, and then ship the results to North American ports in products tankers. A VLCC was chartered from London & Overseas Freighters for the import operation, while Common Brothers was to provide a number of products tankers. The bankruptcy of the refining company left both shipping companies in a difficult position, trying to find new employment for their vessels in an overtonnaged market.[152] The biggest British independent tanker fleet, that of P&O, was quick to reduce its ambitious tanker plans: an order for a 414,000 ton tanker was renegotiated initially into an order for two bulk carriers, and finally for two cargo ships and two ferries.[153] The downturn had by 1976 extended to the dry bulk sector and shipping firms such as Ropner and Lyle struggled in difficult conditions.[154]

How would the British shipping industry react and adapt to this new depression? One reaction was diversification, a strategy that had been growing in importance since the 1950s. Maritime-related diversification, such as a shipping company owning a shipbuilding firm or a marine engine works, was nothing new, but profits in such ventures also depended on the ups and downs of the shipping cycle. Perhaps more useful were initially maritime-related activities which led into new business areas. For example, arranging travel for crews led to investment in travel agencies and the leisure industry, while arranging a shipping firm's insurance and investments led to wider involvement in the financial services field. Such activities could provide profits when the shipping side of a firm was not doing well.[155]

However, non-maritime investments could lead to problems. In 1974 the Court Line collapsed because of problems with its travel and leisure interests at a time when its shipowning and ship-building activities were doing well.[156] Nevertheless diversification into new fields was increasingly attractive for shipping firms. In 1972 P&O had taken over the large construction company Bovis, although only after considerable debate in the boardroom.[157] When a dry bulk carrier operator like Graig Shipping of Cardiff began to feel the effects of the shipping downturn in the mid-1970s, it could look to income from its other activities: a travel agency; commercial property; commodity investments; a share in oil and gas exploration in the Celtic Sea; and even a quantity of vintage port bought as an investment.[158] Graig's interest in offshore oil and gas was an increasingly common new venture for British shipping companies during the 1970s, although usually in the North Sea rather than the Celtic Sea (the waters to the south-west of Britain).[159]

It should not be thought that the problems of British shipowners were theirs alone. Between 1975 and 1988 the UK merchant fleet fell from 50 million dwt to 16.6 million dwt. Between 1975 and 1986 the Norwegian flag fleet fell from 45 million dwt to 11 million dwt; the West German fleet from 13 to 6 million dwt; the French fleet from 18 to 11 million dwt; and the Swedish fleet from 12 to 4 million dwt. By 1986 many West European shipowners, particularly Norwegians and West Germans, were operating their fleets under foreign flags.[160]

Scandinavian shipowners had long been held up as examples to the British of how shipowners with no more advantages than them could modernise and prosper. However, Scandinavian shipping firms were also in serious difficulties after 1973. Two long-established Norwegian firms were Norwegian America Line (NAL) and Wilhelm Wilhelmsen (WW). By the 1970s NAL was out of the transatlantic passenger trade and was using its passenger liners for cruising. The company could not afford full containerisation of its cargo services so it tried to carry on with palleted cargoes in its conventional cargo liners. This proved unrewarding and by the late 1970s the company was in serious financial trouble.[161] Although operating in a number of shipping sectors, WW had invested in tankers up to the early 1970s and suffered when the market collapsed. Even the firm's hybrid ro-ro/container ships in the liner trades were experiencing problems by 1980. The company's great support during the 1970s was its investment in offshore oil and gas activities in the North Sea, where it owned both rigs and supply vessels.[162]

Of the two main Swedish liner companies based in Gothenburg, Brostrom and Transatlantic, the former had large shipbuilding interests, substantial tanker and bulk carrier activities, and bought the Holland America Line with borrowed money in 1974. The world shipping and shipbuilding crisis from the mid-1970s hit Brostrom hard and in the early 1980s the firm was taken over by its rival Transatlantic. The latter had followed a more circumspect policy in the boom and bust conditions of the 1960s and 1970s. Both companies had joined Cunard and other foreign firms in the ACL consortium running hybrid ro-ro/container ships on the North Atlantic route.[163]

Thus it can be seen that the sufferings of British shipowners were not unique to them because of some particular British failings. It was a world shipping depression and even their best Scandinavian rivals found it hard to adapt successfully to the new adverse conditions. All shipowners hoped the downturn was just temporary, and there were some slight signs of improvement at the end of the 1970s, but then the new oil crisis of 1979–80 led to a continuation of the shipping depression. One of the most significant signs of the decline of British shipping was the sale in 1980 of Furness Withy, long one of the leading British liner shipping groups, to C.Y. Tung, the Chinese shipping magnate based in Hong Kong. Its activities were soon integrated into his worldwide operations and its fleets reduced.[164]

The consortia which were a feature of the expansion of the British merchant fleet in the late 1960s and early 1970s now began to unravel or be taken over by one participant. The Seabridge bulker consortium was wound up in 1981, and the OCL container consortium became solely owned by P&O in 1986.[165] The collapse of smaller bulker consortia brought down firms such as Sir William Reardon Smith in 1985 and Lyle Shipping in 1987.[166] Many of the great liner shipping groups of the past now began to disappear or move out of shipping: British & Commonwealth left shipping in 1986; Ellerman was taken over by Cunard in 1987; and Ocean moved out of deep-sea shipping in 1989.[167]

In this time of troubles could British shipowners look to government for some support as they had done in the 1930s and the 1960s? The answer was definitely in the negative. Rather than assist British shipping, the Thatcher government inflicted another blow on it with the 1984 budget, which ended free depreciation on new ships and removed certain tax concessions to seafarers.[168] As consequences of these changes orders of new ships for the UK register dried up and shipowners sought to flag out their vessels to reduce crew and other costs. Admittedly most ships moved to British subordinate registers like the Isle of Man or British dependent registers like Bermuda rather than foreign countries, but by 1987 for the first time most British-owned shipping was not on the main UK register.[169]

The decline in the size of the UK merchant fleet was a matter of growing concern in some quarters by the late 1980s, but the Conservative government stuck to one refrain. The size of the fleet must be left to market forces, and, in the words of the Department of Transport, 'Any case for assistance to the shipping industry . . . must be strategic; it has no compelling economic basis.'[170]

In 1988 a strongly worded report by the House of Commons transport committee argued that there were economic as well as strategic reasons for preserving a UK-registered merchant fleet, but the government declined to change its policy.[171] In 1990 came the Parkinson/Sterling report on British shipping, a unique collaborative study by the government and the industry. This report did concede that there might be some economic justification for having a national merchant fleet, such as its contribution to the balance of payments, but generally the report followed the line that only defence needs justified a UK-registered merchant fleet.[172]

The Parkinson/Sterling report was published in September 1990, at the start of the confrontation with Saddam Hussein, and included the statement: 'The Gulf crisis has brought back into sharp focus our strategic defence needs for British ships and British seafarers.'[173] Sadly the British merchant fleet, whose only *raison d'être* in government eyes was for defence purposes, contributed only five of the 162 ships chartered to support British forces taking part in the Gulf conflict.[174]

By the beginning of the 1990s the UK-registered merchant fleet was but a pale shadow of the fleet which had dominated the world in 1914. Some decline had always been inevitable as new national fleets arose to provide additional competition on the world's oceans. External factors such as the period of wars and depression from 1914 to 1945 had also played an important part in undermining the strength of British shipping. However, world shipping enjoyed unparalleled opportunities in the long boom from 1945 to 1973. For too long British shipping was reluctant to seize these opportunities by adapting to changing markets and new technologies. Only in the late 1960s and early 1970s did British shipowners fully embrace new ship types such as container vessels, bulk carriers and supertankers.

Then came the shipping depression after 1973 which reduced the fleets of all maritime nations, but hit Britain especially hard. Government aid to British shipping had peaked in the second half of the 1960s and then steadily declined until it was largely ended in 1984. A nationally based merchant fleet began to look increasingly unviable by the 1990s.

In the past maritime commercial competition had been between national merchant fleets, usually owned, built, manned and registered in one country. What finally undermined the UK flag merchant fleet—and most other national merchant fleets in the developed world—was the triumph of the flag of convenience merchant fleets, a triumph which has made international shipping the first truly global industry. A shipowner can now base himself in any country, build a ship in any country, register his ship in any country and obtain his crew from any country or countries. He is the true multinational capitalist.[175] With cheap ships, low or no taxes to pay and low-wage crews, he has successfully undercut the old nationally based merchant fleets. Flag of convenience shipping, or open registry shipping as it is more politely termed, now makes up more than half of the world's merchant tonnage and its continued growth seems inevitable if world sea transport is governed only by the economics of the free market.

Originally the creation of American business interests, the flag of convenience ships can only thrive under the pax Americana. Only if war, terrorism or piracy render the major ocean trade routes insecure will flag of convenience shipowners suddenly find the security offered by the national flag of a naval power attractive once again.

3

Losing the Market
Shipbuilding 1918–1990

'There are few important industries where the predominance of British manufacturers has been more marked than in shipbuilding and marine engineering', observed the Booth committee in 1918.[1] Those twin industries were among the largest British manufacturers, employing over 200,000 workers before the First World War. Capital invested in them was put at £35 million and their annual output exceeded a gross selling value of £50 million. The figures would be even greater if the output of the Admiralty dockyards was also included.[2] In 1913 British shipyards had produced 1,932,000 gross tons of new merchant shipping, more than the output of all the world's other shipbuilding nations put together and more than four times the output of Germany, Britain's nearest rival.[3]

The Booth committee had been set up in 1916 to consider the likely challenges to British shipping and shipbuilding in the postwar world, especially from increased foreign competition. The committee's consideration of shipbuilding touched on points which were to be raised again and again over the next fifty years. Foreign competition, particularly from the USA, Japan, the Netherlands, Italy and Scandinavia, was likely to increase after the war, but this would not be a problem as long as British shipbuilders and marine engineers 'retain and develop their energy and enterprise, and take steps to bring their works and employees to the highest possible pitch [of efficiency]'.[4]

The committee noted that 'the tendency of the world appears to be in the direction of larger economic organisations', citing the rise of liner shipping groups as one sign of this trend. Shipbuilders should remember that while 'individualism has been of inestimable advantage in the past, there is reason to fear that individualism by itself may fail to meet the competition of the future in shipbuilding . . . We are convinced that the future of the nation depends to a large extent upon the increased co-operation in its great industries.'[5] Standardisation of ship types for easier construction was pointed out as a good idea in peace as well as war, while the committee believed 'that everything should be done to promote industrial research and to encourage the adoption of improved methods' throughout the shipbuilding and marine engineering industries.[6]

The Booth committee had thus pointed out the need for shipbuilders to invest in the most efficient use of capital goods and labour; to co-operate among themselves with a view to creating larger units of production; to standardise the production of ships; and to carry out research to improve production methods. The Geddes committee would be hammering away at almost the same points in its report on the shipbuilding industry fifty years later. Had British shipbuilding completely failed to adapt to the changes in world shipbuilding in the intervening half century?

Interwar Slump

The British shipbuilding industry's response to the challenge of the Great War was hampered by the fact that it quickly came under the control of the Admiralty. Naval construction and repair received priority over merchant work with the result that by late 1916 merchant construction could no longer keep up with losses inflicted by German submarines. Such losses increased dramatically in the first half of 1917 and desperate efforts were now made to increase British merchant ship production. Private yards expanded their capacity and standard ship types were built to raise output. The government decided to set up new, state-owned shipyards, but these were not completed before the end of the war. If Britain made a greater effort in merchant ship production, her new American ally took only a comparatively short time to set up the world's greatest shipbuilding operation, although its full output did not come until after the peace. In 1919 Britain produced 1,620,000 gross tons of new merchant shipping, some 300,000 tons less than the 1913 peak, while the USA produced 3,580,000 tons, half of all world output in 1919.[7]

The American shipbuilding effort continued for a few postwar years, then faded away as economic realities reasserted themselves, with the USA unattractive as a high cost shipbuilder. However, other nations had also expanded their shipbuilding capacity during the war and further extended it during the postwar shipping boom of 1919–20. Compared with 1914 world shipbuilding capacity had doubled by 1920. Britain in 1920 produced 2,055,000 gross tons of merchant shipping, a figure that was never to be exceeded, but the total shipbuilding capacity of her yards was thought to be twice that amount.[8]

The supply side of world shipbuilding had reached a new peak, but hopes that demand would match it were soon dashed. From 1921 world shipping entered a long period of depression because seaborne trade slumped at a time when the world merchant fleet had greatly expanded. Demand for new ships fell and shipyards around the world were soon in bitter competition for what orders were available. The British shipbuilding industry suffered additional problems. Before the Great War about 20% of British output was for foreign buyers, but new shipyards abroad took a large proportion of those orders after 1918. Similarly 25% of British prewar output had been Royal Navy warships during the Anglo-German naval race. Naval orders were cut once peace returned and cut again after the Washington Treaty of 1921 sought to curb naval armaments. Until rearmament began in 1935, naval work ceased to be of major importance to British shipbuilders. The reduction in export and naval orders threw British shipbuilders back on the home merchant ship market, always their principal support, but even this was cutting back. During the interwar period the total size of the British merchant fleet did not increase greatly, and the tramp sector, whose orders had kept many N.E. England shipyards in business, experienced a definite contraction. Thus British shipbuilding would have suffered anyway from the basic mismatch of supply and demand in the world shipbuilding market, but special factors made its position even worse.[9] How was the industry to adapt to this major change for the worse?

The shipbuilding market had always been highly volatile, so many shipbuilders hoped the downturn in 1921 was only temporary and that the good trading conditions of pre-1914 would soon return. In the meantime there seemed to be hope of temporary encouragement of new demand through the Trade Facilities Act of 1921 (and later extensions of it during the 1920s). The government would guarantee loans for capital projects which would promote employment in Britain. The Act was intended to be a short-term measure and was open to all industries, but in fact a third of the guarantees went to shipbuilding projects. The government of Northern Ireland issued similar loan guarantees which were of assistance to Belfast shipbuilders.[10] Lord Pirrie at Harland & Wolff co-operated with Lord Kylsant of the Royal Mail shipping group in making use of the loan guarantees to fund a large programme of new building.[11] Furness Withy used the Act to obtain over £2 million to pay for twelve new ships for various of its companies.[12]

It was Furness Withy that provided a salutary shock to British shipbuilders in the mid-1920s and showed they were in a world very different to that before 1914. In March 1925 it was announced that a contract to build five new ships for Furness Withy's Prince Line had been given to German shipbuilders in Hamburg. This was the first major order placed by a British shipowner with a foreign shipyard and it caused an outcry. One reaction was the formation of a joint committee of inquiry by the Shipbuilding Employers' Federation and the shipyard unions to assess why British ships were now more expensive than foreign products and to see how work practices might be changed to overcome this problem.[13] Such employer-union co-operation had been rare in the past and it is a measure of how seriously the prospect of the loss of British orders to foreigners was taken.

If the mid-1920s saw new co-operation between shipbuilding employers and unions (albeit short-lived), it also saw the start of co-operation between shipbuilding companies with a view to re-stricting supply by reducing overcapacity in the industry. The move started among the naval builders in 1925 and they agreed on how to divide up what little work was available by a scheme beginning in 1926. The following year a wider grouping of shipbuilders met with the aim of reducing cut-throat competition among firms desperate for orders, and in 1928 this led to the setting up of the Shipbuilding Conference. This organisation saw a reduction in building capacity as its first priority and in 1929 began discussions with the Bank of England about setting up a body to purchase and 'sterilise' such berths.[14]

When the National Shipbuilders Security Ltd. (NSS) was set up in 1930 to carry out this task, the UK shipbuilding industry comprised about 800 building berths of all sizes with a maximum annual capacity of almost four million gross tons (in 1930

British shipyards produced only 1,470,000 gross tons of merchant shipping). During the 1930s (with most closures carried out by 1936) the NSS sterilised 216 building berths with a total capacity of 1,400,000 gross tons.[15] Unfortunately the world depression from 1929 onwards hit shipbuilding very hard, with British output down to a mere 133,000 gross tons in 1933, so that even when the NSS had finished its work much excess capacity remained. Nevertheless the shipbuilders had shown themselves capable of co-operation to stop the worst cut-throat competition in very difficult times.

However, this adaptation to change had strict limits. The NSS was not a full-blown attempt to rationalise the shipbuilding industry. Shipbuilders saw little reason to change the basic structure and practices of their industry. There were few amalgamations into bigger units, the merger of Armstrong Whitworth and Vickers in 1927 and Lithgow's acquisition of Fairfields in 1935 being exceptions, and investment in expensive new plant was avoided. Among factors of production, the emphasis was still on labour rather than capital. Large workforces were left to construct vessels on a craft system. This allowed for maximum flexibility. Craftsmen could turn their hands to a wide variety of vessels and could be easily laid off when the volatile shipbuilding cycle turned down.[16] Thus it is hardly surprising that in the poor trading conditions of the interwar period unemployment among shipyard workers reached very high levels, with about 60% of insured workers in the industry unemployed in the period 1931–33.[17]

British shipbuilders, like British shipowners, have been condemned for failing to move fast enough into new techniques and ship types in the interwar period, but this criticism is only partly true. It was a British yard, Cammell Laird at Birkenhead, which produced the first all-welded ship, the coaster *Fullagar*, in 1920, and made a heavy loss on the contract. The high costs of introducing welding, initial problems with the process, and doubts entertained by the ship classification societies did not encourage British shipbuilders to make a major shift to the new process. There was more welding during the 1930s, but riveting remained the preferred construction method.[18]

Lord Pirrie of Harland & Wolff had bought the British rights to the Danish Burmeister & Wain marine diesel engine before the First World War, and after the conflict he and Lord Kylsant of Royal Mail began building a series of motorships.[19] The shipbuilders Doxford developed the only successful British marine diesel engine in the interwar period and claimed that British failure to win foreign orders was largely due to the reluctance of many British shipyards to build motorships.[20] Nevertheless Britain was the largest builder of motorship tonnage between the wars. The foreign advantage was that a greater percentage of their output was made up of motorships. Over the whole period 1920–39 motorships made up 27.8% of British shipbuilding output compared with 41.9% of foreign shipbuilding output. Similarly, while tankers were about the same percentage of British output as of foreign output during the 1920s, in the following decade tankers (which were often motorships) made up a greater share of foreign output (1930–38: tankers were 23.8% of British output and 32.6% of foreign output).[21] However, tanker-building was important to British shipbuilders in this period. The largest customer (by tonnage ordered) of British shipyards in the interwar years was not P&O or Cunard but the British Tanker Company, the shipping arm of the Anglo-Persian Oil Company (later BP), and of the top five customers two were tanker operators: British Tanker Co. and Anglo-Saxon Petroleum (later Shell).[22] Well might J.R. Robertson, the chairman of British Tanker Co., point out with pride in 1937 that during the past twenty years his firm had ordered ninety-seven tankers from British shipyards, costing a total of £19 million, and had often placed orders at times when they were most needed to keep shipyards in business.[23]

By the mid-1930s British shipping was in almost as dire a position as British shipbuilding, and the government provided a subsidy to tramp shipowners in the British Shipping (Assistance) Act of 1935. The Act also included a 'scrap and build' scheme by which tramp shipowners disposed of old tonnage in return for government loans to build new ships in British yards. In fact the scheme was only partially successful. Some fifty new ships totalling 186,000 gross tons, and costing £3.5 million, replaced ninety-seven old ships totalling 386,625 gross tons which were scrapped. However, as freight rates began to recover during the course of the scheme, British shipowners were reluctant to get rid of their own old ships and most of those scrapped were specifically bought abroad to take advantage of the scheme.[24] The British Shipping (Assistance) Bill of 1939 offered government loans to British shipowners for new building without the scrapping requirement, and although the outbreak of war killed the Bill, the government did give loans to those firms which had ordered new ships in expectation of the Bill becoming law.[25]

Even without government loans to encourage new building of merchant ships in British yards, economic conditions were beginning to improve for shipbuilding in the second half of the 1930s, with naval rearmament one important factor.[26] Nevertheless foreign competition was increasing. Partly this was because of subsidies to foreign shipyards and autarchic regulations. Blocking currency movements out of Germany was one way the Nazis persuaded foreigners to have ships built in German shipyards. For example, Unilever had eight ships built in Germany in 1936–37 for the firm's services to West Africa.[27] However, a more worrying reason that some British shipowners were ready to order abroad was that foreign yards could provide modern ship types more cheaply. For example, in 1937–39 Hunting had three motor tankers built abroad, two in Denmark and one in Sweden.[28]

The British shipbuilding industry faced a profound depression in the interwar years and had little hope of regaining the level of dominance it had achieved before 1914. The industry's problems were mostly external: the collapse of world trade cut demand for new ships and the expansion of foreign shipbuilding capacity increased supply, producing a mismatch that British shipbuilders could do little to overcome. The British government gave some assistance to the industry via the Trade Facilities Act in the 1920s and the scrap and build scheme in the 1930s, while the industry itself did something to reduce overcapacity through the activities of the NSS. These efforts provided some help to the industry in difficult times, but there was no attempt to change its basic structure and methods. Shipbuilders were interested in cost-cutting not investing and they were content to leave unchanged the old system of working, with craft gangs in charge when there were ships to build and most workers laid off when there were not. Investing in new, more efficient ways of building ships seemed pointless when the demand for more new ships was simply not there. (For principal British shipbuilders in interwar period see Table 3.1.)

The performance of British shipbuilding in the Second World War is a matter of some dispute. Its efforts have been seen as 'the fossilisation of inefficiency' by some commentators, while others believe it performed better than in the Great War.[29] The British shipbuilding industry at the peak of its power produced 1.6 million

Table 3.1: Principal British Shipbuilders by Merchant
Tonnage Launched, 1920–1939
(thousands of gross tons)

Company	Location	Tons	% of UK output
Harland & Wolff	Belfast & Clyde	1983	10.0
Swan Hunter	N.E. England	1448	7.3
Lithgows	Clyde	1017	5.1
Wm. Gray	N.E. England	810	4.1
Armstrong Whitworth	N.E. England	693	3.5
Cammell Laird	Birkenhead	657	3.3
Furness S.B. Co.	N.E. England	629	3.2
Barclay Curle	Clyde	591	3.0
Workman Clark[1]	Belfast	551	2.8
Palmer's S.B. Co.[2]	N.E. England	530	2.7
Vickers Armstrong	Barrow	523	2.6
John Brown	Clyde	522	2.6
Doxford & Sons	N.E. England	507	2.5

1. closed 1935.
2. closed 1931.
Source: A. Slaven, 'British Shipbuilders: Market Trends and Order Book Patterns
Between the Wars', *Journal of Transport History*, Sept. 1982, p. 47.

tons of warships in the first four years of the First World War; the
shipbuilding industry of the 1940s, exhausted and reduced by
twenty years of depression, produced 1.7 million tons of warships in
the first four years of the Second World War. Similarly in 1915–18
3.8 million tons of merchant ships were built in Britain, but in
1940–43 the 'fossilised' industry produced 4.5 million tons of
merchant shipping.[30] The efforts of British shipbuilding were
somewhat retarded in the first war because of confused Admiralty
control, but given the condition of the industry at the start of the
second war, its achievements seem all the more impressive.

However, this is not to deny that the shipbuilding industry was a
cause of concern in the Second World War. In 1942 the Barlow
report on shipyard labour noted the lack of skilled workers as a
result of the interwar slump, a serious problem in an industry
that depended on labour rather than capital for its productivity.
Next came the Bentham report which highlighted the antiquated
machinery in most shipyards. The government organised a £6
million investment in new machinery in the yards between 1942

and 1944, perhaps the biggest capital investment programme in them for a quarter of a century. Yet in the last years of the war shipyard productivity failed to increase significantly, probably because of the inability of management to organise the best use of the new equipment and because of the opposition of trade unions to new methods.[31]

But this was only a capital replacement programme. It did not imply any change in the basic organisation of British shipbuilding. The prefabrication and flow production methods of the huge Liberty ship programme in the USA were not copied in Britain where 'shipbuilding suffered from that universal Victorian industrial hangover . . . of individualistic fragmentation.'[32] Looking forward to the postwar period in 1944 a Cabinet committee expected British shipbuilding to do well for the first eight or ten years and hoped this period would be used to improve the efficiency of an industry whose management and workforce 'tended to be conservative', whose shipyards were often 'cramped and ill-sited', and whose trade unions tended 'to resist the introduction of new methods and to impose demarcation rules to a degree which impeded progress'.[33]

Short-Lived Prosperity and Missed Opportunities

After the return of peace in 1945 the British shipbuilding industry escaped nationalisation by the new Labour government and, unlike 1918, found itself with few foreign rivals in any condition to meet immediate postwar demands for new tonnage. As in 1918 the US shipbuilding industry had vastly greater capacity, but it was a wartime growth that could not be commercially viable in peace-time. Of the other principal shipbuilding nations, only Sweden had shipyards undamaged by war. Yet despite Britain's unique position, her shipbuilders remained pessimistic about the future. They feared there would be a short-lived postwar boom, then a return to the shipbuilding slump of the interwar years. Such a gloomy outlook made them reluctant to invest in new machinery for the shipyards.[34] The government to some extent shared these fears and hoped to use naval orders to cover the apparently inevitable downturn in the shipbuilding cycle, thus preserving employment.[35]

The pessimists proved to be wrong. World shipbuilding ex-panded almost continuously for thirteen years after 1945. In 1948 world shipbuilding output had reached 2,480,000 gross tons; in

1958 it was to be 9,270,000 tons, almost four times the 1948 total.[36] British shipyards enjoyed a prosperity they had not seen since before 1914. In 1948, with an output of 1,300,000 tons, Britain produced 51% of world output.[37] Back in 1946 the government had set up the Shipbuilding Advisory Committee to oversee the future development of an industry about which it had some concern, but the postwar boom conditions in shipbuilding soon reduced government worries about the industry's future.[38]

Unfortunately the seller's market encouraged complacency among British shipbuilders and they were slow to carry out modernisation recommended and begun during the war. The first stage of modernisation required the adaptation of yard facilities for welding and prefabrication. The methods had been the basis of the huge US output of merchant ships during the war. However, British shipbuilders, like many British shipowners, still had their doubts about welding as opposed to riveting.[39] In 1948 one shipyard owner spoke of being 'forced' to spend money on new welding equipment because of 'a highly competitive market which calls for the building of mainly welded ships'.[40] The preference was to meet increased demand with the old labour-intensive construction methods as much as possible, since too much expenditure on new equipment would lead to over-capitalisation and an expensive burden when the feared downturn came.

That the old methods would no longer do was demonstrated dramatically in 1956. Even before the end of the year it was already clear that Japanese shipyards would produce more new tonnage than British ones.[41] This was the first peacetime year since 1920 in which Britain had not been the world's leading shipbuilding nation. It was a shock to British shipbuilding prestige to match Furness Withy's German order in 1925. The shock was all the greater since Japan, like West Germany, now rivalling Britain for second place, had only come back into large-scale shipbuilding at the start of the 1950s. Commentators blamed much of Britain's failure to keep ahead on the reluctance of British shipbuilders to invest in new plant and equipment. Between 1951 and 1954 German and Japanese shipyards had gone in for large-scale re-equipment, but British shipbuilders spent only about £4 million on their fixed assets, a low figure for an industry producing an average of £120 million a year at this time.[42] Rather than being provoked into new investment by the Japanese success, many British shipbuilders took comfort in the view that most Japanese output was made up of large

3. Launch of the *Kepwickhall* at Doxfords, Sunderland in 1956. Built by William Doxford and Sons for West Hartlepool Steam Navigation Co. Ltd., this motorship was a high-class tramp also intended for charter to liner shipping companies.
(Photo: Tyne & Wear Archives Service 1811/170/162. Reproduced by permission of the Chief Archivist, Tyne & Wear Archives Service)

bulk carriers, ore carriers, and tankers, relatively simple vessels to construct with low values per ton. The British preferred to concentrate on building high-value passenger and cargo liners, demanding substantial labour input and unsuited to the mass production methods of the Japanese. Unfortunately the growing world demand was for the vessel types favoured by the Japanese.[43]

What British shipbuilders failed to appreciate was the important change in the world shipbuilding market which took place during the 1950s. Previously the output of most shipbuilding nations had been closely linked to their own national merchant fleet's requirements, with export orders as an added bonus. Even the success of Swedish shipbuilding was based very much on a 'local' market—not just the small Swedish fleet, but the larger Norwegian merchant marine. Shipowners like the Norwegians and the Greeks, who had little or no home shipbuilding industry, were exceptional in their need to get most of their new ships from other countries. In the

1950s such non-national customers for new ships grew in numbers. On one side were the newly independent ex-colonies, seeking to build up their own national fleets but largely without their own shipyards. On the other side, and much more important, were the 'flag of convenience' fleets, often owned by Greeks and Americans, who had no linkages to national shipyards. The flag of convenience shipowners not only wanted big new tankers and bulk carriers, but were prepared to order them in large numbers, encouraging economies of mass production. Such owners could shop around the world and choose the best shipyard capable of meeting their needs. It was by meeting the needs of this new market, rather than just rebuilding their own national merchant fleets, that Japan and West Germany made such rapid progress as shipbuilding nations after 1950. By the late 1950s shipbuilding was Japan's chief export industry.[44]

British shipbuilders made no great effort to get into this new market, although, for example, Vickers at Barrow did build two very large (for that time) tankers (32,000 dwt each) for Stavros Niarchos in 1951–52.[45] They might have been drawn into it via the Norwegians, Britain's principal export customers for new ships, who were rapidly expanding their fleet and moving into the new, larger vessel types. However, Britain's hold on the Norwegian market began to slip during the 1950s. Sweden had always been a major rival for the business, but she was now joined by West Germany, Japan and Norway's own growing shipbuilding industry. Disputes over credit terms, prices and delivery dates began to undermine Anglo-Norwegian links. In 1949 Britain had 44% of the Norwegian market for new ships, but by 1958 her share had fallen to only 8.5%.[46]

British shipbuilders claimed not to be greatly concerned about their failure to retain a large share of the world ship export market. British shipowners had always been their principal loyal customers and close links had been forged between particular British ship-owners and shipyards, such as Cunard with John Brown on the Clyde. However, the British merchant fleet, although still the world's largest, did not expand much during the 1950s, while the traditional loyalty of British shipowners to British builders began to wear thin in some cases by the end of the decade, when 28% of ships for UK registration were built abroad.[47]

The success of foreign shipbuilding rivals was due to them setting up modern production facilities, involving welded construction of prefabricated sections on something like an assembly line. The Japanese had turned against welding in the late 1930s after the loss of several naval vessels, but postwar they took it up again with enthusiasm. They benefited from free access to the latest American shipbuilding methods, especially through the activities of Daniel K. Ludwig's National Bulk Carriers Ltd. (NBC). In 1951 NBC took over the old naval dockyard at Kure and set up a very modern shipbuilding operation, geared to the production of large bulk carriers and tankers, some of over 100,000 dwt. During NBC's time at Kure (1951–62) some fifty-two ships, totalling 2.36 million dwt, were built there by Japanese workers using Japanese steel, and the latest shipbuilding methods spread from Kure to the rest of the Japanese shipbuilding industry.[48]

Sweden witnessed a similar expansion of new, capital-intensive shipbuilding facilities, which stood in marked contrast to the continuing labour-intensive basis of British shipbuilding. Welding had been commonplace in Sweden since the interwar period, but it was the growing size of ships which compelled the Swedes to set up new production facilities on greenfield sites. For example, using profits generated by the Suez tanker boom of 1956–57, the Uddevalla shipyard laid out a new yard, Sorvik, next to the old, with a huge slipway to make possible the building of supertankers. At Gothenburg the Gotaverken firm built a new shipyard at Arendal, completed in 1963 at a cost of around £40 million, which could produce tankers up to 120,000 dwt. The expense of these new specialised facilities was substantial, so the Swedes had to ensure a constant large volume of business by internationalising their market rather than just relying on Swedish and Norwegian orders.[49]

As noted above, the Suez crisis of 1956 drove up tanker charter rates and led to a boom in tanker orders. British shipyards derived some benefits from such orders, but they had no intention of carrying out modernisation on the scale of the Arendal project so that they could build the ever-bigger tankers being demanded by some owners. Between 1945 and 1958 British shipbuilding invested about £8 million p.a. in modernisation, which if averaged out among the thirty-one main shipyards meant each was spending only £260,000 p.a. on modernisation. Of course modernisation was not so spread, with only a few yards making a major effort in that direction. Vickers Armstrong had been alone in spending £2.25 million in reconstruction in the immediate postwar years. Cammell Laird began an £18 million modernisation at Birkenhead in 1956.

For most shipyards, however, modernisation was a piecemeal process rather than a matter of major change, and shipbuilding's capital investment during the 1950s fell well below that of other British industries.[50]

As long as world shipbuilding orders kept expanding, British shipyards could still get by, largely depending on the old production methods, but in 1958 world merchant tonnage finally exceeded the demands of world trade. Orders for new ships dried up and a shipbuilding recession lasted until 1961. When it ended, world shipbuilding began to revive rapidly, but British shipbuilding did not. With the downturn in 1958 its underlying fragile condition was quickly exposed, and by 1959 it was clear that shipyards were likely to close, with many job losses. Suddenly thoughts turned back to the 1930s and the government feared it might have to intervene to prevent a serious collapse. (For average shipbuilding output 1958–60 see Table 3.2.)

Early in 1959 government took the view that the British shipbuilding industry 'did not seem to fully recognise the critical situation which would shortly develop'. If the industry did not improve its efficiency even British shipowners might start to order new ships abroad on a large scale. 'Many of the difficulties stemmed from bad labour relations within an industry which covered some forty different trade unions. Shipbuilding was probably the worst and most outmoded of our industries in this field.' There were faults on both sides in the industry and neither showed any enthusiasm for tackling the problem.[51]

An internal government report later in 1959 did 'not consider the prospects of the United Kingdom shipbuilding industry becoming competitive in the near future can be rated very high'. The industry's management had not attracted the best people during the interwar slump, and although new blood had come in since 1945, such men, while often well-educated in naval architecture, were ignorant of production engineering and management techniques needed for efficient modern shipbuilding.[52]

British shipyards had made some efforts to invest in new processes and modern equipment. Gross investment in shipbuilding between 1951 and 1957 averaged £8.5 million per year, representing only about 2% of turnover, which was not a high rate judged by the record of other industries. In 1957 investment was estimated to be £15 million and it was likely to remain at that level until 1961 when the modernisation plans of the big shipyards were

Table 3.2: Shipbuilding in the UK: Annual Average of
Tonnage Launched 1958–1960
(Thousands of gross tons)

Locality	Tonnage Built	% of UK Output
N.E. England	646	46
Tyne	259	19
Wear	243	17
Tees	144	10
Clyde	406	29
Belfast	138	10
Birkenhead	55	4
Forth	34	2
Barrow	25	2
Tay	22	2
Dee & N.E. Scotland	21	2
Humber	19	1
Others	30	2
Total	1,395 (16% of world output)	

Source: J. Bird, *The Major Seaports of the United Kingdom* (London, 1963), p. 45.

expected to be completed. However, the British were having to compete with new, capital-intensive shipyards in West Germany, Japan and Sweden. Comparatively little money was spent on ship-building research in Britain and that research concerned ship design rather than production methods and how to reduce the cost of the product.[53]

The report then turned to the vexed question of industrial relations. 'Although the effect of labour difficulties can be exaggerated, there is no doubt that they are a restrictive element of importance in the industry', both directly and because of bad publicity for the industry at home and abroad. Labour relations were generally characterised by 'a tradition of toughness' by both management and workers. Both sides took up entrenched positions and underrated the value of consultation and negotiation. 'If the competitive efficiency of British shipbuilding is to be restored . . . improvement in labour relations is a sine qua non.' There should be no question of government aid to the industry until it sorted this problem out itself.[54]

After considering the report, the economic policy committee of the Cabinet concluded that government intervention in the ship-building industry was not yet required and the government should seek to discourage any agitation for subsidies. Shipbuilding research bodies were to be supported and the two sides of the industry were to be encouraged to come together to improve industrial relations.[55]

Sir Graham Cunningham, chairman of the Shipbuilding Advisory Committee (SAC), tried to form a sub-committee to examine the problems of the industry, but obstruction by the shipbuilders finally caused an exasperated Cunningham to resign. The govern-ment appointed a new chairman and forced the SAC to begin the inquiry that Cunningham had desired. While the inquiry was taking place, the report of the Department of Scientific and Industrial Research on research and development in the ship-building industry was leaked to *The Times* in October 1960. The report noted that productivity in shipbuilding had increased by only 1% since 1945, only limited modernisation had taken place in the shipyards, production control was primitive, and research and development was insufficient, with little of it directed to pro-duction and management problems.[56]

In 1961 the SAC delivered its report on the industry, but full agreement was only achieved on one point: the need for government assistance via a credit scheme, the only kind of aid that avoided government intervention in individual shipyards. The government then asked for a report from accountants Peat, Marwick, Mitchell analysing why British owners were increasingly ready to have ships built abroad. Peats pointed out the four main areas in which British shipbuilders were not competitive with their foreign rivals: British prices were often higher and there was a reluctance to quote fixed prices; British delivery dates were longer and often not met; credit facilities were usually more favourable abroad; and bad labour relations delayed production, raised costs and damaged the industry's reputation. The report believed a government ship-building credit scheme would not be helpful. Taking all the reports into consideration, the government decided against intervention.[57]

Meanwhile the crisis in British shipbuilding became increasingly apparent. Between 1957 and 1961 employment in the industry fell from nearly 81,000 to 63,500, and between 1958 and 1963 seventeen shipyards closed, including famous firms such as William Gray at West Hartlepool (in 1962) and William Denny at Dumbarton (in 1963).[58] The government had been trying to avoid intervention since 1959, but as British shipbuilding had failed to

Table 3.3: Shipbuilding Output of UK, Japan, Sweden and
West Germany, 1954–1973
(Thousands of gross tons)

Year	UK	Japan	Sweden	W. Germany
1954	1409	413	544	963
1955	1474	829	526	929
1956	1383	1746	489	1000
1957	1414	2433	661	1231
1958	1402	2067	760	1429
1959	1373	1723	857	1202
1960	1331	1732	711	1092
1961	1192	1799	742	962
1962	1073	2183	841	1010
1963	982	2367	888	971
1964	808	3764	1034	827
1965	1282	4886	1266	1035
1966	1074	6495	1130	1158
1967	1188	7217	1361	1041
1968	1047	8349	1097	1211
1969	828	9168	1263	1787
1970	1327	10011	1532	1311
1971	1235	11119	1864	1978
1972	1191	12860	2028	1355
1973	1062	14662	2289	1922

Source: Chamber of Shipping of UK, *British Shipping Statistics*, 1968–69 and 1974.

match the revival of world shipbuilding after 1961, it seemed some action had to be taken. Although the option had been rejected by the Peats report, the government chose a shipbuilding credit scheme, which lasted from 1963 to 1964. [59] The government was originally only going to provide £30 million for loans to British shipowners to have vessels built in British shipyards, but the sum was finally raised to £75 million. In all sixty-seven ships totalling 892,000 gross tons were ordered.[60] Unfortunately once the scheme was over, orders for British shipyards slumped back to low levels.

Between 1962 and 1964 world shipbuilding revived rapidly, reaching an output of over ten million gross tons in the latter year, which exceeded the previous postwar high of nine million tons in 1958. The Organisation for Economic Co-operation and

Development (OECD) noted that most shipbuilding countries in the world had a higher output in 1964 than in 1954, the chief exceptions being the USA, the Netherlands, and the UK. The USA was a special case, its industry largely kept going by government subsidies and protection, while the Dutch share of world output had fallen from 8% in 1955 to 2.6% in 1964. The real loser was the UK, its share of world output slumping from 27.8% in 1954 to 9.3% in 1964. In 1963 and 1964 the Scandinavian shipbuilders, and especially the Swedes, achieved outright production records. However, Japan was the big winner. In 1954 it had 8.2% of world shipbuilding output, but that share had risen to 39.5% in 1964. In the latter year Japan produced over half the ships for export built in the world.[61] It would take more than the shipbuilding credit scheme of 1963–64 to stop British shipbuilders slipping even further behind their foreign rivals. (See Table 3.3.)

In the introduction to the British shipbuilding industry handbook for 1962 it was claimed that the industry followed 'modern practice, embracing the latest automatic equipment and productivity methods', but also offered 'a wealth of experience and craftsmanship'.[62] The problem for British shipbuilding in the first twenty years after the end of the Second World War was that it brought in too little of the former and preserved too much of the latter. Despite an unprecedented market for new ships and its order books overflowing, the British shipbuilding industry was incapable of expanding output to any great extent in the good years up to 1958. Expecting the worst in the postwar period, the industry seemed incapable of fully grasping the opportunities offered by boom conditions. As a new global market for ships emerged, the British shipyards were content to rely primarily on their own almost stagnant domestic market. Modernisation was largely a slow and piecemeal process, leaving foreign rivals to reap the benefits from establishing modern construction facilities to meet the needs of the expanding global market. Yet even if British shipyards had modernised to a greater extent, it is unlikely they could have made the best of the new opportunities unless new production planning and work practices were introduced.[63] Little progress had been made in those areas, especially in industrial relations, and the shipbuilders seemed to be looking to government to save an industry they were unwilling or unable to save themselves.

Geddes Report and Government Intervention

When Labour came to power in 1964 it decided to set up a public inquiry under Reay Geddes, the chairman of Dunlop, into the shipbuilding industry. This began in early 1965, but the closure of shipyards continued: six in 1964 and four more in 1965. A fifth yard, Fairfields on the Clyde, also went into liquidation in 1965, even though it had an order book worth £32 million and had nearly completed a £5 million modernisation scheme.[64] Political considerations forced the government to act over Fairfields and a million pound loan was made available. In December 1965 the firm was reconstructed as Fairfields (Glasgow) Ltd., with the state having a half share and the other half involving the trade unions and private capital. Not only had the government intervened directly in a shipyard for the first time, but the new Fairfields was to see an 'experiment' in improved labour practices in the industry with the aim of increasing productivity. Unfortunately before any clear results could be achieved, Fairfields was merged with other yards in Upper Clyde Shipbuilders as a consequence of the Geddes report.[65]

The Geddes committee had been appointed in February 1965 'to establish what changes were necessary in organization, in methods of production and any other factors affecting costs to make the shipbuilding industry competitive in world markets'. In 1966 its report recommended a fundamental change in the structure of the industry, aiming at reforming production, marketing and industrial relations so that more orders could be secured. However, adoption of the new methods, especially provision of staffs for design, research, production control and marketing, would not be possible unless the existing yards were joined together in groups. Each group should have a group headquarters and a number of specialised yards employing 8-10,000 workers and with an output capacity of 400-500,000 gross tons a year. Five groups were initially suggested: two on the Clyde, two in N.E. England, and one in Northern Ireland. Naval orders were to be concentrated on a few yards so that the others could take advantage of the economies of specialisation in merchant ship production.[66]

The Labour government largely accepted the Geddes recommendations and embodied them in the Shipbuilding Industry Act of 1967. A Shipbuilding Industry Board (SIB) was set up to encourage reorganisation and to dispense government financial assistance, which included £35.5 million for reorganisation and modernisation and £20 million to cover the losses of shipbuilders during the period of reorganisation. In addition £400 million was available through SIB to guarantee loans on favourable terms to shipowners who would order new ships from British yards. These measures coincided with the devaluation of the pound sterling in 1967, which aided exports, and between 1967 and 1969 the British order book rose from 1.1 million gt to 3.3 million gt. No privately owned industry had previously enjoyed such lavish state support, and some commentators worried that this investment was being wasted on an industry with only limited potential for future growth.[67]

On Clydeside five shipyards—John Brown, Charles Connell, Fairfield, Alexander Stephen and Yarrow—agreed to merge as Upper Clyde Shipbuilders (UCS), but only Yarrow, a warship builder, had a good order book and by 1969 the group was already in financial difficulties. On the lower Clyde a number of shipyards came together to form Scott Lithgow Ltd. and this group made plans to provide facilities for building supertankers and other large vessels. On the east coast of Scotland three small yards came together to form Robb Caledon. On the Tyne and the Tees a number of yards were linked to form Swan Hunter and Tyne Shipbuilders, which, like Scott Lithgow, was intending to build large vessels. The Wear, in N.E. England, produced two groups: Doxford and Austin and Pickersgill. About 40% of UK ship-building capacity remained outside these groups, including large firms such as Cammell Laird at Birkenhead, Vickers at Barrow, and Harland & Wolff at Belfast, the latter making big investments to build supertankers.[68]

The passion for mergers to provide the advantages of size was a common feature of British industrial policy during the 1960s, the belief being that economies of scale would provide greater efficiency. However, the Geddes committee and the government exaggerated the advantages of size and underestimated the difficulties of making mergers work.[69] The government provided new money, but most of the old shipbuilding management remained, as did most of the old labour problems. Nor did modernisation get very far. Of the seven yards in the Swan Hunter group, only two—Wallsend (for building supertankers) and Haverton Hill (for building oil/bulk/ore carriers)—had been modernised to any great extent and facilities at the other five yards were poor. Even the modernised Wallsend yard had only three hammerhead travelling

4. SD14-type cargo ship *City of Exeter*, originally built in 1974 by Austin & Pickersgill Ltd., Sunderland, for P&O as the *Strathdare*. The vessel was renamed *City of Exeter* in 1976 to enable Ellerman's City Line to carry out their share of a joint service with P&O. In 1980 the vessel was sold to a Greek owner.
(Photo: FotoFlite, Ashford, Kent)

cranes lifting 60 tons each to move prefabricated sections for supertanker construction, compared with a gantry crane lifting 225 tons at the Scott Lithgow supertanker building berth on the Clyde.[70] As early as 1970 it was becoming clear that too much government money was being used to stave off shipbuilding company insolvency, rather than being spent on modernisation and new facilities.

One of the aims of the post-Geddes reorganisation was to create shipyards producing a standard product meeting the needs of the world shipbuilding market. Only one British shipyard achieved this goal and its success had little to do with government intervention in the industry. In 1957 London and Overseas Freighters (LOF), the London Greek dry cargo and tanker shipping firm, bought a half share in Austin and Pickersgill (A&P), a shipbuilding firm on the Wear. LOF's connections with the worldwide Greek shipping

71

community were important in the mid-1960s for identifying a growing market for new general cargo ships to replace the Liberties and other war-built tonnage that were rapidly becoming obsolete. A&P came up with a shelter-deck design of 14,000 dwt (hence SD14) which would lend itself to series production and it was marketed to Greek and other owners.[71]

The first SD14, the *Nicola*, was completed in 1968 for Greek interests and the first for the British flag, the *Rupert de Larrinaga*, appeared in the following year. By the end of 1969 some sixty-two SD14s were on order from A&P, its associated yard Bartram & Sons, and a Greek shipyard which built them under licence.[72] Between 1968 and 1985 A&P and its licensees in the UK, Greece, Brazil and Argentina were to turn out no less than 207 SD14s. It was the most successful British ship design of the post-1945 period.[73] Matching the product with the market soon proved profitable for A&P. In 1969 the firm made a net profit before tax of £1,829,000. In the same year the Swan Hunter group had a loss of £3,449,000, while Cammell Laird (£7,974,000 loss) and Harland & Wolff (£8,330,000 loss) were in such dire financial condition that government intervention in their affairs was soon needed.[74] The success of A&P showed what could be done when the right product was aimed at the right market. It also showed, since A&P management had no special deal with the trade unions, that shipyard industrial relations, a favourite excuse for the failings of British shipbuilding, did not necessarily prevent a British shipyard from adapting successfully and profitably to the needs of the world shipbuilding market.[75]

In 1970 British shipbuilding was still producing outstanding vessels: the 253,000 dwt supertanker *Esso Northumbria* completed by Swan Hunter was the largest vessel ever built in the UK; the *Naess Enterprise* (134,400 dwt) produced by Scott Lithgow was the largest vessel ever built in Scotland; and the *Furness Bridge* (167,000 dwt) from Swan Hunter was the biggest OBO carrier ever built in the UK or Europe.[76] Nevertheless such vessels were few in number, and while total British output in the year (1,327,000 gross tons) was similar to that of West Germany and Sweden, it was far behind Japan's ten million gross tons. The most sobering statistic was that while UK shipowners received 913,000 gt of new ships from British shipyards in 1970, the best figure since 1965, they received 1,551,000 gt from foreign shipyards (compared with 187,000 gt in 1965).[77] Despite all the government money poured into British

Table 3.4: Ships Delivered to UK Owners, 1963–1973
(Thousands of gross tons)

Year	From UK shipyards	From foreign shipyards
1963	784	267
1964	590	290
1965	1020	187
1966	752	181
1967	444	671
1968	435	1620
1969	578	2250
1970	913	1551
1971	948	2466
1972	900	2623
1973	623	3236

Source: Chamber of Shipping of UK, *British Shipping Statistics*, 1968–69 and 1974.

shipbuilding its condition still seemed precarious, and it was soon to plunge back into crisis. (See Table 3.4.)

The Conservative government which came to power in 1970 claimed to be determined not to assist 'lame duck' companies and showed its opposition to state intervention by abolishing the Shipbuilding Industry Board. However, after Upper Clyde Shipbuilders became insolvent in 1971, the political consequences forced the government to act. The warship yard, Yarrow, was separated and regained its independence, the Clydebank yard of John Brown was sold to Marathon to build oil rigs, and the remainder of UCS was relaunched as a wholly owned government company, Govan Shipbuilders Ltd., in 1972. Financial crises at Cammell Laird and Harland & Wolff brought government intervention in those firms as well, with further expenditure of taxpayers' money.[78]

Thus by the end of 1972 government intervention in shipbuilding had moved from providing financial support to actual ownership of three firms. Perhaps to clarify its view, the government also commissioned in 1972 a study of the shipbuilding industry by consultants Booz-Allen and Hamilton. Their report was depressingly similar to that produced by the Geddes committee six

Table 3.5: Annual Building Capacity of Principal
UK Shipbuilders, 1974
(Thousands of gross tons)

Company	Locality	Capacity
Swan Hunter	Tyneside	500
Harland & Wolff	Belfast	250
Scott Lithgow	Greenock	200
Doxford & Sunderland	Wearside	200
Cammell Laird	Birkenhead	100
Govan Shipbuilders	Govan	100
Austin & Pickersgill	Wearside	100
Vickers*	Barrow	80
Robb-Caledon	Dundee/Leith	75
Appledore	Bideford	50
Vosper Thornycroft*	Southampton	50
Yarrow*	Scotstoun	10

*warship yards.
Source: K. Warren, *Steel, Ships and Men: Cammell Laird, 1824–1993*
(Liverpool, 1998), p. 296.

years earlier. The industry was still handicapped by weak management, poor marketing, outdated equipment and poor labour
relations. The shipbuilders had particularly complained of excessive
and unfair subsidised competition by European and Japanese builders, backed by their governments. However, while the report
recognised that nearly a third of the free world's demand for ships
was not open to international competition, that still left two-thirds
for British builders to seek to win. Anyway, British shipyards were
still too dependent on the home market, even though the majority
of British shipowners now preferred to obtain their new ships from
abroad. Between 1967 and mid-1972 British governments had
poured almost £160 million into shipbuilding, of which over £47
million had gone to Cammell Laird, Harland & Wolff and UCS/
Govan. Only 34% of the £160 million had gone on capital
expenditure; most of the rest went to cover losses. In return for this
large expenditure, government had seen little improvement in the
industry's economic performance.[79] (See also Table 3.5.)

Nationalisation and Privatisation

The world shipbuilding picture changed dramatically after 1974. The oil price rises of 1973–74 caused a collapse of the tanker market (about half the world shipbuilding market), with orders drying up and owners trying to cancel vessels already on order. World shipbuilding output peaked at thirty-six million gt in 1975, then fell by 60% to fourteen million gt in 1979.[80] The European and Japanese shipyards battled for the few remaining orders and tried to reduce their excess capacity. In 1978 the Japanese government decided to reduce the capacity of its national shipbuilding industry by 35% and set up the Shipbuilding Stabilisation Society, similar to Britain's interwar NSS, to oversee this reduction. The target was achieved by 1980, with little assistance from public funds, but Japanese building capacity was still well above world demand.[81] Some European shipbuilders chose even more radical solutions. Sweden, for example, decided to get out of large-scale merchant shipbuilding altogether. The principal shipyards were nationalised in 1977 and closed one by one between 1979 and 1986.[82] British yards might have hoped to avoid such massive reductions in capacity since they had not expanded their output in the boom years, but the world shipbuilding market collapse meant it would be very difficult to get any new orders for the ailing industry. Further government intervention seemed to be the only solution.

Thus the Labour government's nationalisation of the shipbuilding industry in 1977 was not something unique to Britain. Sweden did the same in 1977, while the Japanese government intervened in its shipbuilding industry in 1978. However, Labour's commitment to nationalisation had existed before the collapse of the tanker market and had been an election pledge when they came to power in 1974. It was political opposition that prevented the Aircraft and Shipbuilding Industries Act from being passed until March 1977. The Act set up a public corporation, British Shipbuilders (BS), which took control of seventeen merchant shipbuilding and composite yards, three warship building yards, five marine engine builders, and six ship repair companies, with a total workforce of 87,300, of whom 65,000 were engaged in shipbuilding. Harland & Wolff operated separately from BS, but was also state-owned.[83]

Nationalisation brought more bureaucracy to shipbuilding, and there was little attempt to integrate the shipyards. This would have been hard anyway because some were modernised and some not. Wage rates were, however, integrated at high levels, and there were assurances of no compulsory redundancies. Nevertheless it was soon clear that in the greatly depressed world market capacity would have to be cut, with large and expensive redundancies. Despite the desperate world situation BS yards were expected to compete against each other as well as foreign rivals for the few orders available. Government subsidies did something to reduce the wide gap between British prices and those of foreign yards, but during its whole existence BS never made a profit, its losses varying from a high of £160.9 million in 1984 to a low of £19.7 million in 1982.[84]

In 1977 the yards which had expanded facilities to get into the big ship business—Swan Hunter, Scott Lithgow and Harland & Wolff—produced their last supertankers.[85] Nevertheless BS continued to try to pick up orders for 'simple' ships like bulk carriers when high-value niche markets like cruise ships offered better prospects. Back in the 1950s British shipbuilders had been the world's principal builders of 'high class' ships like passenger liners and looked down on ships like tankers and bulk carriers which were in great demand. In the 1960s British shipbuilders belatedly tried to compete with foreign rivals in the 'simple' ship market, but those rivals had already perfected mass production shipbuilding facilities and the British found it hard to get market share. The British began to neglect the more sophisticated sectors of shipbuilding, such as container ships (of OCL's first six ships, five were built in West Germany and only one in Britain) and cruise ships (Cunard's first purpose-built cruise ships in the early 1970s came from Dutch and Danish yards). Even after the collapse of world shipbuilding in 1975, the British still concentrated on the 'simple' ship market, while a firm like Wartsila in Finland, with little past shipbuilding experience and comparatively little state support, built itself up as a leading world supplier of high-value cruise ships.[86] Work for the offshore oil and gas industry seemed to offer one way back into sophisticated construction, but even that was not without its perils. The loss-making merchant yards Scott Lithgow and Cammell Laird were to undertake work for the newly created Offshore Division of BS, building craft such as semi-submersible drilling rigs, but within a few years they were running up even bigger losses on this new work.[87]

By 1980 there were a few signs of revival in world shipbuilding, but less so for BS than others. British output of 244,000 gross tons in 1980 was the lowest since 1933 and the third lowest total ever recorded. BS had a loss of £109.9 million in 1980.[88] In 1982 it was noted that since nationalisation nine shipyards, thirty-eight building berths, three engine building works, and three ship repair companies had been closed by BS, with the loss of 20,700 jobs.[89] By 1983 the slight revival in world shipbuilding was over and Britain's Conservative government was tired of pouring money into shipbuilding. It passed the British Shipbuilders Act which gave it the power to privatise the remaining yards.[90] The building capacity of BS had been reduced to 600,000 tons by 1983, compared with the pre-nationalisation maximum capacity of 1.5-2 million gross tons, a figure which had been maintained for the previous fifty years or so.[91] Yet the cut in capacity was of little help to British shipbuilding. Not only was the world shipbuilding market still depressed, but new, low-cost shipbuilding nations were forcing their way into it. The most successful newcomer was South Korea, whose output was second only to Japan by the mid-1980s.[92]

The first shipyard to be privatised in 1984 was Scott Lithgow, the biggest loss maker in the BS group. It was sold to Trafalgar House, but was largely to cease production within a few years.[93] In July 1984 it was announced that the warship yards were to be privatised. However, Swan Hunter and Cammell Laird, mixed merchant and warship yards, were included with the principal warship yards of Yarrow, Vosper Thornycroft and Vickers. This meant that Swan Hunter and Cammell Laird were no longer eligible for EEC shipbuilding support funds as these funds were not available to purely warship yards. Unable to compete with the established warship builders and totally uncompetitive in merchant shipbuilding, the two firms seemed doomed, Cammell Laird being merged with Vickers in 1985.[94] By 1987 BS had only a handful of merchant shipbuilding yards and 8,600 workers, yet its loss for that year (£147.5 million) was the second highest recorded since nationalisation ten years earlier.[95] North East Shipbuilders (formed by a merger of Sunderland Shipbuilders and Austin and Pickersgill a few years earlier) closed in 1988, despite having very modern facilities such as the 'ship factory' at Pallion, and in the same year Govan shipyard was sold to Kvaerner of Norway. Harland & Wolff, state-owned but always separate from BS, was privatised in 1989 via

Table 3.6: British Merchant Shipbuilding, 1914–1990
(Thousands of gross tons; ships over 100 gt; wartime excluded)

Year	UK output	As % of world output
1914	1648	59.0
1919	1620	22.6
1920	2056	35.0
1921	1538	41.8
1922	1031	41.2
1923	646	39.2
1924	1440	64.1
1925	1085	49.5
1926	640	38.2
1927	1226	53.0
1928	1446	53.6
1929	1523	54.5
1930	1479	51.2
1931	502	31.1
1932	188	25.8
1933	133	27.2
1934	460	47.5
1935	499	38.3
1936	856	40.4
1937	921	34.2
1938	1030	34.0
1948	1176	51.1
1949	1267	40.5
1950	1325	37.9
1951	1341	36.8
1952	1303	29.6
1953	1317	25.8
1954	1409	26.8
1955	1474	27.7
1956	1383	20.7
1957	1414	16.6
1958	1402	15.1
1959	1373	15.7
1960	1331	16.0
1961	1192	15.0
1962	1073	12.8

Year	UK output	As % of world output
1963	928	10.9
1964	1043	10.2
1965	1073	8.8
1966	1084	7.6
1967	1298	8.2
1968	898	5.3
1969	1040	5.4
1970	1237	5.7
1971	1238	4.9
1972	1233	4.6
1973	1017	3.2
1974	1281	3.6
1975	1304	3.6
1976	1341	4.3
1977	1119	4.6
1978	813	5.2
1979	610	5.1
1980	243	1.7
1981	339	1.9
1982	528	3.0
1983	526	3.5
1984	190	1.0
1985	144	0.8
1986	237	1.5
1987	45	0.4
1988	31	0.2
1989	43	0.2
1990	28	0.1

Source: Lloyd's Register of Shipping, annual shipbuilding returns.

a management buy-out, supported by Fred Olsen of Norway. BS was finally wound up in late 1989. In the period 1979–89 it had absorbed no less than two billion pounds of public money and returned nothing but losses.[96] By 1990 British merchant shipbuilding had been reduced to a very small remnant of a once great industry, just as the world shipbuilding market finally began to recover.[97] (For decline in British share of world output see Table 3.6.)

The revival of British shipbuilding in the late 1960s associated with the post-Geddes reorganisation of the industry and lavish government financial aid had been faltering even before the world shipbuilding market collapse after 1975 dealt it a severe blow. The shipbuilding groups produced by mergers failed to achieve much integration and too much of the public money put into them went to cover their losses rather than invest in modern equipment and techniques. Labour's nationalisation of the shipbuilding industry in 1977 did little to improve the situation. One national, state-owned group seemed as incapable of co-ordinating change in the industry after 1977 as several regional, privately owned groups had been in the 1967–77 period. After 1977 building capacity was reduced in a piecemeal fashion, which only seemed to prolong the agony, with losses being recorded year after year. Perhaps a definite state-planned ending of merchant shipbuilding, as in Sweden, would have been quicker and cheaper than the slow wasting away between 1977 and 1989. The few merchant shipbuilding yards left in 1990 seemed to have no future and even the profitable warship yards became concerned about their prospects after the ending of the Cold War in 1989–91.

Shipbuilding: Paradigm of Decline?

The fall of the British shipbuilding industry from world leader in 1914 to the edge of extinction in 1990 has been a favourite subject of those scholars working on the economic decline of Britain during the twentieth century.[98] The two main schools of thought about the decline of British shipbuilding have been described as the 'institutional' and the 'entrepreneurial'. The first group of scholars take the view that certain aspects of the structure of the ship-building industry were key elements in its decline. These aspects include the small scale of British shipyards, the extent of family ownership, the craft structure of the work process, and the trade unions.[99] The entrepreneurial explanation prefers to concentrate on the failings of management, on why the shipbuilders failed to alter the structure of their industry by adapting it to change. Scholars favouring this viewpoint have drawn attention to the failure of management to make sufficient investment in modern construction facilities, to assess the changed nature of the world shipbuilding market after 1945 and to produce the type of ships the market required.[100] Consideration has also been given to the role of government in the industry's fortunes, considering whether it should have intervened earlier and whether its intervention helped change or delayed it.[101]

These various studies of the decline of British shipbuilding have emphasised certain aspects of a complex process which occurred over a considerable period. A general overview must seek to interweave these factors to understand how British shipbuilding failed to adapt to changing times in the world shipbuilding industry.

The industry structure cited by the 'institutionalists' as a prime cause of failure had arisen during the boom period of 1870–1914 when British shipbuilding achieved world dominance. It was admirably suited to the conditions of the period and, most of all, to dealing with the vagaries of the shipbuilding cycle. Shipyards tended to be small, with limited output, produced by gangs of craftsmen who had a variety of trade unions and were often allowed by management to arrange the work process as they wished, provided the ships were built. Shipyard owners did not invest much in capital equipment since production was labour intensive. When the market turned down, the workforce was simply laid off until better times returned.

The problem in the 1920s and 1930s was that it seemed that good times would never return. The governing reality was the collapse of world demand for ships and there was little the shipbuilders could do about that. Shipyard workers were laid off for years at a time and although some interest was taken in tankers and motorships, there was little money available to invest in new shipbuilding technology. Although the industry did much to reduce building capacity through the NSS, this did not amount to a reorganisation of the basic structure of the industry, nor did belated government assistance in the 1930s have a great impact. The problems of the interwar period were basically due to a failure of demand which changes in the industry's structure, its management and government assistance could not have altered to any great degree.

In 1945 British shipbuilding emerged from thirty years of war and depression facing a new world of full order books, but bitter memories of the past did not allow shipbuilders to adapt quickly enough to what soon became the longest shipbuilding boom in history. Despite some modernisation of facilities, the basic working structure of the industry was much the same in 1954 as in 1914 and with full order books most shipbuilders saw little reason to alter it in any major way. The shipbuilders completely failed to appreciate the fundamental changes in the world ship-building market that took place between 1945 and 1965. Mass-produced 'simple' ships like tankers and bulk carriers were required by a new class of global shipowners who were no longer linked to any particular shipbuilding nation, but ordered wherever their ships could be most cheaply produced. Nations like Japan and Sweden built new 'ship factories' to meet this rising demand, but British shipyards increasingly fell back on orders from the British merchant marine. After 1958 even this support began to disappear as British owners looked to foreign yards for cheap, modern ships.

This entrepreneurial failure to appreciate a vital new market had serious consequences in the early 1960s, when the rest of the shipbuilding world began to recover from the 1958–61 recession but British shipyards continued to decline. The government was at first reluctant to intervene, but after the Geddes report of 1966 it poured money into shipbuilding as the industry sought to restruc-ture. Although output improved in the late 1960s, it was probably too late to save the mass of the industry. Britain was at least a decade too late in re-equipping to meet the needs of the new world market. Even before the world shipbuilding market collapsed after 1975, the British government was having to move from financial incentives for restructuring to actual ownership of failing shipyards. Nationalisation in 1977 was just the logical conclusion of this process. Unfortunately the government spent too much time and money propping up a dying industry rather than overseeing its rationalisation: either closing it entirely like Sweden or concentrat-ing on niche shipbuilding markets.

It is clear that the crucial period for British shipbuilding was 1945–65 when by sticking to the old ways and the old markets the shipbuilders passed the lead in world shipbuilding to Japan, which provided the construction facilities and the products that the new global market required. The antiquated structure of British ship-building undoubtedly hindered adaptation to this change, but management showed little appreciation of the need to adapt at all. Could government have intervened to force a change? This was unlikely during the good years of 1945–58 and when it became obvious from 1959 that things were going wrong a fear of raising the ghosts of the 1930s depression made government reluctant to impose any rationalisation from above. By the time government and management felt compelled to act in the late 1960s, the opportunity had passed and no matter how the structure of the industry was altered, it seemed beyond help, even before the collapse of the world shipbuilding market after 1975.

4

Breaking with the Past
Ports 1918–1990

> To anyone making no more than a cursory study of our ports it must
> surely seem that had we set out to devise the most difficult way to
> work our ports we could not have succeeded better than the existing
> state of affairs in which labour has no regularity of employment, in
> which there is excessive fragmentation in cargo handling, unco-
> ordinated transport to and from ports, a multitude of clearing
> and forwarding agencies and, within all this, the inertia of long
> established custom.[1]

Thus did Sir Arthur Kirby, a leading figure in British transport,
characterise the state of the nation's ports in 1965. He was
not the first to express such sentiments about the situation
in British ports. In 1960 the Minister of Transport had told
Cabinet colleagues that the ports were 'neither adequate nor
efficient' and that 'both [the] management and equipment of
United Kingdom ports is [sic] old-fashioned and labour relations
bad'.[2] In 1962 the Cabinet was told that 'British shipping has the
disadvantage of being the largest user of British ports.'[3] Port
congestion in the autumn of 1964 was so bad it held up exports
and led to the setting up of a special docks committee by the
Cabinet.[4]

In January 1965 the Cabinet docks committee took the view that
'the movement of goods in and out of the country represented one of
the least efficient parts of our economy'. The basic problems were
'inadequate facilities, particularly for access to the docks; the
multiplicity of the different interests involved in the handling and
transport of goods; and the legacy of difficult labour relations

bequeathed by the past history of the docks.'[5] Later the Minister of Transport told the committee that

> ideally the docks problem will be solved only when cargoes are transported by road/rail and into ships under some form of co-ordinated control. There are too many middle men and what we must aim at is to cut out unnecessary links in the chain from the manufacturer to the ship's hold.[6]

The intense exasperation with the state of the British port transport industry was nothing new in the first half of the 1960s. It was a feeling that had been growing since the end of the Second World War.[7] However, a veritable revolution in cargo handling which had been gathering pace since the late 1950s now added to domestic pressures for changes in port facilities, port administration and port labour.[8] The unit load—the container—was to revolutionise cargo handling, whether it was lifted on and off a ship (lo-lo) or towed on and off by a motor vehicle (roll on, roll off, ro-ro). Faced with the challenge of unit load traffic, British ports could no longer cling to a system of working created in the Victorian period.

Under the old system cargo was laboriously loaded and unloaded from a ship's hold in small batches. Then it was often stored or sorted in a warehouse before being distributed by the inland transport system. The port acted not so much as a conduit for trade but as a potential bottleneck, where action by any of the wide variety of people handling the break-bulk cargo could delay or disrupt the transport process.

Unit load cargo traffic offered a revolutionary alternative to the old break-bulk system of handling general cargo. The use of a container was intended to cut out almost all unnecessary links in the chain of transport between manufacturer and overseas customer. The cargo was loaded ('stuffed' in the new jargon) into the container at the factory, or an inland depot which brought together ('grouped') potential container cargoes. Then, provided customs and other documents were in order, there was no need to open the container until the cargo was removed ('stripped') on arrival at the customer. The new system would make a large number of port workers, including cargo agents, warehousemen and dockers, redundant. Only a handful of men were needed to load and unload containers from ships, and even they would not be required when containers rolled on and off vessels on motor vehicles. The port, and the ship, were now just stages in an integrated transport process promising the uninterrupted movement of cargo from seller to buyer.[9]

The unit load revolution—and the related postwar changes in the handling of bulk cargoes such as oil, iron ore and grain—provided a massive challenge to the existing British port transport system in the early 1960s. Britain had too many port authorities, with inadequate resources for financing the capital investment needed for the new methods of cargo handling. Dock labour was still largely casual, under the control of a multitude of mostly small employers, and working practices often differed widely from port to port. The industry was fundamentally fragmented and old-fashioned. Change and adaptation were unlikely to come from within, so the government felt compelled to take a hand.

First came the official inquiries to establish the parameters of the problem. Lord Rochdale's inquiry into the major ports of Great Britain reported in 1962. It called for the government to set up a national body to supervise port development, to reduce the number of port authorities by amalgamation, and to advise on the allocation of government loans for construction of new port facilities.[10] Lord Devlin's inquiry into dock labour delivered its report in 1965 and recommended the ending of casual employment in the ports. In return for this, the dockers were to agree to new working practices which would permit the efficient use of the new cargo handling systems.[11]

After 1965 the British port transport industry was to be transformed. This transformation was not without its problems, chiefly in terms of industrial conflict, but it represented adaptation to fundamental changes in cargo handling technology. However, before detailing this transformation it is necessary to outline the old ports system and the first efforts made to reform it.

The Old Ports System

First it must be made clear that the old ports system was anything but systematic. Its principal characteristic was diversity, with port administration, facilities and work practices varying from port to port. However, the two common features of British ports in the Victorian and Edwardian periods were the massive expansion of port facilities and the establishment of the casual labour system for dockers.

The nineteenth century and the early twentieth century, up to the First World War, was the great period of expansion in the history of British ports.[12] Seaborne trade grew year after year, the number of vessels using ports increased, and the ships themselves grew in size, particularly after the coming of the iron steamer, demanding ever larger and deeper docks. The great dock systems of London and Liverpool were the finest achievements of the dock engineer, but all around the coast existing ports were being improved and expanded while new ports were created, often by railway companies to handle the booming coal export trade.[13] Manchester was a completely new port established by the local cotton interests, while an existing port such as Grimsby was so altered by an enterprising railway company that it might rank as a new creation.[14]

There was no shortage of new facilities to match the expanding trade, but by 1900 certain changes were becoming clear. Trade was becoming increasingly concentrated at the larger ports, such as London and Liverpool, and at those ports new docks and quays were being built away from the inner city docks, at sites with space for bigger and deeper berths, such as Tilbury on the Thames estuary. Also, with so many ports in competition and expanding their facilities, it was probable that if trade expansion faltered there would be serious over-capacity in the British ports industry.

If expansion was a feature common to nearly all ports, port authorities overseeing those changes showed considerable diversity. Britain had over 300 ports and of these perhaps one hundred were of commercial significance. Some were run by municipal authorities and others by private companies, while others were controlled by public trusts. During the Victorian period the public trust emerged as the favoured model of port administration, following the example of the Mersey Docks and Harbour Board set up in 1858 to run the docks of Liverpool and Birkenhead.[15] These were non-profit making bodies which paid for port improvements by taking out long-term loans, the interest on which was paid from port dues. When private companies could no longer run Bristol docks effectively, the city council took them over, but when the private dock companies in London were on the verge of collapse, it was a public trust, the Port of London Authority, which took them over in 1909.[16]

One curiosity of British port authorities was that very few of them controlled the labour working in their docks. They provided the docks, quays, warehouses, cranes, etc., but the men working them, and labouring on the ships, were usually provided by private employers. In many ways this suited the shipowners, who feared being at the mercy of monopolistic port authorities, but it fragmented the control of working practices within the ports. Similarly, the boards of the port authorities were often dominated by user interest groups, such as merchants and shipowners, who put their own welfare before that of the port as a whole. Also, port authorities were often obsessed by local rivalries, such as those between Hull and Grimsby or Liverpool and Manchester, and there was no question of a national ports policy which transcended local concerns.

Victorian technical innovations such as hydraulic cranes were important, but loading and discharging ships still remained a labour-intensive business. As trade grew, so did the demand for dockers. Some of the early London dock companies had tried to keep permanent staffs, but the volatile nature of demand for dockers soon made a system of casual labour seem preferable.[17] Contrary winds might keep sailing vessels out of port for days. Then, when the wind changed, the ships all came in together, all demanding labour to unload them. Trades such as timber were highly seasonal, with deal porters inactive during the winter, but busy once the ice broke on the Baltic and the St Lawrence.[18] With the coming of the steam-ship a rapid turn-round in port was essential to maximise the use of a considerable capital investment. Labour had to be available immediately, and, although some shipowners later set up their own stevedore companies to work aboard ship, casual dock labour was seen as essential for the successful working of the ports.

Most dock work was unskilled, so any able-bodied man could be a docker. Each day men would assemble outside the dock gates for the 'call'. The employers chose the number of men needed for the day's work and the others were sent home. Even those given work might only be employed for half a day at a time. The life of most dockers was notoriously insecure and impoverished, but the men compensated with the formidable solidarity of dockland communities, and, when in work, their gangs main-tained rigid demarcation rules and stretched out work as long as possible.

Casualism was believed to be the only way to match supply and demand in dock work, but its deleterious effects were not solely on the workers' side. Most employers of dockers were small middle-men, offering their services to the shipowners. These small employers found it difficult to unite even within ports let alone on a national basis, and this undermined their bargaining power after the rise of docker trade unions from the 1880s onwards. Casualism was common to nearly all ports, but wage rates and working practices could differ widely from port to port and within different sections of the same port.[19]

Although trade unionism was making progress among dockers by 1870, the traditional turning point for this type of 'new unionism' is said to be the London dock strike of 1889 and the struggle for the 'Dockers' Tanner'.[20] It is interesting to note that the apparent success of the dockers provoked a response not from the port authorities or the port employers, both of whom lacked national organisations, but from the shipowners, who set up the Shipping Federation in 1890. Its primary purpose was to co-ordinate strike-breaking efforts around the country against the dockers' union and Havelock Wilson's union of seamen.[21] The Shipping Federation had some success against the dockers and the struggle was not renewed in earnest until 1911 when Ben Tillett took the initiative in setting up the National Transport Workers' Federation. The great industrial struggles of 1911–14 brought some improvement for dockers, but more was achieved during the First World War, when for the first time dockers found both government and employers anxious to consult them.

One objective of the docker trade unionists was the setting up of registration schemes. Once employers agreed to recruit only from a pool of registered dockers, this would prevent them bringing in labour off the streets to undercut union men. The first docker registration scheme had been introduced at Liverpool in 1912, and similar schemes were set up at other ports during the Great War.[22] Dockers could look forward to the coming of peace with some hope that their conditions might be improved.

Attempts at Reform, 1918–1960

Building on progress made during the First World War, dockers in 1919 made their first claim for a national wage rate, in place of the various rates within ports and between ports. The claim was for sixteen shillings per day, for a payment to 'maintain' men who were available to work but not hired at the daily call, and for a standard working week of forty-four hours. The leading figure on the trade union side was Ernest Bevin and his successful handling of the claim was to make him a national figure, and eventually led to his leadership of the Transport and General Workers' Union (TGWU), which was set up in 1922.[23]

Bevin decided to pursue the claim through the new machinery of the Industrial Courts Act instead of by strike action. A court of inquiry was set up under Lord Shaw of Dunfermline. Before the court Bevin made an eloquent condemnation of casual dock labour, earning him the nickname 'the Dockers' KC', and the Shaw report and award of 1920 seemed to be a great victory for the dockers.[24] Shaw conceded sixteen shillings per day and recommended more docker registration schemes, the provision of maintenance money, and payment of wages by the week instead of daily. The report called for a National Joint Council (NJC) for port transport to be established with full bargaining machinery at port level. Finally, it proposed that the NJC deal with any points arising from the report which could not be ratified in direct negotiations.

The NJC and local port committees were set up for collective bargaining between dockers and employers. This compelled the latter to set up their own national organisation, the National Association of Port Employers. This body was supposed to be independent of the Shipping Federation, but in fact it came to include shipowners as well. (The port authorities had set up their own national association in 1917.) The monetary element of the Shaw award was sanctioned by a national agreement.[25] However, much of the Shaw award was a dead letter as early as the mid-1920s. The fall in levels of seaborne trade meant problems in the ports and wages soon fell to ten shillings per day, not to return to the Shaw level until the Second World War. The Shaw report had set out a goal of decasualisation in the docks which it would take more than forty years to achieve.

The main progress made by the dockers in the interwar period related to registration. By the start of the 1930s thirty-one major ports had docker registration schemes, and twenty-five of these were jointly controlled by employers and dockers. The schemes meant that registered dockers were given priority in the allocation of work. The problem was that by the early 1930s work was a scarce commodity even for registered dockers, and unemployment reached 30–40% among dockers in the worst years of the depression. Registration also revealed for the first time a feature of docker behaviour that was to become common in later years. While most trade unionists saw registration schemes as progressive, some dockers objected to them as being ways employers could impose discipline and curb the dockers' independence.[26]

If port employees started the interwar period with high hopes that were soon to be dashed, the port authorities themselves were to have a similar experience. As in other areas of British economic life, the ports hoped to return to prewar conditions and continue the port expansion that had been almost continuous since the Victorian period. The Port of London Authority (PLA) opened the new King George V Dock in 1921, making the Royal group of docks the largest in the world. The PLA also carried out new works at the Surrey Docks and Tilbury up to 1930. At Liverpool the new Gladstone Dock was opened in 1927. At Southampton, between 1927 and 1934, the new dock extension (in fact a deep-water quay) was built and the King George V Graving Dock, the largest in the world, was opened.[27]

Such new construction was impressive, but it was already clear by the mid-1920s that the volume of traffic at British ports had fallen and showed little sign of reviving. Particularly hard hit were the coastal trade and the coal export trade, which showed considerable drops compared to prewar traffic, but world trade in general had declined, hitting even great ports such as London and Liverpool. South Wales coal ports such as Cardiff, Barry and Penarth suffered badly (Penarth dock was closed), as did coal ports in Scotland and N.E. England. The drop in coal exports also hit the trade of ports such as Goole and Grimsby.[28]

Nevertheless, when the Royal Commission on Transport presented an overview of British ports in its 1930 final report it tried to present a positive picture.[29] Britain had around 330 ports, employing 100,000 people. Non-profit making local commissions or trusts, established under statutory authority, ran 110 ports, seventy were run by municipal authorities, fifty by railway companies, and one hundred by harbour companies or individuals. The Dock and Harbour Authorities Association consisted of forty-seven undertakings whose port facilities handled over 70% of British port traffic. Another 25% of such traffic was handled by railway-owned ports.

The commission was in no doubt which was the best type of port authority: 'The efficiency of many of the undertakings controlled by these public trusts cannot be denied.' The PLA, the Mersey Docks and Harbour Board (MDHB) and the Clyde Navigation Trust were the great examples of 'statutory authorities which have done a very great deal to provide the most modern and convenient accommodation for shipping both ocean and coastwise'. However, the commission also praised the work of municipal port authorities such as Bristol, railway companies such as the Southern Railway at Southampton and hybrids like Manchester docks, run by a private company, the Manchester Ship Canal Company, but with Manchester Corporation having a majority of the directors.

Nevertheless the commission had to admit that the ports faced problems. The volume of world seaborne trade was still below the level of 1914, and some British ports, especially the smaller ones, had 'been allowed to fall into decay'. However, during the 1920s continental ports such as Rotterdam and Hamburg had prospered and their success could not be solely blamed on subsidies from local or central government. Perhaps many British ports were simply getting too small for modern ships. Certainly the commission noted that only twelve British ports could accommodate large ocean liners and that 'the bulk of our imports and exports go through those twelve ports'.

Some witnesses had blamed the decline of the smaller British ports on the policies of the railway companies, who were said to offer freight rates that undercut coastal shipping and also provided inferior berths for such vessels at railway ports. The companies were also said to obstruct road access to ports. While accepting that it was 'undesirable that one form of transport should own docks and harbours to which access is essential to other means of transport', the commission felt the railway companies were not guilty and should not lose control of their ports. Most railway ports were for coal exports or passenger traffic. Only two, Hull and Southampton, were important general ports, and the commission noted of Southampton that 'its wonderful development in recent years has been largely due to the enterprise of the London & South Western (now Southern) Railway'.

While not ready to strip the railway companies of their ports, the commission reiterated its opinion that 'the best kind of authority to own docks and harbours is a public trust'. Yet even with regard to trusts the commission had a reservation: 'it would appear to be greatly to the public interest that such trusts should not be confined to single ports, but should control all the harbours in a particular district.' This was the germ of the idea later put forward by the 1962 Rochdale report that ports should be linked in estuarial groups under a single authority.

If the picture of British ports in the interwar years is generally one of stagnation in trade and only limited new works, the period did see one major change, namely the growth in port facilities to handle oil. Before 1914 crude oil was largely refined at the place of production and refined products were shipped to markets like Britain. Demand was at first small, so most major British ports only offered an oil jetty where cargoes could be landed and stored before distribution. Thames Haven, sited well down the Thames estuary by order of the PLA, was the largest of such depots, but others included Fawley on the Solent. After the Great War the demand for oil products grew rapidly and so ports had to offer increased facilities for tankers. Further impetus to development was given by the establishment of oil refineries in Britain.

Former coal docks became tanker terminals when the Anglo-Persian Oil Company (later BP) opened refineries near Swansea (1922) and at Grangemouth (1924). In 1923 a dock specifically built for tankers was opened at Avonmouth. The previous year a

Table 4.1: Ports of the United Kingdom arranged in order of net registered tonnage of ships arriving with cargo and in ballast, foreign and coastwise, annual average, 1936–1938 inclusive (Thousand tons)

London	30965
Liverpool	17467
Southampton	13366
Glasgow (including Greenock)	9899
Newcastle	9066
Belfast	7561
Cardiff	7269
Hull	6178
Plymouth	5908
Manchester	3941
Bristol	3782
Swansea	3464
Middlesbrough	3135
Newport	2344
Grimsby (and Immingham)	1969

Source: J. Bird, The Major Seaports of the United Kingdom (London, 1963), p. 24.

Table 4.2: Ports of the United Kingdom arranged in order of the value of their foreign trade, imports, exports and exports of imported merchandise, 1936–1938 inclusive
(£ thousand)

London	556,217
Liverpool	320,074
Hull	89,059
Southampton	66,728
Manchester	62,870
Glasgow (including Greenock)	60,279
Bristol	31,534
Newcastle	28,569
Harwich	27,422
Swansea	21,348
Grimsby (and Immingham)	18,997
Leith	16,694
Cardiff	15,646
Goole	14,376
Belfast	13,888
Dover	12,475

Source: Bird, p. 26.

similar dock had been built at Stanlow, after the Manchester port authority refused to allow an oil berth inside the city. Shell-Mex opened a refinery at Stanlow in 1933.[30] All these oil facilities were part of or linked to pre-existing ports. Demand for oil did not yet justify building a major new port devoted solely to oil, as Milford Haven would be later. Indeed no major new port was built in Britain between the opening of Manchester in 1894 and the inception of Milford Haven in 1957. (For port traffic in the late 1930s see Tables 4.1 and 4.2.)

At the outbreak of the Second World War it was not expected that Britain would be short of port capacity, but the decision in September 1940 to reduce the use of south coast ports and of east coast ports south of the Humber because of the danger from enemy air attacks meant a large transfer of shipping to the west coast of Britain. With London handling only about a quarter of its usual traffic, a heavy burden was placed on west coast ports, particularly those around the Mersey and the Clyde. By December 1940 port congestion was considerable on the west coast, with delays in port as great a threat to the efficient functioning of British shipping as attacks by U-boats at sea. As part of the solution to this problem the government established what Churchill called 'port dictators' on the Clyde and the Mersey. Robert Letch, the port director appointed on the Clyde, was particularly successful at ending port congestion and his methods were followed elsewhere. By the summer of 1941 the ports situation had improved considerably. Serious port congestion did not re-occur, although London and other east and south coast ports were not fully reopened until the summer of 1944.[31]

If shipping had to be redirected to west coast ports, so would dockers, and wartime relations with that group of workers were smoothed by Churchill's appointment of Ernest Bevin as Minister of Labour in the summer of 1940. In June 1940 Bevin made the registration of dockers compulsory and made them subject to transfer from port to port if required. The port congestion during the winter of 1940–41 made it essential that dockers should be closely controlled, but they would never accept such control if it was exercised solely by the employers. Bevin persuaded the dockers to accept control by the Clyde and the Mersey port directors set up by the government, and in return the casual labour system was in effect ended. Dockers had to be available for work, but if none was provided they would receive a weekly minimum wage. The scheme began on the Clyde and the Mersey in March 1941. In September of that year it was extended to all ports and was run by the National Dock Labour Corporation. After 1941 the ports generally worked well, although absenteeism and strikes among dockers began to increase as victory came nearer.[32]

The end of the Second World War and the election of a Labour government committed to wide-ranging nationalisation caused some alarm among port authorities. There were fears that they might not recover operational control from the Ministry of War Transport and that ports would remain under government control. In the immediate postwar years this did not happen: operational control returned to the port authorities, and although the Ministry of Transport retained residual powers in relation to the ports, it chose to remain in the background.[33]

Nevertheless the Labour government was committed to an integrated national transport policy, at least as far as inland transport was concerned. The Transport Act of 1947 nationalised a number of transport systems, including the railways and the canals.

5. Break-bulk cargo handling: unloading oranges from the *Dunbar Castle*
at South West India Dock, London, in 1945.
(Photo: courtesy of Museum in Docklands, PLA Collection)

Since railway and canal ports amounted to a third of Britain's port
capacity this in fact amounted to quite a large-scale taking of ports
into public ownership. These nationalised ports were to be run by a
division of the British Transport Commission (BTC). Furthermore,
section 66 of the 1947 Act gave BTC powers to amalgamate port

authorities into estuarial groups (including non-nationalised ports), to reconstitute the internal organisation of port authorities, and to prepare a national ports plan. These powers seemed to pose a threat to the freedom of the non-nationalised port authorities.[34]

Yet before any further changes in administration could be made, the ports first needed to have wartime damage repaired. It proved a slow process. There was no question of wholesale rebuilding and modernisation. Piecemeal improvement was the order of the day and the government kept a tight rein on public money provided to achieve even that. Some £13.5 million was to be invested in the ports in 1949, yet the port of Liverpool alone—'the most congested port in the country'—had suffered war damage of over £13 million. In Hull and Southampton two-thirds of the war damage was still awaiting repair. By 1950, even after five years of peace, Britain had still failed to equip itself with a single port comprehensively up to date in layout and equipment.[35]

As noted earlier, the 1930 Royal Commission on Transport had already suggested amalgamation of port authorities into estuarial groups, and Lord Cooper's 1945 inquiry into the Clyde ports made similar recommendations. Between 1948 and 1950 BTC carried out a survey of British trade harbours with a view to organising amalgamations, e.g. on Tyneside, and reconstituting port authorities such as the PLA to give greater worker representation. The trade harbours report was published in 1951, but the return to power of the Conservatives saved the port authorities from change. The Transport Act of 1953 abolished section 66 and so stripped the BTC of its powers to pursue a national ports policy.[36]

The ports outside BTC had preserved their autonomy, but were they functioning efficiently? Time and money was spent on repairing war damage, but relatively few new facilities were opened, especially in the impoverished smaller ports. Seaborne trade began to increase and government was determined to boost exports, but it soon became clear that the ports were not working well. Immediate postwar problems might be put down to problems of adjustment to peacetime working, but by 1950 turn-round times for ships using British ports were worse than those achieved in the late 1930s. The turn-round problem was to trouble port authorities throughout the 1950s.[37]

One solution to the problem seemed to be increasing mechanization in the ports and American methods, first seen during the war, were investigated. It was not yet the age of the container, but innovations such as mobile cranes, fork lift trucks and moving cargo on pallets promised considerable productivity gains. The Ministry of Transport set up an advisory committee on port mechanisation, but obstacles to its implementation were still considerable in the 1950s. The dockers were largely hostile, port authorities did not have the money to invest in new equipment, and the layout of many ports was so congested that such machines could not be employed to the best advantage.[38]

Some commentators felt that the mechanisation of the ports was hindered by the great number and variety of port authorities. This was true even among the nationalised ports, especially after their control was split in 1962 between three bodies: the British Transport Docks Board, running ports on Humberside, in South Wales and at Southampton; the British Railways Board, which ran ferry ports such as Holyhead, Folkestone and Parkeston Quay at Harwich; and the British Waterways Board, with small ports such as Sharpness and Gloucester. Other commentators saw the multiplicity of ports as a spur to competition, but it also led to a waste of capital resources and made overall national port policy impossible. However, it seemed to the general public that the chief cause of problems in the docks was not too many ports or the lack of new equipment, but rather the militancy of dock labour.[39]

After the end of the Second World War the Labour government continued the 1941 dock labour scheme while dockers and their employers negotiated a peacetime version. However, such negotiations proved slow and difficult, so finally the government forced the two sides to accept the 1947 dock labour scheme, which was very similar to the wartime one. The scheme originally applied to 78,500 dockers in eighty-four ports. It had five main features:

1. The scheme was to be administered by the National Dock Labour Board (NDLB), with local boards in the ports. Employers and dockers were to be equally represented on the boards, establishing a system of joint control.
2. All port employers and dockers were to be registered.
3. Registered employers could engage only registered workers as dock labourers, thus creating a closed shop.
4. Any registered daily worker, when not given employment under the scheme, went into a reserve pool under the control of the Board and received attendance money. In 1947 only 12% of

dockers were permanent (weekly) workers, but it was hoped the scheme would eventually increase their number.

5. The NDLB (which came under the Ministry of Labour not the Ministry of Transport) was also to look after the training, welfare, recruitment, discipline and discharge of dockers.[40]

Thus when Ernest Bevin died in 1951 it seemed that all he had fought for at the Shaw enquiry of 1920 had finally been achieved. The worst features of casualism seemed to have been dealt with —dockers had work or maintenance—and there were high hopes that the growth in permanent jobs would end casualism altogether. However, if it was thought that the 1947 scheme would bring peace to the docks, the reality turned out to be rather different. In 1947 there were seventy-seven stoppages in the docks with a total of 132,470 days lost; in 1951 fifty-nine stoppages with 339,878 days lost; and in 1955 112 stoppages with 693,209 days lost. Dockers had become perhaps the most strike-prone group among British workers.[41]

The spate of strikes led to a number of official inquiries. The Leggett report of 1951 put the blame for the industrial unrest on the 1947 scheme. Its benefits were disguised because the postwar period had turned out to be one of growing trade and almost full employment, while the obligations and discipline of the scheme irritated men used to the prewar freedom to pick and choose a job. Also the vital importance of exports at this time allowed militants, including Communists, to exploit the situation, even under a Labour government. None of the stoppages was made official by the dockers' unions.[42]

In 1955 Lord Devlin first became involved with the industrial relations problems of the ports. He headed a committee of inquiry into the working of the 1947 scheme. The port employers made a strong plea for an end to joint control of the scheme, but Devlin was unsympathetic. The view of the committee was that there was little wrong with the scheme. It was up to both dockers and employers to make it work, and the employers in particular had been failing to make the effort.[43]

The great area of growth in the port industry during the 1950s was in the petroleum trade, whose separate terminals employed comparatively few workers and were largely immune to industrial action. Increasing political problems abroad made it expedient for oil companies to transfer refining from producer to consumer countries. Between 1938 and 1957 the capacity of Britain's oil refining industry, then the largest in Europe, grew from 2.5 million tons per annum to 31 million tons per annum. Esso opened new facilities at Fawley in 1951, making it the largest refinery in Europe; British Petroleum opened a new refinery on the Isle of Grain in Kent in 1953; and Mobil opened one at Coryton on the Thames in 1954. In 1956 it was decided to build a major new, deep-water oil port at Milford Haven in S.W. Wales, with a new refinery there and a pipeline to the older refinery near Swansea. A similar scheme in Scotland involved a deep-water terminal at Finnart and a pipeline to the Grangemouth refinery. By 1963 Britain had nineteen oil terminals, but only six were capable of taking tankers of 50,000 dwt or more and only two of these, Finnart and Milford Haven, could handle the new big tankers of 100,000 dwt.[44]

During the 1950s seaborne trade grew steadily from year to year, but the problems of Britain's ports remained, with little improvement in turn-round times. The employers were still unhappy about

Table 4.3: Ports of the United Kingdom arranged in order of net registered tonnage of ships arriving with cargo and in ballast, foreign and coastwise, annual average, 1958–1960 inclusive (Thousand tons)

London	42279
Southampton	24816
Liverpool	19743
Glasgow (including Greenock)	9499
Manchester	8118
Newcastle	7555
Belfast	7448
Bristol	6017
Hull	5919
Dover	5694
Middlesbrough	5090
Swansea	4977
Harwich	3736
Cardiff	3336
Grimsby (and Immingham)	3008

Source: Bird, p.22.

Table 4.4: Ports of the United Kingdom arranged in order of the
value of their foreign trade, imports, exports and exports of
imported merchandise, 1958–1960 inclusive
(£ thousand)

London	2,605,555
Liverpool	1,656,475
Hull	411,045
Manchester	386,564
Southampton	310,458
Glasgow (including Greenock)	295,244
Bristol	194,463
Harwich	124,683
Swansea	112,114
Dover	109,813
Newcastle	106,624
Middlesbrough	83,832
Grimsby (and Immingham)	71,160
Belfast	66,716
Goole	66,522

Source: Bird, p.23.

joint control, while dockers were dissatisfied with the working of
the scheme. It had made casualism less painful, but it had only
limited success in increasing the number of permanent workers.
Even by the end of the 1950s the percentage of dockers in
permanent employment had only risen from 12% in 1947 to 23%
in 1959.[45] Dockers remained resentful of the disciplinary elements
of the scheme and were hostile to most kinds of mechanisation in
the ports. (For port traffic in the late 1950s see Tables 4.3 and 4.4.)

Given their feelings about mechanisation, it can be understood
why in 1960 British dockers were shocked by the news from the
United States. By the so-called West Coast agreement the long-
shoremen (dockers) in Pacific coast US ports had 'sold the rule book'
in return for $5 million compensation and agreed to new working
practices in new kinds of mechanical cargo handling involving unit
loads. How soon would it be before such new cargo handling
systems reached Britain, and what would be the reactions of both
port authorities and dockers' unions to them?[46]

The Rochdale Report (1962) and Containerisation

If the start of the container revolution caused the US West Coast agreement of 1960, it was the other great change in cargo handling since 1945 that influenced the British government when it reviewed the situation in British ports in the same year. This change was the ever-increasing size of bulk cargoes, such as oil, iron ore and grain, and the need for modern harbour facilities to handle them and the huge vessels in which they arrived. In December 1960 the economic policy committee of the Cabinet expressed concern that because bulk cargo handling facilities at continental ports such as Rotterdam were much superior to those at British ports large bulk vessels would go there and only part cargoes would go on to Britain in smaller tonnage, with a consequent loss of revenue to British ports. This concern led the government in early 1961 to appoint a committee under Lord Rochdale to examine the adequacy and efficiency of the major ports of Great Britain.[47]

The Rochdale committee decided to look at fifteen major British ports, chosen on the basis of their foreign dry cargo trade: London, Southampton, Bristol, Newport, Cardiff, Swansea, Liverpool, Manchester, Glasgow, Grangemouth, Leith, Newcastle, Middlesbrough, Hull and Immingham. Between them these ports handled about 70% of Britain's imports and exports and their share of coastal traffic was almost as high. Surveying these ports led the Rochdale committee to take a critical view of the port transport industry in its 1962 report, but the committee took the view that 'the industry has developed piecemeal in ways that may have met the requirements of the time, but which are inappropriate to today's rapidly changing conditions'.[48]

Once it had rejected the idea of the complete nationalisation of the ports, one of the Rochdale committee's first and most important proposals was for the creation of some central organisation to undertake national planning and co-ordination of ports policy, in effect a non-operational national ports authority. This body would advise, urge and in the last resort compel port authorities towards greater efficiency, particularly through more investment in modern facilities. Among other things, the authority would seek to carry through 'a national plan of port development' by encouraging investment at some ports and discouraging it at others.[49]

After surveying the major British ports, Rochdale felt there was no need for new ports, save some iron ore and oil terminals. Indeed the ports had an excess of old-fashioned capacity such as coal docks. What were lacking were modern deep-water berths, not just for bulk cargoes, but also for general cargo. In Britain 'no single additional deep water berth for general cargo has been started since the 1930s, apart from those now nearing completion at Teesport'.[50]

The lack of such facilities was highlighted when the Rochdale committee visited Antwerp, Rotterdam and Hamburg. All these continental ports had made major investments in new facilities to handle both bulk and general cargoes and development was continuing. The new Europoort project at Rotterdam was to cost £70 million, excluding private investment in installations. In contrast the total capital investment by all major British ports since 1945 came to only £150 million. Most of this had gone on repairs and minor works, with only the Langton/Canada dock scheme at Liverpool costing as much as £10 million. The continental ports were well-equipped with deep-water berths. Antwerp alone had well over twice as many berths with a depth of over thirty-five feet as all the major British ports put together. Indeed only five British ports had any berths of that depth at all.[51]

New development was clearly needed at British ports, but the Rochdale committee wanted it to be concentrated at a few selected ports on the south and east coasts of Britain, namely Southampton, London (Tilbury), Middlesbrough (Teesport) and Leith. Although the committee stressed its interest in oceanic trade, this choice of ports seems to reflect a consciousness, at a time when the country was making its first (abortive) attempt to join the Common Market, that trade with Europe was becoming ever more important to Britain. The committee openly disapproved of major developments planned at Liverpool, still Britain's second most important port, and Bristol. While conscious of the growing importance of the ports of the Stour and Orwell estuaries—Ipswich, Harwich and Felixstowe (known collectively as the 'Haven Ports')—the committee still preferred development in that area to be concentrated at Tilbury in the port of London.[52]

To finance deep-water berths and other developments in the ports, Rochdale suggested that the government, advised by the new national ports authority, should provide loans. In general, however, ports were to be left to function as private commercial entities and not receive local or central government subsidies as was the case with a number of continental ports. However, Rochdale was aware that other new developments in cargo handling—especially the unit load—might require even greater capital investment in British ports if they were to compete with foreign rivals.[53]

Containers were already being carried on the short sea route between Liverpool and Belfast, while in their roll on, roll off (ro-ro) variant there were shipping services carrying them between Tilbury and the continent and between Preston and Northern Ireland. Yet Rochdale observed: 'It is a regrettable fact that British ports, and probably British shipowners, have been less forward-looking than some overseas interests in developing systems for the carriage of general cargo in containers.' The port of New York was spending $275 million on container facilities. Would British ports be able to match such massive capital investment?[54]

Like the Royal Commission on Transport back in 1930, the Rochdale committee pressed for the amalgamation of port authorities into estuarial groups under one controlling body. Any ports which were not financially viable were to be closed rather than subsidised by more profitable ports in the group. The new national ports authority would oversee these amalgamations, and it was also to reform the administrative organisation of port authorities, many of whose governing statutes had been unchanged since the nineteenth century. To aid its planning activities, the authority was to collect better port statistics and persuade port authorities to adopt standard financial accounting procedures. Additionally, Rochdale called for the complete decasualisation of dock labour and for improved road access to ports.[55]

Even before the Rochdale report was published, the government had agreed to set up the national ports authority it suggested. This body, the National Ports Council (NPC), began on a non-statutory basis in 1963 and received statutory authority by the Harbours Act 1964. Section 9 of that Act stipulated that all proposed port developments costing more than £500,000 (£1 million from 1971) were to be submitted for approval to the Minister of Transport, who would take advice from the NPC. While section 11 of the Act permitted the government to make loans to finance such projects, the advice of the NPC was to be obtained before approval was given. During the first ten years of its existence 170 port development schemes, with a total estimated cost of £125 million, were referred to the NPC for consideration.[56]

The work of the NPC will be examined in a later section, and consideration will now be given to how far Rochdale's strictures on the blindness of British port authorities to the approaching container revolution applied to Britain's premier port, London. Between 1945 and 1959, its fiftieth anniversary year, the PLA had spent about £11 million on capital investment in the docks under its control. Even this not particularly great investment had exhausted the PLA's capital reserves by 1957 and after then the authority had to finance all improvements by borrowing. The PLA made its first mention of the container in its fiftieth anniversary annual report, but the authority's immediate concern was to provide more deep-water berths.[57]

Conscious that 'the majority of the authority's docks and quays were constructed before 1914', the PLA decided in 1961, when the Rochdale committee was still taking evidence, to undertake a major modernisation scheme over the next six or seven years which would cost at least £30 million, nearly three times its capital investment between 1945 and 1959. The principal element of the modernisation would be four deep-water berths at Tilbury. Two would be suitable for the fork-lift/pallet handling of general cargo for India and Pakistan, while the other two would handle ro-ro traffic to the continent. Construction began in 1963 and the first berths were ready in 1966.[58]

Even as the construction of Tilbury Phase I began, the PLA applied to the government for permission to undertake the Tilbury Phase II scheme, which would involve the construction of seven more new deep-water berths. These were intended for 'unitised' traffic. Two were quickly allocated to handle packaged timber, but the question in 1964-65 was whether the others would be equipped as lift on, lift off (lo-lo) container berths. In 1965 the PLA commissioned the Martech report on the pattern of UK trade on ocean routes and what proportion was suitable for containerisation. The report revealed that a quarter of Britain's total export trade originated within thirty miles of London and more than half within 105 miles of the capital. On the basis of such information, the PLA decided it would have to provide container services to all parts of the world, or it would end up just providing a feeder service to container routes based on continental ports like Rotterdam. By the end of 1966 the PLA was committed to making Tilbury Britain's chief container port for both short sea and oceanic services.[59]

The Wilson government was conscious of the quickening pace of the container revolution and set up a Cabinet committee on containerisation in September 1967, largely to consider its impact on the development of British ports. That it would mean a cut in dock labour was obvious, but it was also clear that ocean container services could be concentrated at only a few ports. Lo-lo container handling facilities were costly and to achieve economies of scale had to be assured high traffic flows, as well as being part of a wider integrated transport system. High traffic flows could only be achieved by concentrating oceanic container operations on a handful of ports. Ro-ro container traffic on short sea routes posed less of a problem since ramps were comparatively cheap and so any suitable port could afford them. The Cabinet committee expected most general cargo on the Western Europe/East Coast of North America route to be containerised by 1970.[60]

In January 1968 the PLA opened a deep-water short-sea container berth at Tilbury and it was used by European Unit Routes Ltd., a subsidiary of P&O, for a container service to the continent. The immediate success of this service showed the danger that London might just run a container feeder route to a continental port like Rotterdam. Then in June 1968 Tilbury's first deep-water oceanic container berth opened. The United States Lines vessel *American Lancer* was the first transatlantic container ship to use Tilbury's berth 40. It took only thirteen hours for fifteen dockers to unload and load containers on the ship before she sailed on the next tide. Had the cargo been handled in the traditional break-bulk fashion the operation would have taken 176 dockers (ninety-six on the ship and eighty on the quay) some four or five days. This was a major achievement for Tilbury, but the PLA was well aware that competition was growing. Liverpool and Southampton were building container berths for transatlantic services, while by the end of 1968 both Rotterdam and Antwerp were said to be handling 1,250 containers every week.[61]

In 1965 various leading British shipping lines (P&O, British and Commonwealth, Ocean and Furness Withy) had set up Overseas Containers Ltd. (OCL), Britain's first oceanic container line. The first OCL service was to be from Europe to Australia. Tilbury was to be the UK terminal and operations were to commence in February 1969. A new container berth (no. 39) was made ready and flexible working practices were agreed with the unions similar to those already in place at berth 40. Then came disaster. In connection with wider wage negotiations in the port, the TGWU told its members at the start of 1969 not to operate any new berths until the negotiations were completed. With berth 39 closed, OCL had to begin its Australian services from continental ports and no OCL ship came to Tilbury until May 1970. The union intervention did serious damage to Tilbury's growing reputation as a container port. OCL was to start another container service to the Far East in 1971, and when in November 1969 the company decided on its UK terminal for that service it chose Southampton instead of Tilbury.[62]

In 1962 the Rochdale report had been sceptical that British port authorities could meet the challenge of the container, but London at least had proved equal to that challenge. At considerable expense but in a relatively short time, the PLA had turned Tilbury into Britain's leading container port, only to have that success undermined by dock labour problems. This was ironic at a time when the Devlin report and its consequences seemed to have finally ended decasualisation and satisfied the dockers' long-standing grievances.

The Devlin Report (1965) and Decasualisation

'It was the Devlin committee's task to find a means of adapting a volatile, conservative industry to the container age.'[63] Thus did one commentator characterise the underlying aim of Lord Devlin's inquiry which was set up in October 1964 to examine the problems of dock labour. Such an intention was not obvious from the committee's terms of reference. Rather did it seem that Devlin would once again grapple with the old docker grievances and try at last to end casual labour.

Yet whatever the outward appearances, it was the demands of the new cargo handling methods which made full decasualisation more urgent than ever before. Containerisation demanded large capital investment and the new container berths could only repay such investment if they were kept in regular use and were manned by a small permanent staff of dockworkers ready to accept flexible working practices. Devlin was to hammer out the deal by which dockers would be given permanent employment in return for accepting new working practices to use the new technology. Surplus dockers would be encouraged to leave the industry by generous severance payments.

At first the Devlin deal seemed a good compromise, but it soon became clear that containerisation and other new cargo handling technology were making dockers surplus to requirements much faster than anybody had expected. The old fear of underemployment in the casual system was replaced for dockers by the fear of unemployment in the post-Devlin period. The problem of dock labour had changed from fluctuating demand to permanent surplus. Decasualisation led to an increase in port industrial unrest rather than a decrease. After 1970 the dockers fought back with two demands: that the dock labour scheme should be extended to non-scheme ports which had been growing rapidly in recent years, and that a broader definition of 'dock work' should be agreed so that dockers could be guaranteed jobs in other areas such as cold stores and container groupage depots.

However, these troubles were unforeseen when the Devlin committee delivered its report in August 1965. It recommended that all registered dock workers should be employed on a permanent basis. In return dockers were to agree to new working practices. The changes called for by Devlin were to be overseen by a National Modernisation Committee. The number of port employers was to be reduced by a licensing scheme run by the port authorities. The Devlin proposals were given statutory authority by the Docks and Harbours Act 1966, leading to a new dock labour scheme in 1967, although it was still largely controlled by the National Dock Labour Board. In future all registered dock workers would be allocated to a permanent job with a licensed employer. Those men still unable to find work would be put on the temporarily unattached register (TUR) to await permanent assignment.[64]

Decasualisation (Devlin Phase I) came into effect in September 1967, and was to be followed by negotiations in the ports for local modernisation agreements on new working practices (Devlin Phase II). Docker reaction to decasualisation was an immediate wave of strikes. This was because some dockers resented the disciplinary restrictions attached to permanent employment, while others feared they would inevitably lose their jobs in the new conditions. The need to shed labour was obvious, but severance schemes to encourage men to leave were slow in being organised. The port of London instituted such a scheme in 1967, concentrating on old and sick dockers. Given that the average age of British dockers was in the mid-forties, a large number seemed suitable for severance on grounds of age. Agreeing a national severance scheme proved difficult, largely because the port employers would have to pay for it. Those employers who were also port authorities, such as the PLA, were already burdened with the heavy cost of servicing loans incurred for investment in new cargo handling facilities. Nevertheless the employers finally agreed to a national scheme in 1969. Between 1967 and 1970 the number of registered dockers fell from

56,161 to 44,588, with about 10,000 taking severance at a cost of almost £14 million.[65]

By 1969 the port employers and port authorities had more to worry about than docker severance schemes as the Labour government had announced its intention of nationalising the port transport industry. Labour had made an election commitment to nationalisation and a 1966 party report had pushed for full public ownership and 'a major extension of the industrial democracy that already exists in the running of the industry'.[66] Port employers had long resented the joint control of the industry by them and the unions and they would not welcome its further extension. In June 1966 the government made a definite commitment to nationalise the ports, but did not in fact bring forward a bill to do so until 1969.

The government had decided that an advisory body like the National Ports Council was not sufficient to carry out a radical reorganisation of the ports. Instead a National Ports Authority would own and run the major ports with annual traffic of more than five million tons of cargo. These ports would include London, Liverpool, Bristol, Manchester and Teesport, as well as the already nationalised ports (including Hull and Southampton) previously run by the British Transport Docks Board. The nationalised ports run by the British Railways Board and the British Waterways Board were not initially to be taken over by the new authority.[67]

The government's proposal was said to be a reaction to the great changes taking place in the port transport industry. The principal changes were the use of larger ships; the introduction of rapid throughput facilities for bulk cargoes; the development of unit load techniques (notably containerisation of general cargo); and the growth of through transport. The National Ports Authority was to manage such change by ensuring that new investment and rationalisation of facilities produced the best services at the right places. In addition port management was to include effective worker participation. Only public ownership and national co-ordination could save the industry from 'the present diffusion and misdirection of resources'.[68] However, the port nationalisation bill was lost when a general election was called in 1970 and the Conservatives won. When Labour returned to power in 1974 they were still committed to port nationalisation, but no further action was taken in the matter.

While the shadow of the ports bill lay over the port authorities and employers in 1969, the dockers became increasingly concerned about the impact of containerisation. The OCL container ban at Tilbury was largely a tactical move in negotiations about modernisation within the port of London, but there was a more general fear among dockers that containerisation meant large-scale unemployment for them. The dockers felt that they should be given priority for new job opportunities being created at container groupage depots near (but not in) the docks. The government set up the Bristow committee to examine whether the terms 'dock work' and 'in the vicinity of the port' could be stretched to make work in container groupage depots the exclusive preserve of registered dockers. Bristow proposed the creation of a five-mile corridor on each side of the Thames in which all container depots must employ registered dockers. The fall of the Labour government in 1970 put paid to such ideas for the moment, but they were to be revived later in the 1970s.[69]

Decasualisation in 1967 had been followed by increasing unrest in the docks, with Liverpool beginning to replace London as the most militant port. The situation on Merseyside was not helped by the financial collapse of the Mersey Docks and Harbour Board in 1970. Indeed 1970 was to be a turning point in all ports since July saw the first official national dock strike since the General Strike of 1926. The cause of the three-week stoppage was a wage dispute rather than fears of unemployment due to new technology, and a compromise settlement was eventually reached. However, the strike showed that the leadership of unions such as the TGWU were increasingly ready to take major strike action, if only to upstage the militants active in many ports. More constructive was union consent to the first Devlin Phase II modernisation agreement, in the port of London in September 1970, which was followed by similar agreements in all the other major ports over the next two years.[70]

Even after 1967 a non-permanent element remained in the dock labour scheme. This was the temporarily unattached register (TUR), and dockers feared that the employers would use it as a reserve pool or back door way to dismiss surplus labour. By mid-1972 the number of men on the TUR had grown to 1,650 (4% of the total registered labour force). London and Hull had most TUR men, and docker unrest on the issue was growing. In an attempt to resolve the problem a non-statutory committee of inquiry was set up, under the joint chairmanship of Lord Aldington, chairman of the PLA, and Jack Jones, General Secretary of the TGWU. Its interim

6. Unit load cargo handling: unloading containers from the Norwegian vessel
Tarago at the new roll on/roll off terminal, Tilbury Docks, London, *c.* 1973.
(Photo: courtesy of Museum in Docklands, PLA Collection)

report called for all those on the TUR to be reallocated to other employers.[71]

However, by the time the interim report appeared, another national dock strike was in prospect. In London the dockers had taken exception to the use of unregistered labour in a Hackney cold store, claiming such work should be reserved for dockers. Five dockers were arrested in July 1972 for refusing to comply with an order from the Industrial Relations Court to cease picketing the cold store. The committal of the 'Pentonville Five' to prison led to all Britain's 42,000 dockers agreeing to come out on strike. At the last moment the five were released, but the strike went ahead. It lasted for three weeks and was finally resolved by the intervention of the Aldington/Jones committee. Among their recommendations were guarantees of jobs for dockers at certain inland container depots and assurances that cold store work in London would be reserved for dockers. Aldington/Jones also outlined a special severance scheme for dockers in 1972–73, which went ahead after the government provided the money, and proposed an inquiry into the non-scheme ports.[72]

The latter inquiry was carried out by the National Ports Council, which reported in 1973. The reason the dockers were so concerned about the non-scheme ports, that is ports not subject to the national dock labour scheme, was that they had been handling an increasing proportion of British trade. By the early 1970s the non-scheme ports handled 20% of Britain's port traffic, and from 1965 to 1970 their tonnage of dry cargo handled rose by 11.5% per annum compared with an annual increase of only 0.5% at the scheme ports. Scheme port dockers alleged that non-scheme ports were under-cutting them through having inferior labour conditions, but the NPC found no evidence of this. More than two-thirds of regular workers in the non-scheme sector were employed by the ports of Dover, Felixstowe, Portsmouth and Shoreham, and the ports controlled by the British Railways Board.[73]

Despite the NPC's findings, the Aldington/Jones committee's final report in April 1974 still called for the curbing of unfair competition from the non-scheme ports. The committee also called for container groupage work to be reserved for registered dockers and for the number of men on the supplementary register (for seasonal dock work) to be kept down lest it be exploited in the way the TUR seemed to have been, that is as a way of forcing dockers out of the industry. Aldington/Jones reinforced the view that there should be no compulsory redundancies among dockers, no matter how great the number of surplus workers became.[74]

However, if dockers were guaranteed jobs, the port employers were not guaranteed survival. During the 1970s more and more stevedoring companies and other employers of dockers went out of business. Under the scheme their former employees were reallocated to other employers. But the number of available employers declined rapidly, so the port authorities were forced to employ surplus dockers themselves. Many of them became substantial employers of dock labour for the first time. The PLA had been one of the few port authorities that had always directly employed a large number of dockers, but during the 1970s its workforce grew rapidly as private employers disappeared. In 1975 Scruttons, the largest private employer of dockers in London, went out of business and its men passed to the PLA. Only one important private employer of London dockers remained (it went out of business in 1979), leaving the PLA as the largest single employer of dock labour in Europe. The problem was that functioning as employer of last resort imposed a heavy financial burden on port authorities already heavily indebted from capital investment in new facilities. The authorities had to pay the men even if there was no work for them, and even if dockers took severance, the employers also had to meet most of that cost. As a consequence of the financial collapse of the MDHB in 1970 the Harbours (Loans) Act of 1972 had been passed to allow the government to give some assistance to ports in financial difficulties. Nevertheless by the mid-1970s many port authorities were under financial strain and the future looked grim.[75]

The National Ports Council

Given statutory authority by the Harbours Act of 1964, the National Ports Council (NPC) had the tasks of advising the government on port development projects and of trying to formulate a national ports plan. However, for much of the 1960s, the NPC worked under difficult conditions. It did not have a good working relationship with the British Transport Docks Board, which controlled the main group of ports already under state control, and between 1966 and 1970 the shadow of complete nationalisation of the ports hung over the NPC and made its future insecure.[76]

When the ports nationalisation bill was put before parliament in 1969 the NPC seemed doomed, so the council reviewed what had been achieved since its foundation in 1964. A number of major port developments had been approved: the deep-water berths (including those for container ships) and the grain terminal at Tilbury; the Seaforth development (including container berths) at Liverpool; the container berth at Southampton's west dock extension; the container berth at Greenock on the Clyde; and the ro-ro and container berths at Felixstowe and Harwich (Parkeston Quay). In addition many new ro-ro berths had been opened at ports on the south and east coasts of Britain. Since some of these ro-ro developments had been cheap enough to avoid the need for NPC approval, the council feared there might soon be an over-provision of such facilities.[77]

One important task the NPC had completed by 1969 was the reorganisation of port authorities into estuarial groups. The council intended that such amalgamations should include, where appropriate, the nationalised BTDB ports, such as Southampton and those on Humberside. Amalgamations leading to single port authorities were achieved on the Clyde, Tees, Forth, Humber, Medway and Tyne estuaries and at Southampton. Less success was achieved on the Thames, Severn, Mersey and Stour/Orwell estuaries, where various port authorities fought for their autonomy, although both the Thames and the Mersey had one authority that was clearly dominant. The various amalgamations were not however linked to any national ports plan, which the NPC admitted in 1968 was proving difficult to prepare despite the mass of new port statistics collected since 1964.[78]

The NPC received a reprieve when the ports nationalisation bill was killed by the decision to call a general election in 1970. The new Conservative government was obviously opposed to nationalisation and still believed the NPC had a role to play in advising on port development, but any idea of preparing a national ports plan was given up. Container and ro-ro traffic had been the big challenge for British ports in the 1960s. In 1971 the NPC pointed out the two challenges for the ports in the coming decade: first, the effects of Britain joining the Common Market (scheduled for 1973), and secondly, the consequences of the development of the North Sea oil and gas industry. With regard to EEC membership, the NPC expected traffic through south and east coast ports to the continent to rise and that there would be some decline in deep-sea trade, but the council underestimated how quickly these changes would take place. The NPC had surveyed ports between the Humber and Southampton and believed they had sufficient capacity to handle foreseeable increases in trade.[79]

With regard to North Sea oil, two questions arose. Would there be sufficient port capacity available to support exploration and exploitation operations in the North Sea? New development might be needed at the ports adjacent to the oil fields. Secondly, would obtaining oil from the North Sea greatly reduce imports of foreign crude oil (Britain's biggest import item) and so render some existing oil ports redundant? Although North Sea operations were still at a comparatively early stage, the NPC concluded in 1971 that North Sea oil would not greatly reduce oil imports in the near future, but the need to export North Sea oil would require the building of new outward shipment port facilities. There was expected to be a rapid rise in traffic at ports near the oil fields, so the NPC saw a need for some new developments at those places.[80]

The biggest import item after oil was iron ore, but port developments during the 1960s seemed to have provided all the capacity needed for that trade. New iron ore terminals had been built at Port Talbot and Redcar, while Immingham had developed iron ore import facilities. The new iron ore terminal proposed at Hunterston on the Clyde should, thought the council, be the last. With regard to container berths, the NPC felt Britain now had enough in both the deep-sea and the short sea trades. However, if further container berths were needed the council believed they should only be built if the port authority had already tied a user to them by contract. Because container berths were so expensive to build they should not be provided on a common user basis. The need to tie a shipping company to a berth by contract was highlighted by the fact that the new container consortia were more ready to move from port to port than the old liner shipping companies.[81]

The 1960s had seen a reduction in the number of port authorities through estuarial groupings. In the 1970s the NPC began the task of overhauling the management structures of the reduced number of port authorities. The principal targets were the trust ports, many of which had constitutions dating back to the nineteenth century. The NPC proposed to reduce management boards to between eight and ten members; to include a substantial minority of full-time executive officers; and to ensure that non-executive board members were appointed for their knowledge and experience rather than because they were from a particular interest group. Between 1970 and 1978 the boards of the Forth, Clyde, Tyne, Medway, Tees, Ipswich and Dover port authorities were all reconstituted along these lines. The PLA was also reorganised early in 1976, although with more board members than the NPC recommended. The Milford Haven board was altered largely as the NPC proposed, though it retained a measure of representation for certain interest groups.[82]

During 1973 the world price of oil began to rise rapidly and this underlined the need for Britain to develop North Sea oil and gas as quickly as possible to reduce dependence on expensive foreign oil and hence ease pressure on the balance of payments. Major pipelines were proposed to bring much of the oil ashore in Britain. Oil from the Norwegian Ekofisk field would be piped to the Tees estuary and exported from there. Piped oil from the Forties field would come ashore at Cruden Bay in N.E. Scotland, then be piped to Grangemouth refinery and to the new oil export facility at Hound Point on the Forth. Occidental wanted a pipeline from the Piper field to an oil shipment facility at Flotta in Scapa Flow, Orkney Islands. Shell planned a pipeline from the Brent field to a new oil shipment port at Sullom Voe in the Shetland Islands. It seemed likely that Sullom Voe would eventually handle more oil

Table 4.5: Traffic through the Principal Ports of
Great Britain, 1965–1985
(Million tonnes)

Port	1965	1975	1980	1985
Sullom Voe	—	—	28.5	59.0
London	64.6	50.3	54.2	51.7
Milford Haven	24.8	44.9	39.3	32.5
Tees and Hartlepool	12.1	20.2	39.4	30.6
Grimsby and Immingham	8.3	2.0	22.2	29.1
Forth	6.1	8.4	28.8	29.1
Southampton	24.4	25.3	23.9	25.2
Orkney	—	0.4	15.4	16.1
Liverpool	31.7	23.4	12.3	10.4
Medway	22.3	21.7	17.2	10.4
Felixstowe	—	4.1	5.4	10.1
Dover	1.4	3.7	6.7	9.3

Source: COI, *Britain 1988*, p. 318.

traffic than Britain's main existing oil port, Milford Haven, which had thrived during the 1960s.[83] (See Table 4.5.)

With regard to port facilities to support offshore operations, the gas fields of the southern North Sea had been served by Great Yarmouth and Lowestoft since the 1960s. The new oil fields in the northern North Sea were necessitating the construction of new port facilities at Leith, Dundee and Montrose, with the biggest works at Aberdeen and Peterhead. A new harbour authority had been created at Cromarty to oversee port development there. In the Orkneys the old naval facility at Lyness was being turned into an offshore support base. At Lerwick in the Shetlands there were various developments, with Ocean Inchcape setting up a support base at North Ness and Norscot a facility at Greenhead. Elsewhere in the Shetlands, Hudson Offshore was setting up a base at Sandwick.[84]

In 1974 the NPC looked back over ten years of great change in the port transport industry. In that time 170 port development schemes, with a total estimated cost of £125 million (of which £84 million was on new schemes), had been referred to the council. Most had been approved, and over the period new facilities built to cater for unit load traffic included twenty-two deep-sea container berths,

MAIN UK PORTS, 1974

SCOTLAND

NORTH SEA

Aberdeen

Dundee

Finnart
Grangemouth
Greenock
Glasgow
Leith
(Edinburgh)

NORTHERN
IRELAND
Belfast

Newcastle upon Tyne
Sunderland
Teesport
Middlesbrough

IRISH SEA

IRELAND

Hull
Immingham
Grimsby
Liverpool
Manchester
Stanlow

ENGLAND

WALES

Great Yarmouth
Lowestoft

Ipswich · Felixstowe
Harwich

Milford Haven
Swansea
Llandarcy
Shellhaven
Tilbury Coryton
Port
Talbot
Cardiff
Newport
Avonmouth
London
Isle of
Grain
Dover
Bristol
Folkestone

Southampton
Shoreham
Fawley
Poole
Portsmouth
Newhaven
Plymouth

English Channel

FRANCE

▽Main oil refineries

Map by András Bereznay; www.historyonmaps.com

fifty short sea container berths and seventy-six ro-ro berths, with a total throughput exceeding twenty-eight million tonnes, and a theoretical maximum of much more. This technological progress had not been without its cost. Over the ten years the number of registered dockers had fallen from 64,600 to 34,600, while other port workers had declined from 64,000 to 38,000.[85]

Not only had port technology changed, but so had the direction of trade. By 1975 EEC traffic was the fastest growing sector of the UK's non-fuel trade. It had risen from 14.5 million tonnes in 1965 (16% of the total) to 31.5 million tonnes in 1975 (33% of the total). In the same period passenger movements on near and short sea routes had grown from 8.2 million to over 15 million. Many passengers went via Dover, but changes in freight movements at that port were even more impressive. Road freight transport vehicles passing through Dover had increased from 54,000 in 1969 to 253,000 in 1974. The growth in EEC traffic was more rapid than the NPC had expected and it was concerned that south and east coast ports should be properly equipped to handle it.[86]

In June 1975 the first North Sea oil was brought ashore. In October the Ekofisk/Tees and Forties/Cruden Bay pipelines began to operate, and in November the first British crude oil was exported from the Hound Point facility on the Forth. The NPC was involved in sorting out problems relating to the oil shipment facility at Flotta in the Orkneys, while difficulties had also arisen about Sullom Voe. The development plan for that port, estimated to cost £24 million, had been put forward, but there were disputes between the port authority, the Shetland Islands Council, and the oil companies. The NPC endeavoured to act as a mediator in those disputes.[87]

In 1976 the NPC noted that there were now relatively few port development projects coming forward and this seemed to indicate that UK general cargo facilities were probably sufficient for existing needs. New container facilities were, however, being built at Southampton (for South African trade) and at Tilbury (for Australasian trade). Although traffic was becoming increasingly concentrated at ports like these two, the NPC hoped the UK could maintain its dispersed patterns of trade and not concentrate traffic on a few giant ports like Antwerp, Rotterdam and Hamburg on the continent.[88]

The NPC made a comparison of UK non-fuel exports in tonnage and in value terms, comparing 1970 with 1975, and came up with

Table 4.6: Growth of the Haven Ports (Felixstowe,
Ipswich and Harwich) 1966–1990
(Traffic in thousand tonnes)

Year	Fx	Ip	Hw	Total HP	HP *as* % *of UK port traffic*
1966	814	2142	816	3772	1.2
1972	2670	2303	2470	7443	2.0
1978	4769	2783	3286	10838	2.7
1984	9311	4111	3731	17153	3.7
1990	16448	4692	4225	25365	5.2

(Traffic at Mistley and other quays on the Stour and the Orwell rivers excluded)
Source: Port Statistics 1994.

some surprising results. By both measures London and Liverpool
remained the top two British ports for exports, although their share
of the trade had declined over the period. More surprising was the
fact that if taken together the Haven Ports (Ipswich, Felixstowe and
Harwich) ranked second only to London in both value and tonnage
terms of non-fuel export traffic. (See also Table 4.6.) Also, Dover,
which was essentially a ro-ro port, had become the third most
important British port (after London and Liverpool) in terms of the
value of non-fuel exports passing through it. Whatever the hopes of
the NPC, it was clear that British port traffic was becoming
increasingly concentrated in a 'golden triangle' in S.E. England,
with its apexes at Southampton, Dover and the Haven Ports.[89]

Towards the end of 1976 the first North Sea oil was shipped out
from Flotta in the Orkneys. The pipeline from the Brent field to
Sullom Voe was not yet complete, but the first Brent crude was
shipped out during 1976 with tankers loading from the Brent Spar
on the field itself. Terminals to deal with gas from the northern
North Sea were built at Sullom Voe, Scapa Flow, Grangemouth and
Teesside, and a large new facility was planned at Braefoot Bay on
the Forth. In March 1978 the Sullom Voe harbour agreement was
finally signed by Shetland Islands Council and the oil companies,
after NPC mediation between the parties. In November of that year
Sullom Voe shipped its first crude oil. During 1978 oil production
from the North Sea reached 53 million tonnes, over half the UK's
national petroleum consumption.[90]

In 1979 the Conservative government of Mrs Thatcher came to power committed to de-regulation of industry. In December of that year it was announced that the NPC was to be wound up. The responsibility for the efficiency of the port transport industry was to be put firmly on the ports themselves. The council tried to persuade the government that there was still a role for a national advisory body on port development, but to no avail. Yet in its annual report for 1979, looking back over the fifteen years of its existence, the NPC seemed ready to accept that its task was at an end and that it had helped the ports through a period of unparalleled change.[91]

The number of port authorities had been reduced by estuarial groupings in the 1960s and their constitutions had been overhauled in the 1970s, all under NPC supervision. Originally set up just to control the building of the deep-water berths called for by the Rochdale report, the NPC had gone on to oversee the port developments required by the container and ro-ro cargo handling revolution. The council had played a role in ensuring sufficient port facilities were available to support the new North Sea oil and gas industry. It had also been involved in the creation of three of the four entirely new British harbours created since 1945. These were Cromarty, Flotta and Sullom Voe, the fourth, Milford Haven, having been begun before the NPC's creation in 1964.[92]

Nevertheless, for a body originally intended to provide some form of centralised port planning, the NPC had been a failure. After the interim national ports plan of 1965, the council had largely given up its wider planning functions and had chiefly been an agency for vetting port development plans put forward by others. The port authorities exerted influence on the NPC from one side, while on the other side political considerations could easily override its plans. For example, in 1964–70 proposals to expand the port of Bristol (at Portbury) were held up, despite having NPC approval, because Labour ministers heeded the opposition from the South Wales ports which were afraid of losing trade to Bristol.[93]

The NPC, writing in 1979, believed that the surge of port investment was now largely complete and expenditure on port facilities had now fallen in real terms to its pre-1964 level. There now seemed to be an adequate supply of modern facilities for every category of traffic. The NPC was only exaggerating a little when it said it had been concerned with port investment at a particularly significant period 'when the ports had to adjust to new cargo handling systems and new cargo directions and in general cope with change on a scale unequalled since the sailing ship was replaced by the steam ship'.[94]

Mrs Thatcher and the Ports

Dockers were, after coal miners, probably Mrs Thatcher's least favourite people. However, she was not prepared to embark on a decisive confrontation with them until 1989, ten years after she came to power and only a year before she resigned as prime minister. However, changes in the British port transport industry in the ten years between 1979 and 1989 were to shift the balance of power decisively from unions and labour to government and employers, so that the final confrontation was to be something of an anti-climax.

The three principal developments undermining the dockers' position were: first, the steady decline in their own numbers; secondly, the consolidation of their employers into a few large bodies, stronger and better organised than the multitude of small employers in the past; and thirdly, the continued shift of trade from dock labour scheme ports to non-scheme ports. Between the national dock strikes of 1972 and 1989 the number of registered dockers fell from over 40,000 to a little over 9,000. The employers, often backed by government loans, encouraged dockers to take severance, but many in an ageing workforce refused to exchange a guaranteed job for almost certain unemployment. In 1979 nearly 13% of registered dockers were surplus to requirements, but the employers still had to pay them.[95]

When Lord Devlin recommended a reduction of the number of port employers in 1965 he cannot have expected the scale of the reduction which took place. By 1980 there was no large independent employer of dock labour in the port of London, leaving the PLA as the sole employer of most dockers. Traditionally the port authority on Merseyside had employed few dockers, but by the end of the 1970s the Mersey Docks and Harbour Company (MDHC) had become the principal employer. Indeed in 1980 port authorities employed 11,000 registered dockers (48% of the total) and the nationalised British Transport Docks Board (privatised in 1983 as Associated British Ports (ABP)) another 5,000 (21% of the total). Barely 30% of the workforce was left under independent employers. By 1989 only 137 employers employed registered dockers on a full-time basis and they were dominated by the big three employers: the PLA, MDHC and ABP. Such organisations, with government support, presented a more formidable challenge to dockers than the numerous and weak employers of the past.[96]

The growing success of the non-scheme ports was obvious by the mid-1970s and commentators believed it was largely due to better and more flexible industrial relations than in the scheme ports. The unions wanted the dock labour scheme extended to the non-scheme ports, and the 1976 Dockwork Regulation Act seemed to hold out this possibility, as well as getting dockers into container depots. However, the Act was pretty much a dead letter and the non-scheme ports continued their seemingly inexorable rise. In 1965 they had only 8% of UK non-fuel port traffic; by the mid-1970s it was 20%; and by 1989 over 30%. By the latter year Felixstowe was Britain's leading container port and Dover the leading ro-ro port. Both were outside the dock labour scheme. In 1947 only 1.5% of Britain's dockworkers were in non-scheme ports. By 1972 the figure was 6.6% and by 1989 a massive 31.3%.[97]

In 1980 the TGWU, the principal dockers' union, asked for an extension of the dock labour scheme to non-scheme ports under the terms of the 1976 Act. The government refused to allow this and only narrowly avoided a national dock strike, chiefly by providing more government money to the employers to fund more severance schemes. The unions and the employers had negotiations about reforming the scheme, but could find no common ground. In July 1984 there was the first national dock strike since 1972. It was in protest at the use of unregistered labour at Immingham and the strike enjoyed considerable support in both scheme and non-scheme ports. The use of unregistered labour at Hunterston led to a second national dock strike in August. It was well supported in Scotland, but less so elsewhere. A quarter of registered dockers refused to strike and no dockers in non-scheme ports gave their support.[98]

In 1987 the last deep-sea container line moved its operations out of Greenock on the Clyde. This withdrawal seemed to mark the end of the Clyde as an important port, though that hardly seemed to matter since 80% of Scottish manufactured goods were exported from English ports anyway. Greenock had suffered along with other northern ports from both the decline of manufacturing and the shift from North American to European trade. Most Greenock dockers took severance and the employers tried to ease out the rest. The union threatened a national strike if the men were forced out and the employers backed down. In October 1988 the union balloted dockers over a national strike in a dispute about more holidays, but the men rejected the strike call.[99]

By the end of 1988 it seemed to the government and the port employers that it was now time to take on the dockers. The union would no doubt fight to defend the dock labour scheme, but the limited response to the second national strike in 1984 and the failure of the 1988 ballot seemed to show that support for the union was no longer complete or automatic. With victories over the miners (1985) and the seamen (1988) behind it, the government was now ready to act. On 6 April 1989 it was announced that the dock labour scheme was to be abolished and the bill to do this was expected to be law by July.[100]

The government announcement led to a rash of unofficial strikes, but the TGWU stopped these while it challenged the government's decision in the courts. When the courts backed the government there were further unofficial strikes in June. In the same month the National Association of Port Employers (NAPE) said it was pulling out of the National Joint Council, the industrial relations forum of the port transport industry since 1920. On 3 July the dock work bill received royal assent and on the following day the first dockers were made compulsorily redundant. The employers announced they were winding up NAPE so there would be no national body with which the union could negotiate. At midnight on 10 July 1989 the national dock strike began.[101]

The strike lasted for three weeks. Cargoes for strike-bound ports were diverted to the non-scheme ports and the TGWU could not prevent them coming ashore and being distributed without breaking the law. Docker solidarity was weakened when the employers offered generous terms to those who would take voluntary redundancy. In early August the TGWU gave in and called off the strike. Over 3,000 men, a third of the old registered dock labour force, had been made redundant during the strike, and those men returning to work did so entirely on the employers' terms. *The Economist* exulted: 'a national dock strike was once a national crisis. When the T & G spoke, prime ministers trembled . . . Mrs Thatcher has drawn the union's teeth [and] snapped the solidarity of labour across her handbag.'[102]

Not More Ports, but Better Ports?

Before 1914 British port facilities had expanded enormously and the casual dock labour system had become entrenched. The rise of docker trade unionism was challenging the latter, and received a powerful boost during the Great War. Initially the interwar period seemed to promise a continuation of port expansion and a better deal for dockers after the Shaw award of 1920. In fact the stagnation of international trade, increased by the world depression after 1929, discouraged further port development and inflicted serious unemployment on dock labour.

The Second World War, like the First, compelled the government to give dockers better conditions of employment to ensure their co-operation in the war effort. The ports themselves were often badly damaged by enemy bombing and their equipment was worn out by excessive working. After 1945 dockers held on to their wartime gains through the 1947 dock labour scheme, while the new era of full employment gave added weight to their further demands. The port authorities faced the challenge of rebuilding the ports, but should they merely repair old facilities or embark on totally new developments? Financial constraints largely compelled the former choice, and the only 'new ports' of the 1950s were oil and iron ore terminals to cater for the great expansion in bulk cargoes.

Nevertheless, by 1960 it was becoming clear that muddling through with a patched-up version of the old Victorian ports system was no longer possible. Above all the new cargo handling technology of the unit load—the container—promised large gains in productivity in return for large capital investment and flexible working practices. Unfortunately the British port transport industry was in no condition to adapt rapidly to the new challenge. Port authorities were numerous and impoverished; port employers were largely small firms geared to the old break-bulk system of cargo handling; and dockers and their unions were reluctant to embrace change, especially as the period since 1945 had brought them previously unknown power and influence. Left to itself the British port transport industry would have had great difficulty in adjusting to the new technology, so, as with other maritime industries such as shipbuilding, the government intervened during the 1960s to assist ports in their passage from one age of cargo handling to another.

However, unlike shipbuilding, government intervention in the

124

ports between 1965 and 1975, particularly through the National Ports Council, was largely successful. The new ro-ro and container facilities were constructed, often thanks to government loans, and port development kept pace with the expansion of trade, its changing direction (increasingly to Europe), and new challenges such as the North Sea oil and gas industry. The chief area of failure was with regard to dock labour. Job losses had been expected, but their size and the speed with which they became necessary took all those involved by surprise. Viewed in retrospect it might have been better if a single agreement 'buying out the rule book' had been possible, on the lines of the US West Coast agreement of 1960, but the port authorities and employers never had the finance to undertake such a major initiative. Instead from 1967 onwards surplus dockers were slowly eased out of the industry, largely through severance schemes which depended increasingly on government money.[103]

By 1979 the National Ports Council had probably outlived its usefulness and the Thatcher government's decision to wind it up and encourage de-regulation and privatisation in the ports was not unreasonable. The problem was the continued existence of the dock labour scheme, but changes in the industry had already undermined the scheme even before it was abolished in 1989 and the resulting national dock strike was easily defeated. The British port transport industry, described in 1965 as 'one of the least efficient parts of our economy', is now largely modern and efficient. An island nation like Britain could survive the loss of a maritime industry like shipbuilding, but efficient ports are a basic requirement for the nation's trade and prosperity.

5

Maritime Opportunity?
North Sea Oil and Gas 1964–1990

In September 1977 Britain's prime minister, James Callaghan, observed: 'God has given Britain her best opportunity for one hundred years in the shape of North Sea oil.'[1] In the following year his government went into more detail: 'North Sea oil provides a unique opportunity for Britain to improve her economic perform-ance, raise her living standards, move forward to full employment, and develop a socially just society.' [2] However, the turn of the political wheel passed the benefits flowing from the North Sea to the Conservatives, and 'without oil the Tory "economic miracle" of the 1980s would have been impossible'.[3]

Politicians of all parties were aware that the riches from North Sea oil and gas offered Britain an unrepeatable opportunity to break out of the cycle of economic weakness and balance of payments crises that had afflicted the country since 1945. North Sea oil was Britain's 'third industrial revolution' and represented 'the biggest industrial development for Britain since the railway boom of . . . the 1840s'.[4] Gas production started in 1967 and oil production in 1975. As early as 1977 North Sea oil output exceeded half of the UK's oil consumption, and by 1981 output exceeded domestic consumption, providing a surplus for export.[5] (See Tables 5.1 and 5.2.)

By the time that Britain's North Sea oil and gas industry reached its twenty-fifth anniversary in 1989, its achievements were on a massive scale. There were thirty-six offshore oilfields and twenty-six offshore gas fields in production, with twenty-one new fields under development. The fields were served by 150 offshore installations and 3,500 miles of pipeline. The industry's cumulative production (up to the end of 1988) amounted to approximately nine billion barrels of oil and over 23.5 trillion cubic feet of gas. Total investment in the industry since 1965 amounted to approximately £50 billion, plus expenditure of a further £14 billion on exploration (all at 1988 prices). British government revenues from North Sea oil and gas since production began exceeded £65 billion.[6]

Potentially the North Sea bonanza offered British industry a wide range of new opportunities. In this chapter consideration will be given to how Britain's maritime industries reacted to these opportunities. The maritime industries were in various degrees of decline or difficulty by the 1960s, the decade in which the North Sea oil and gas industry was born. The oil companies which began exploration in the North Sea usually hired drilling rigs and supply boats from contractors, and although the oil companies owned the later production platforms, those structures were built by outside suppliers.

Could British shipyards find new business by building drilling rigs and supply boats, and even platforms? Could British shipowners diversify into the operation of drilling rigs and offshore

Table 5.1: UK North Sea Oil and Gas Production, 1977–1990

Year	Crude Oil (million tonnes)	Natural Gas (million tonnes oil equivalent)
1977	38.3	35.4
1978	54.0	33.9
1979	77.9	34.2
1980	80.5	32.0
1981	89.3	32.4
1982	103.2	33.0
1983	114.9	34.0
1984	125.7	33.2
1985	127.3	37.1
1986	126.5	39.0
1987	123.4	40.8
1988	114.5	39.3
1989	91.7	38.3
1990	91.6	42.2

Source: Harvie, *Fool's Gold*, p. 363, with corrections.

Table 5.2: UK Offshore Oil Production/UK Crude Petroleum
Imports and Exports, 1976–1986
(Million tonnes)

	1976	1981	1984	1985	1986
Offshore oil production	11.5	89.3	125.7	127.3	126.5
Crude petroleum exports	3.3	52.5	75.9	79.6	82.1
Crude petroleum imports	87.0	33.0	25.0	26.9	32.6

Source: COI, *Britain 1988*, p. 276.

support vessels? Could British ports provide the necessary base facilities to support the offshore industry in the North Sea? Could British deep-sea fishermen, driven out of their distant-water fishing grounds during the 1970s, find new work for their trawlers as safety standby vessels among the offshore installations? If the British maritime industries could make a success of their involvement in the North Sea, they would have the products and the expertise to offer in the emerging offshore energy markets around the world.

Norway has the second largest oil and gas sector in the North Sea and the policies of its government and industry have been held up by some commentators as examples of how best to exploit the North Sea opportunity.[7] Among existing Norwegian expertise which is said to have been crucial in seizing that opportunity was its 'seafaring and shipbuilding tradition'. Britain's tradition in those areas was equal, indeed superior, to that of Norway, so why did one British observer in 1983 claim that 'we have not extended our maritime heritage into this new area of marine technology'?[8] First a general outline of the development of Britain's offshore oil and gas industry will be given, followed by closer consideration of British performance in the construction and operation of drilling rigs, production platforms and offshore support vessels.[9]

The Development of Britain's North Sea Oil and Gas Industry

The Second World War showed the vital strategic importance of oil. The United States had been the principal supplier of oil to the allied nations, but there was concern about the future production of American onshore oil fields. Companies had been drilling offshore for new deposits of oil in the Gulf of Mexico since the 1930s. In 1945 the United States government took the unilateral decision to extend the USA's claims to offshore natural resources beyond the three-mile limit and cover the whole of the contiguous continental shelf. This was done by the so-called Truman Proclamations. One claimed jurisdiction for the USA over natural resources on the continental shelf, while the other claimed the right to establish fishery conservation zones across areas of the high seas bordering American coasts. Other maritime countries followed the American example and made similar claims.[10]

Britain was unhappy about the Truman Proclamations. They undermined the previous view that three miles was the limit of national sovereignty off coasts; they challenged the concept of the freedom of the high seas; and, if widely accepted, they would make life difficult for British deep-sea fishermen working off distant foreign coasts. However, it soon became clear that most maritime nations wished to claim the continental shelf as an area for economic exploitation. The 1958 United Nations conference on the law of the sea accepted the American position on the status of the continental shelf, and by 1964 sufficient nations had ratified the UN Convention on the Law of the Sea to make it international law.

By 1964 British views on the exploitation of the continental shelf had changed considerably. In 1959 large deposits of natural gas were discovered onshore around Groningen in the Netherlands. Geologists then came to the conclusion that similar deposits might exist offshore in the continental shelf between the Netherlands and Britain. Marine seismic surveys began in the early 1960s and it soon began to be suggested that oil as well as natural gas might be found beneath the North Sea. Changing international law and the lure of new energy sources beneath the sea led the countries bordering the North Sea to agree in 1964 on a division of the area into national sectors for the purposes of economic exploitation. Britain received the largest share (35%) of the North Sea and her control was embodied in the Continental Shelf Act of 1964.[11]

The United Kingdom continental shelf (UKCS) was divided into blocks and these were allocated to oil companies for exploration. Unusually in the international oil business, such blocks were not to be auctioned to the highest bidder, but allocated after government consideration of the finances, experience and plans of the consortia applying for them. This virtually free allocation of blocks, plus a generous tax regime, was intended to encourage oil companies to begin operations on the UKCS as soon as possible and to counter-balance the negative factors of North Sea operations. These were that offshore drilling would take place in deeper waters than ever before; that North Sea weather was notoriously bad, with strong winds and high waves; that operational costs would be very high; and that there was a high risk factor, doubts still being expressed about finding anything, especially oil. Nevertheless there was no lack of companies applying for the blocks in May 1964. In September of that year the government awarded the first licences, covering 348 blocks of the UKCS, to groups containing fifty-one companies.[12]

In the mid-1960s the world oil industry was dominated by seven major companies, the so-called 'Seven Sisters'. Five of these companies were American, one was British (British Petroleum), and one was Anglo-Dutch (Royal Dutch Shell). British Petroleum (BP) was largely owned by the British government and a smaller and older British oil company, Burmah. The American companies largely dominated the world offshore oil industry, based on their experience in the Gulf of Mexico, but other companies had also operated offshore, such as BP's drilling offshore in the Persian Gulf and off Trinidad. However, the seven majors, along with other oil companies, realised that the North Sea would be a particularly difficult and expensive area of operations. This fact caused them to band together in various consortia to share the costs and the risks. Of the first twenty-three groups to obtain blocks on the UKCS in 1964 and 1965 most were made up of American and other foreign oil companies. British interests featured in only five groups: Shell joined with the American company Esso in one group; the British Gas Council was with Amoco and other American companies in another group; Burmah and the British chemicals giant ICI were in a group with American companies; the British mining company Rio Tinto Zinc and the British newspaper group Northcliffe joined American oil company Hamilton; and BP stood alone.[13]

British Petroleum had initially been unenthusiastic about the prospects of finding oil and gas in the North Sea. As the principal explorer for oil on mainland Britain, the company's few finds seemed to suggest that hopes of success would be little better offshore. However, the Groningen gas finds did something to increase BP's interest in the possibilities of the North Sea. The company received special treatment in the division of the UKCS blocks in the first round of awards. BP received twenty-two of the thirty-five blocks for which it applied, including block 48/6 in the southern North Sea which was regarded as the best bet for a find.[14]

With seismic surveys completed, exploration drilling began in the southern North Sea during 1965. In October BP's drilling rig *Sea Gem* made the first commercial gas find in block 48/6, a field later called West Sole, some forty miles off the Humber estuary. Sadly the rig was lost in a storm at the end of the year.[15] In 1966 four more gas fields were discovered off the east coast of England, and in 1967 gas production began, with the West Sole field linked by pipeline to a terminal at Easington in Yorkshire. During the next ten years the whole British gas system was converted to use natural gas from the North Sea. The government made the British Gas Council (later the British Gas Corporation) the sole buyer of gas from the UKCS, fixing the price given to producers, and this situation continued until 1982.[16]

No oil of commercial value was found in the southern North Sea, so the quest for oil took drilling rigs into the stormier and deeper waters further north, off mainland Scotland and the Orkney and the Shetland Islands. The jack-up drilling rigs which had dominated the search for gas in the south were now largely replaced by semi-submersible drilling rigs and drillships which were more suited to the new conditions. In September 1969 BP's British-built drilling rig *Sea Quest*, on charter to Amoco, made the first commercial oil find on the UKCS. The oil field, later named Arbroath, was 135 miles from the east coast of Scotland, and the Amoco consortium included the British Gas Council. In 1970 BP discovered the potentially huge Forties oil field. In 1971 the Shell/Esso joint venture found the Auk and the Brent oil fields, the latter apparently almost as large as the Forties field. Also in 1971 the Hamilton group found the Argyll oil field and Amoco the Montrose field. With new fields, both oil and gas, now being found one after the other on the UKCS, the oil companies began to turn their thoughts from exploration to exploitation, from drilling rigs to production platforms.[17]

By the end of 1971 it was clear that Britain would be an important gas and oil producer. The North Sea gamble had paid off for both the oil companies and the British government. The latter now began to consider how Britain could derive most benefit from the new offshore energy industry. In 1972 the International Management and Engineering Group (IMEG) carried out a survey for the government on opportunities for British industry in offshore work. The IMEG report anticipated that by the late 1970s the North Sea market might be worth £300 million if the government pursued a policy of active support, or £100 million without such support. The report recognised that the development of North Sea oil would (or could) provide the most significant opportunity for industrial growth for many years to come and that it would make exceptional demands for advanced technology and ought to promote the development of internationally competitive equipment, supply and contracting industries.[18]

The IMEG report showed that British firms were getting only 20–30% of offshore work and recommended that an organisation should be set up to assist British industry in obtaining more business. The Offshore Supplies Office (OSO) was set up in 1973 to carry out this task. The government also came under pressure from the House of Commons public accounts committee whose 1973 report revealed that the oil companies active on the UKCS had paid little tax since 1964 and were now in a position to make very large profits.[19]

By late 1973 there was general all-party agreement in parliament that the government should assist British industry in obtaining a greater share of offshore work and that heavier taxes should be levied on the oil companies. Then came the Yom Kippur war in the Middle East and the actions of the Organisation of Petroleum Exporting Countries (OPEC) which rapidly increased the world price of oil. On the one hand the 1973–74 oil price rises enhanced the importance of the North Sea as an oil-producing area outside OPEC and the communist bloc and raised potential revenue levels from North Sea oil to match the high costs of production in that oil province. On the other hand, the oil price rises made the British government even more anxious to get North Sea oil into production to cut the ever-increasing cost of importing foreign oil and so relieve pressure on the balance of payments. It seemed that increased taxation of the oil companies and the encouragement of greater British participation in the North Sea might have to be postponed, but in 1974 Labour returned to power committed to both these objectives.[20]

The new Labour government made clear its intentions: to set up a British national oil company; to take a majority share in existing and future licences to UKCS blocks; to extend its power to control physical production and pipelines; and to put additional tax on the oil companies' profits. The non-tax proposals were largely carried

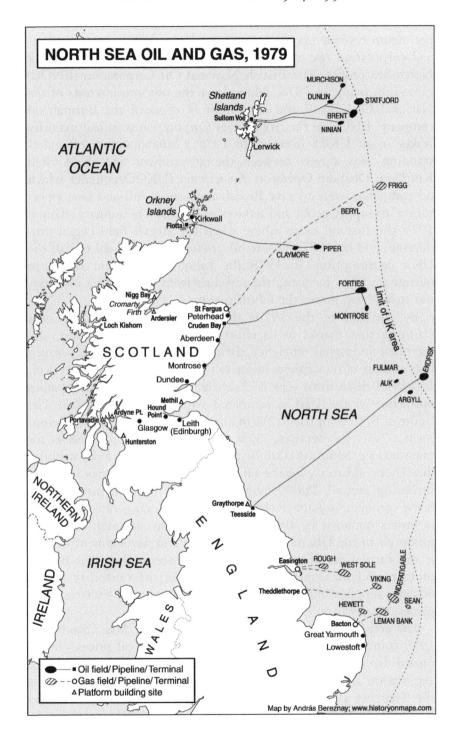

NORTH SEA OIL AND GAS, 1979

MURCHISON
DUNLIN
STATFJORD
BRENT
NINIAN

Shetland
Islands
Sullom Voe
Lerwick

ATLANTIC
OCEAN

FRIGG

Orkney
Islands
Kirkwall
Flotta

BERYL

CLAYMORE
PIPER

FORTIES
MONTROSE

Nigg Bay
Cromarty
Firth
Loch Kishorn
Ardersier
St Fergus
Peterhead
Cruden Bay

Aberdeen

SCOTLAND

EKOFISK

FULMAR
AUK

Montrose
Dundee

ARGYLL

Methil
Hound
Point
Ardyne Pt.
Portavadie
Glasgow
Leith
(Edinburgh)
Hunterston

NORTH SEA

NORTHERN
IRELAND

IRELAND

IRISH SEA

ENGLAND

WALES

Graythorpe
Teesside

Easington ROUGH WEST SOLE
VIKING
Theddlethorpe
HEWETT
SEAN
LEMAN BANK
Bacton
Great Yarmouth
Lowestoft

INDEFATIGABLE

Limit of UK area

■ Oil field/ Pipeline/ Terminal
○ Gas field/ Pipeline/ Terminal
△ Platform building site

Map by András Bereznay; www.historyonmaps.com

out by the Petroleum and Submarine Pipelines Act of 1975, while a petroleum revenue tax was imposed, which together with royalties and corporation tax meant that the government received 70% of North Sea profits. The British National Oil Corporation (BNOC) came into being in 1976, taking over the offshore interests of the National Coal Board and later most of those of the Burmah oil company. BNOC or the British Gas Corporation soon had majority stakes in all UKCS licences. In 1975 a 'memorandum of under-standing' was agreed between the government and the United Kingdom Offshore Operators Association (UKOOA) under which oil companies were to give British industry a 'full and fair oppor-tunity' to supply goods and services to the offshore industry. Also in 1975 the first oil came ashore when the Argyll field began pro-duction, and by 1977 offshore oil production was equal to half the UK's consumption. In 1978 the Labour government began to outline its plans for using the revenues from the offshore industry, but it fell from power the following year.[21]

By the end of the 1970s the Offshore Supplies Office was claiming that thanks to its efforts, the 1975 memorandum, and increased industrial efficiency, British firms were taking a much bigger share of the offshore industry's market for goods and services. In 1981 British firms took 67% of the orders placed by companies operating on the UKCS, compared with 25–30% in 1973. The figure of 67% comprised 75% of orders in connection with develop-ment, 72% for services, 32% for exploration, and 88% for maintenance. Some 100,000 British people were said to be working directly or indirectly for the offshore oil and gas industry in 1981, including around 25,000 employed on the offshore installations. Some commentators have claimed that OSO exaggerated the share of orders obtained by British firms, and that although more was produced in the UK most of the research and development behind it was carried out abroad. Nevertheless it seems clear that British industry did make progress in building up its capability in the offshore supplies industry after initial dominance by overseas com-panies, chiefly from the USA.[22]

The arrival of the Conservative government of Mrs Thatcher in 1979 coincided with another rapid rise in world oil prices, chiefly caused by the Iranian revolution, and this led to a revival of exploration and development in the North Sea. During the 1980s the Thatcher government privatised most of the state's interests in the North Sea and eased the tax burden on the oil companies. In

1982 BNOC's exploration and production activities were split off in the privatised company Britoil, and BNOC itself was abolished in 1985, its residual functions passing to the Oil and Pipelines Agency. In 1983 the British Gas Corporation's oil interests were split off in the privatised company Enterprise Oil. By 1983 Britain was the world's fifth largest oil producer, with an output of more than two million barrels per day, and a third of this went for export, the rest to home consumption. The Forties, Brent and Ninian oil fields had been the major suppliers of UKCS oil, but by the early 1980s they were regarded as mature. New oil was being sought in increasingly hostile areas, notably in the Atlantic west of the Shetlands. British North Sea oil production peaked at 127 million tonnes in 1985, declining in the following year due to the collapse of world oil prices.[23]

Indiscipline among OPEC members led to overproduction of oil and the price collapse of 1986. The price fall precipitated the worst crisis in the short history of the North Sea oil and gas industry. By the end of 1986 some 20,000 workers had been made redundant, drilling rigs and offshore support vessels were laid up, and many companies associated with the offshore industry faced ruin. The oil companies called a halt to further development in the North Sea. Fortunately the industry weathered the storm, with some government assistance, and by 1990 the oil price had made some recovery. Nevertheless the future in the North Sea looked more circumscribed. In 1990 total production was 91 million tonnes, down from 127 million in 1985, and oil exports were just over 6% of the world total, down from almost 10% in 1985. The government directed OSO to reduce its efforts getting work for British firms in the North Sea. Instead OSO was to concentrate on promoting the British offshore supplies industry worldwide. In the North Sea existing fields were more efficiently exploited, new small fields were developed, and great efforts were made on the new oil frontier west of the Shetlands. Britain would remain a major oil and gas producer into the twenty-first century, but the peak period in the North Sea seemed to have passed.[24]

Offshore Drilling Rigs and Production Platforms

When the oil companies came to the North Sea in the mid-1960s the offshore energy industry seemed to be on the verge of major expansion worldwide. George Bush, later President of the United

States, but in 1965 head of Zapata Offshore Company, observed: 'It is positively exhilarating to take a look at a world map and see the places where offshore drilling is underway or planned', but if the North Sea 'hits there won't be enough rigs'.[25] Since the late 1940s the Americans had dominated the offshore industry, but a shortage of rigs and British government pressure led to a large number of the first drilling rigs on the UKCS being built in Britain, although usually to American designs.

There are three main types of offshore drilling rig: the jack-up, the semi-submersible, and the drillship. The jack-up unit is a drilling barge with legs that can be lowered or raised. It is towed to the drilling site, then its legs are lowered to the seabed. It is most suitable for shallow waters up to a depth of 100 metres, and jack-up units were widely employed in exploring the southern North Sea. A semi-submersible drilling rig is a self-propelled working platform supported by vertical columns on submerged pontoons. By varying the amount of water ballast in the pontoons the unit can be raised or lowered in the water. Such rigs can operate in moderately rough seas, being held in place by up to eight large anchors, or by dynamic positioning. The latter system uses computer-controlled directional propellers to keep the craft stationary in relation to the seabed, compensating for wind, wave or current. Semi-submersibles can drill in water depths of 300 metres or more, and they played an important part in opening up the oil fields of the northern North Sea. Drillships have a ship's hull, but with a large aperture through which drilling takes place. They use either anchors or dynamic positioning to maintain station and they are capable of drilling in water over 1,000 metres deep.[26]

Commentators in the mid-1960s felt that the demand for new drilling rigs represented a great opportunity for British industry to move into a new area of construction. Britain's first drilling rig, the *Orient Explorer*, had been built in 1959 at Southampton, being ordered by Shell for drilling off Borneo. However, this jack-up rig had been constructed by an engineering firm rather than a shipyard. In the mid-1960s British shipyards showed some interest in diversifying into drilling rigs. Of the first sixteen drilling rigs operating in the North Sea in 1965 and 1966, half had been built in Britain. The John Brown shipyard at Clydebank had produced three jack-up units and had orders for others. Smith's Dock at Middlesbrough had built two rigs, one a jack-up and the other, the *Ocean Prince* for Burmah, the first British-built semi-submersible.

7. Semi-submersible drilling rig *Staflo*, built in 1967 at Haverton Hill-on-Tees by Swan Hunter. Based in Aberdeen, the rig was owned and operated by Shell (UK) Exploration & Production Ltd. *Staflo* discovered the Brent and the Auk oil fields in 1971 and was withdrawn from the North Sea in 1975.
(Photo: Aberdeen Journals Ltd.)

Harland & Wolff in Belfast produced a very advanced semi-submersible, the *Sea Quest*, for BP in 1966. Two rigs were the products of engineering groups rather than shipyards: the old *Orient Explorer* and the new *Norsmec I*, a jack-up assembled by Dorman Long at Middlesbrough for the North Sea Marine Engineering Construction Co. Ltd.[27]

Construction of drilling rigs by engineering groups showed one of the problems of offshore work. Were offshore drilling rigs vessels or structures? Most were built by shipyards. There was less confusion about the later offshore production platforms. They were left almost entirely to be built by engineering firms. In any case, the enthusiasm of British shipyards for building offshore drilling rigs faded quickly in most cases. It was felt that it would be difficult to integrate rig-building with conventional shipbuilding. Harland & Wolff, for example, did not build another offshore craft until more than twenty years after the completion of the *Sea Quest*.[28]

The IMEG report of 1972 recommended that the government should give support so that at least one British shipyard could concentrate on rig-building. The obvious candidate was John Brown at Clydebank. It had continued to produce jack-up rigs even after it had been absorbed into the Upper Clyde Shipbuilders group. In the restructuring which followed the collapse of that group, the government sold the Clydebank yard to the American firm Marathon specifically as a place to build jack-up rigs. In 1974 some 119 offshore drilling rigs were under construction around the world, but only three were being built in the UK: by Marathon at Clydebank. Norway was building twelve rigs, Finland nine and France five, but Singapore had twenty under construction and no less than forty-six rigs were being built in the USA. (For number of rigs in service in the North Sea in 1977 see Table 5.3.) Clearly Britain was making very little impact on this new industry. In 1980 Marathon sold the Clydebank yard to the French rig-building company UIE.[29]

Apart from John Brown only one other British shipyard made a major effort in building offshore drilling rigs. This was Scott Lithgow, also on the Clyde. After making big losses building supertankers, the yard began to move into building offshore craft in 1974, and its first products, the drillships *Ben Ocean Lancer* and *Pacnorse I*, were launched before the yard was nationalised in 1977. Next the yard produced the emergency support vessel *Iolair* for BP, and in 1980–81 came orders to build two semi-submersible drilling

Table 5.3: North Sea Vessel Requirements, Summer 1977

Jack-up drilling rigs	18
Semi-submersible drilling rigs	36
Deck cargo barges	100
Master construction barges	9
Accommodation/storage units	17
Derrick barges	16
Lay barges	4
Derrick/lay barges	8
Trenching barges	7
Fixed platforms	91
Repair & maintenance units	38
Firefighting units	12
Standby vessels	91
Supply vessels	170
Anchor-handling supply vessels	164
Anchor-handling tugs	158
Pipecarriers	32

Source: Arnold, *Britain's Oil*, p. 216.

rigs, the *Sea Explorer* for BP and the *Ocean Alliance* for Ben Odeco/ Britoil. Unfortunately building was slow and late delivery charges led to heavy financial losses. Scott Lithgow was privatised and sold to Trafalgar House in 1984, but its fortunes did not improve. The oil price collapse of 1986 killed any hope of new orders, and despite the pleas of the Scottish Trade Union Congress to preserve 'a vital facility to service a growth area in the UKCS and export markets', the yard was run down and finally closed in 1990.[30]

Thus there were only two British shipyards which took up the new opportunity of building offshore drilling rigs to any great extent. Did British business do any better in the actual operation of drilling rigs, whether British-built or not? Even if built in Britain, many rigs were in fact operated by American companies. In 1974 out of twenty-nine rigs operating on the UKCS nineteen were American operated, four American/European, three Norwegian, one French, one was operated by Shell and one was operated by BP.[31] There seemed to be an opportunity for British shipowners to get into a new area of business, but few were willing to take the risk. Even a company like Hunting, with an oil tanker fleet and extensive interests in the oil industry worldwide, restricted its North Sea involvement to seismic surveying and specialist technology such as directional drilling.[32] Only a few British shipowners were ready to become operators of offshore drilling rigs.

In March 1974 it was announced that the Ben Line of Leith, well-known operators of deep-sea cargo liners and container ships, would enter into partnership with the major American firm Ocean Drilling and Exploration Company (ODECO) to set up an offshore drilling company, Ben Odeco Ltd. Ben participated in the joint venture via its subsidiary Ben Offshore Contractors Ltd. Ben Odeco took over from ODECO the *Ocean Tide*, a jack-up rig completed at Clydebank in 1971, and also purchased an old drillship, renamed *Ben Ocean Typhoon*. Ben Odeco placed an order with Scott Lithgow for one of the world's most advanced dynamically positioned drill-ships, completed as the *Ben Ocean Lancer* in 1977.[33]

In 1976 Ben Line purchased the Sheaf Steam Shipping Co. of Newcastle, which had a share in the Atlantic Drilling Co. Ltd. (ADC). This firm had been set up in 1974 by partners including Sheaf and the Cardiff shipowners Sir William Reardon Smith & Sons Ltd., and it had ordered two semi-submersible drilling rigs, one from Norway and one from Finland. Smiths had also ordered another semi-submersible from Finland for their Celtic Drilling Co. The various rigs were delivered in 1976 with *Atlantic 1* and *Atlantic 2* for ADC and *Sea Conquest* for Celtic, which chartered the craft to BP. After Ben bought Sheaf, ADC was restructured so that Ben owned one rig and Smiths the other. However, the Cardiff firm eventually decided to get out of drilling: *Atlantic 1* was sold to Ben in 1978 and *Sea Conquest* to its charterer BP in 1979.[34]

The other famous shipping company based in Leith, Christian Salvesen, also took an interest in the maritime opportunities offered in the North Sea. With Norwegian origins, the company was well-known for its shipping, whaling and fishing activities.[35] It provided a number of services to the North Sea oil industry, including the safety/rescue vessels (converted trawlers) of its subsidiary Safetyships of Aberdeen. From 1977 more sophisticated multi-task vessels entered the Safetyships fleet and by the early 1980s interest shifted to pollution control vessels. Renamed Salvesen Marine (Offshore), the firm was asked by BP to design, convert and manage a safety/pollution vessel. This craft, the *Fasgadair*, was delivered in 1981 and began working in BP's Forties field. In 1986 Salvesen Marine (Offshore) was sold to John Wood of Aberdeen.[36]

Christian Salvesen also took an interest in offshore drilling and became the first British company to have sole ownership of a drillship. However, although their acquisition was inspired by North Sea activities, Christian Salvesen's drillships were not intended to operate there. They were to work in medium depths in calm, tropical waters. Salvesen Offshore Drilling was set up in 1971 and in the following year began to convert an American vessel into a drillship. This appeared in 1974 as the *Dalmahoy* and was joined in 1976 by another conversion, the *Dalkeith*. These drillships operated in India, Australia, the Mediterranean and the Middle East. However, difficult market conditions led Christian Salvesen to sell the two vessels in 1979–80, thus bringing to an end what the annual report for 1979 called 'a disappointing venture'.[37]

Another long-established shipping company that became a drilling rig operator was the major liner shipping group Furness Withy, through its subsidiary Houlder Brothers. As early as 1972 Houlder Brothers took a 20% stake in Kingsnorth Marine Drilling Ltd., which had ordered two drilling rigs from Finland. By 1980 Houlders had control of Kingsnorth and its rigs were managed by Houlder Offshore Ltd., set up in 1975. The rigs had been joined by a specialised pipe-connection vessel in 1974 and a dynamically positioned semi-submersible diving support vessel in 1977. In 1980 control of Furness Withy passed to the C.Y. Tung shipping group of Hong Kong. Offshore work became very important to Furness Withy in the early 1980s and Houlder Offshore had new rigs and specialist craft built. These operated not only in the North Sea, but also in Morecambe Bay, the Gulf and the South China Sea. At a time when shipping was making big losses, offshore work was a vital support for Furness Withy. In 1982 the group's shipping operations lost almost £11 million, but offshore activities made a profit of £14.5 million, leaving the group with a small overall profit.[38]

When the C.Y. Tung group ran into financial difficulties in 1985, Furness Withy faced a difficult future and the position of Houlder Offshore was worsened by the oil price collapse of 1986. It is a sign of the very limited success of British offshore drilling companies that in 1986 their trade association had only four members—Atlantic Drilling Co. Ltd., Houlder Offshore Ltd., Jebsen Drilling plc and KCA Offshore Drilling Ltd.—and one of these, Jebsen, was a subsidiary of a Norwegian company. Between them the four companies operated nineteen offshore drilling rigs, of which fourteen were in the North Sea and the remainder overseas. At the start of 1986 95% of the rigs in the North Sea had been employed, but at the end of the year, after the oil price collapse, less than half were working. There was a danger that the British contractors, having spent twelve years carving out 'a small but respected place in the domestic and international market', might have to lay up their rigs. Conditions improved somewhat in 1987, but Houlder Offshore was sold to the Swedish shipping group Stena in 1989.[39]

In Norway some shipping companies moved into the offshore sector more decisively than their British counterparts. One such was the major shipping group Wilhelm Wilhelmsen (WW). Between 1972 and 1986 some eight semi-submersible drilling rigs and thirty-two offshore support vessels of various types were delivered to the firm's offshore subsidiary, and by 1985 64% of WW's total operating results came from offshore activities, an overdependence which hurt the company badly when the oil price collapsed in 1986. WW's first three drilling rigs in the 1970s were all built to the Norwegian Aker design, but only one was constructed in Norway, the others coming from Finland and Singapore. In the 1980s three new drilling rigs came from Sweden, one from Finland and one from Japan.[40]

Thus British shipyards had only limited success in the rig-building business, while British shipowners did not have much greater impact in the operation of such rigs. With regard to the construction of production platforms, the traditional maritime industries were only incidentally involved. The fabrication of platforms was largely the work of engineering and construction companies. It was only in the area of component supply that maritime industries were able to participate. For example, firms that had supplied the declining Clyde shipyards with items such as engines and pumps now found new outlets in the platform fabrication sites. It is unclear how many ex-shipyard workers found employment at those sites. Given the general hostility to trade unions in the offshore industry, men well versed in the restrictive practices of the shipyards would not have been welcome.[41]

The first demand for production platforms was on the gas fields of the southern North Sea, and these were initially provided almost entirely by Dutch manufacturers. For example, production platforms installed by Shell/Esso on the Leman and Indefatigable gas fields between 1967 and 1975 were nearly all built in the

Netherlands, with the only British input being some deck modules. However, between 1977 and 1990 later developments on Leman and Indefatigable and the new Sean gas field had production platforms almost entirely built in Britain, chiefly by Redpath de Groot Caledonian (RGC) at Methil and McDermott Scotland at Ardersier.[42]

The gas production platforms were never as large and complex as those required by the oil fields of the northern North Sea. The first oil produced, from the Argyll field in 1975, went through a converted semi-submersible drilling rig, *Transworld 58*, for immediate transfer to tankers.[43] Most oil fields, however, had fixed production platforms, made of either steel or concrete, and often linked to pipeline systems carrying the oil to shore terminals. By the beginning of 1972, with a number of major oil fields identified, it was clear that large production platforms would have to be built. A hunt began to find suitable platform-building sites on the Scottish coastline, with spacious areas near to deep water as the ideal. The sites were primarily for the construction of the huge 'jackets', the legs or other supporting structures for the platform. The decks and deck modules (for accommodation, power, processing, etc.) could be built elsewhere and then be united with the jacket during the final assembly.

The number of production platforms required was initially overestimated and too many sites were developed. Of two governmentowned sites, Portavadie and Hunterston, both on the Clyde estuary, the former never did any fabrication and the latter only a small amount. The principal sites were Methil in Fife (used by Redpath Dorman Long; Redpath de Groot Caledonian; RGC Offshore); Ardersier on the Moray Firth (used by McDermott Scotland); and Nigg Bay on the Cromarty Firth (used by Highland Fabricators). Other significant British fabrication sites included Ardyne Point on the Clyde (used by MacAlpine/Sea Tank); Graythorpe on Teesside (used by Laing Offshore); and Loch Kishorn in the Western Highlands (used by Howard Doris). Of forty-three oil production platforms on the UKCS at the end of 1987, more than thirty had been built at British fabrication sites. Others came from Norway, France, the Netherlands and Spain, as well as several joint British/ European constructions. Several of the British fabrication firms had foreign participants, such as the American firm Brown and Root in Highland Fabricators and the Dutch firm de Groot Zwijndrecht in Redpath de Groot Caledonian.[44]

In the first half of the 1970s there was an enthusiasm for building concrete production platforms. This preference was partly due to the high cost of steel, but also because building in concrete was easier for construction companies than the more complex engineering skills demanded by steel construction. The Norwegians were the pioneers with their 'condeep' design. Several Norwegian-built condeeps appeared on UKCS oil fields and British firms also ventured into concrete construction, MacAlpine/Sea Tank producing a number of concrete platforms at Ardyne. The most famous British-built concrete platform was that for the Ninian field constructed at Loch Kishorn by Howard Doris between 1974 and 1978. When completed it weighed 600,000 tons and was called 'the biggest movable object on earth'. Seven tugs were needed to tow it to the Ninian field for installation. Concrete platforms then fell from favour for a time, partly because steel had become cheaper, and when they were once again in demand the type was largely a Norwegian monopoly. The Howard Doris yard at Kishorn did not prosper. It shared with Hunterston the building of the platform for the Maureen field in the early 1980s, but the oil price collapse of 1986 forced Howard Doris into liquidation.[45]

As with gas production platforms, after 1980 most new oil production platforms for the UKCS were built at British sites. At the end of 1987 the four production platforms under construction for the UKCS were being built in the UK. (See Table 5.4.) The problem was that platform-building could not be a long-term business since North Sea demand was finite. A shift to floating production platforms from the late 1980s seemed to offer more business, particularly in export markets. However, since floating production platforms closely resembled drillships, it seemed natural that they should be constructed in shipyards. Clearly the future for platform fabrication sites did not look hopeful, especially as the high cost of dismantling redundant fixed production platforms made oil companies more reluctant to build new ones.[46]

If the fabrication of production platforms had been general engineering rather than a specifically maritime industry, the movement of such structures to the fields and their installation was definitely maritime work. However, while British tugs might be involved, the heavy lift vessels and barge cranes usually involved were almost a Dutch monopoly. Pipelines were an important feature of the UKCS, with nearly a dozen gas pipelines and four main oil pipelines (from the Brent field to Sullom Voe; from the Piper

Table 5.4: Oil Production Platforms on the UKCS, 1987

(A) Oil production platforms in place on UKCS, end of 1987.
　　1 floating production facility
　　2 converted drilling rigs
　　7 concrete production platforms
　33 steel production platforms

(B) Where built
　　1 floating production facility—Sweden
　　2 converted drilling rigs—converted in Scotland
　　7 concrete production platforms (all built 1975–78)
　　　　　　　　　　　　　　　　　　　　　　　　　—3 Norway
　　　　　　　　　　　　　　　　　　　　　　　　　　3 Scotland
　　　　　　　　　　　　　　　　　　　　　　　　　　1 Netherlands
　33 steel production platforms—23 Scotland
　　　　　　　　　　　　　　　　　　3 England
　　　　　　　　　　　　　　　　　　2 France
　　　　　　　　　　　　　　　　　　2 Spain
　　　　　　　　　　　　　　　　　　3 France/Scotland

(C) Under construction for UKCS, end of 1987
　　1 floating production facility—building in Northern Ireland
　　1 converted drilling rig—conversion in Scotland/England
　　2 steel production platforms—building in Scotland

Source: The Brown Book 1988, Appendix 10.

field to Flotta; from the Forties field to Cruden Bay; and from the Norwegian Ekofisk field to Teesside). However, British involvement in the laying of these pipelines was not great, being little more than pipe-coating on shore before the pipes were taken out to be laid by American, Dutch or Norwegian pipelaying vessels.[47]

In 1980 the out-going director general of the Offshore Supplies Office, Norman Smith, criticised British industry: 'The UK's worst record is probably in marine activities requiring very large capital investment—drilling rigs, dual-purpose diving support vessels, heavy lift, and pipelaying vessels, for example.'[48] Undoubtedly there was much truth in this observation, with only limited shipyard interest in building offshore drilling rigs or shipowners in operating them. British lack of interest in heavy lift ships and pipelaying vessels has been noted, but Smith's observations in relation to diving support vessels seem inaccurate. There was considerable British interest in diving and other undersea activities on the UKCS.[49] Diving support vessels were often operated by British companies running a range of offshore support vessels. It is these companies that must now be considered, and they represent one area where British maritime industry showed considerable enterprise in response to the challenge of exploiting North Sea oil and gas resources.

Offshore Support Vessels

One of the new areas of opportunity opened up by the North Sea energy industry was the operation of offshore support vessels (OSVs).[50] Without such vessels the drilling rigs and later the production platforms could not function. A wide variety of craft are covered by the term offshore support vessel, including pipelaying vessels, seismic survey craft and diving support vessels, but the principal types treated here are the anchor-handling tug supply (AHTS) and platform supply (PS) vessels. These craft formed the backbone of the North Sea fleet and accounted for more than half of all OSVs.[51]

When exploration began in the North Sea in the mid-1960s the Americans had a virtual monopoly of OSVs, the Tidewater company running the biggest fleet in the world. Nevertheless British companies were not slow to challenge the Americans. In the summer of 1966 twelve oil company groups were employing twenty OSVs in the British sector of the southern North Sea. Nine of these vessels had been built in Britain, seven in the Netherlands and four in the USA. The main British companies operating were P&O Offshore Services Ltd. (partly associated with Dutch, French and Norwegian companies through the joint venture International Offshore Services Ltd.), the construction company George Wimpey (in association with the American construction firm Brown and Root), and Offshore Marine Ltd., owned by North Sea Marine Engineering Construction Ltd. (a consortium of British engineering companies) and the short sea shipowners London & Rochester Trading Co. Ltd. Offshore Marine was later bought by Cunard. The long-established Lowestoft fishing firm of Small & Co. had provided vessels for seismic surveys and after the loss of the rig *Sea Gem* in 1965 it pioneered the safety standby business with former fishing vessels.

Small later bought supply vessels and all its shipping was managed by the subsidiary Suffolk Marine.[52]

When exploration shifted from the search for gas in the southern North Sea to the search for oil off Scotland in the northern North Sea, new opportunities in the OSV sector seemed to be on offer. These were noted in the IMEG report of 1972. The report expected OSV business to double in the next few years. Annual charter rates for a new vessel were reckoned to be around £300,000. Older and smaller vessels could only command rates half that figure. A modern supply vessel could cost up to £1 million, and oil companies insisted on very high technical specification and performance from such vessels. Each drilling rig needed two or three OSVs to keep it supplied while in operation. The report noted that in the summer of 1972 there were eighty supply vessels operating in the North Sea, of which only twenty-five were registered in the UK.[53]

However, even before the IMEG study was carried out, new British OSV operators were coming forward. Ocean Transport & Trading, well known as operators of deep-sea cargo liners (Blue Funnel, Glen and Elder Dempster lines) and container ships (as part of the OCL consortium), decided at the start of the 1970s to diversify into OSV operations in the North Sea. Ocean chose the international trading group Inchcape as its partner in this venture, since their respective subsidiaries Straits Steamship and the Borneo Company had already set up a joint OSV company, Borneo Straits Offshore, in the Far East in 1969. In 1971 Ocean Inchcape Ltd. (OIL) was set up in London to undertake the North Sea operation. Because British shipyards could not guarantee delivery within the required time, OIL's first eight AHTS vessels were designed and built in the Netherlands between 1972 and 1973. OIL's operating bases were to be at Dundee and at Lerwick in the Shetlands.[54]

Since most oil fields were off Scotland, it is not surprising that Scottish shipping companies now became interested in establishing OSV operations. The Glasgow firms of Lyle Shipping Co. and Hogarth Shipping Co. already had close links when, with the assistance of Edinburgh merchant bankers Noble Grossart, they set up Seaforth Maritime Ltd. in Aberdeen in April 1972. Each shipping company took 30% of the initial £1 million capital, and the remainder was held by other Scottish companies. Seaforth made a determined effort to have all its OSVs built in British shipyards, and the first four came from Cochrane's of Selby in 1973–74.[55]

Another Glasgow shipping firm which decided to move into

OSVs at this time was Harrisons (Clyde) Ltd. Although with family links back to the firm of Gow Harrison, the first to own tankers in Scotland, H(C)L had, like Lyle and Hogarth, been chiefly involved with deep-sea dry cargo shipping in the recent past. OSVs represented a diversification, and it was decided in 1973 to use an existing subsidiary, Stirling Shipping, for the North Sea project. Stirling's first four OSVs were to be built by Cochranes, and three would be leased to the company by the Royal Bank of Scotland, with the other being leased to Stirling by H(C)L. The first Stirling OSV became operational in the North Sea in late 1974.[56]

A survey of OSV activity in the North Sea during the summer of 1974 noted 256 vessels, of which the principal groups by flag were British (fifty-nine vessels), American (fifty-three), Norwegian (forty-four), and Dutch (twenty-seven). The number of British vessels had more than doubled from only twenty-five vessels in the summer of 1972. Nevertheless British progress in the OSV sector was being challenged by other European OSV fleets. The biggest British OSV operator, Offshore Marine, had twenty-nine vessels, but the Dutch firm Smit-Lloyd had thirty-nine vessels and the West German firm Offshore Supplies Association (OSA) had fifty-six vessels. It was only the fact that both the latter firms operated chiefly worldwide that blunted their challenge in the North Sea. Of equal significance was the growing strength of the Norwegian OSV fleet. In 1974 the Norwegians had a staggering 113 OSVs on order (compared to the UK's forty on order) and if all these vessels were completed Norway would have an OSV fleet second only to that of the USA.[57]

Only 5.5% (fifty vessels) of the world OSV fleet in December 1974 had been built in British shipyards, the largest number (twenty-one vessels) coming from the Drypool Group, which included the Cochrane yard at Selby. The principal European builder of OSVs had been the Netherlands, but by the end of 1974 Norway had 13.1% of the world OSV order book, not far behind the Dutch share of 14.8%. Britain had only 5.8% of world OSV orders. The major British shipyards had little interest in building OSVs, and, apart from Drypool, orders were scattered around a variety of small British shipbuilders, including Clelands on the Tyne, Appledore in North Devon and Hall Russell in Aberdeen. Each yard rarely received orders for more than one or two vessels. Even Drypool, with a steady stream of orders, could not start series production of a standard OSV design, unlike Ulstein of Norway which produced

8. British and Norwegian offshore support vessels in Aberdeen harbour, *c.* 1978. British OSVs include *Cumbria Shore*, built by Appledore Shipbuilders, Devon, in 1977, and *Hamilton Piper*, built in South Africa in 1976.
(Photo: Aberdeen Art Gallery and Museums Collections)

the UT704 in 1975, the first of the OSV standard types and one which was to be the basic workhorse of the industry for the next ten years.[58]

The building of OSVs in Britain was thrown into confusion when the Drypool Group went into receivership in late 1975. Companies such as Seaforth Maritime and Stirling Shipping still had vessels building at Cochrane's and it was only with difficulty that they had them completed in 1976–77. Seaforth, recognising that the North Sea OSV market was becoming heavily oversupplied with vessels, took advantage of the delay to have its final ship on order completed in 1977 as a sophisticated firefighting and diving support vessel instead. The blow-out on Norway's Ekofisk oil field in early 1977 had shown the need for more firefighting vessels.[59]

By 1976 it was clear that the first peak of oil exploration in the northern North Sea had passed and a quieter time of exploitation and production was beginning. But the rising expectations of the period 1970–75 had led to a serious oversupply of OSVs, particularly by the Norwegians. In search of employment they began to move into the British sector, pushing down charter rates. The Norwegians could do this because the British sector as well as being the largest in the North Sea was also the only one wide open to foreign competition. All the other sectors operated some form of official or unofficial protectionism. In the Danish sector, for example, the government had given exclusive offshore rights for fifty years to the Danish shipping company A.P. Möller.[60] Indeed the British sector of the North Sea was probably unique in the world in the access it allowed to foreign OSVs. Most other countries either operated overt protectionism in offshore energy development, above all the USA, or made foreign participation difficult, as in Australia. In the early 1970s P&O largely withdrew from OSV operations in the North Sea, but to continue OSV operations in Australia it had to set up a subsidiary company there.[61]

Despite increased foreign competition, the British OSV industry was to weather the slowdown of the late 1970s and then enjoy renewed boom conditions after the world oil price rise in 1979–80. Indeed between 1975 and 1985 the UK-registered AHTS and PS vessel fleet doubled in size. Overall between 1980 and 1984 OSV demand in the North Sea area increased by more than 55%, equivalent to one hundred additional vessels. (See Tables 5.5 and 5.6.) This change drew new entrants into the sector, not always from traditional shipping backgrounds. Captain David Grimes set up the Lowline OSV company in 1981, but much of his financial assistance came from the venture capitalists Investors in Industry (3i). Between 1975 and 1985 the OSV sector was the only area of the British shipping industry that was growing.[62]

While new firms joined the OSV sector, some older companies disappeared or were restructured. The former leading British OSV firm Offshore Marine had been sold to the American OSV operator Zapata and lost its independent existence. In 1983 Inchcape sold its interest in OIL to its partner Ocean, which now became sole owner of the firm but left the company name unchanged because of the memorable initials.[63] As in the boom of the first half of the 1970s, that in the first half of the 1980s had led by 1984 to an oversupply of OSVs. Stirling sought to find a use for its older, surplus OSVs by converting them into safety standby vessels and setting up the Haven Shipping Company to manage them.[64]

By 1985 the boom conditions were ending and British OSV owners became increasingly resentful of foreign craft operating in the British sector of the North Sea. The chief interlopers were the Norwegians, either under their own flag or through UK-based

Table 5.5: Number of AHTS and PS Vessels Employed
in the North Sea by Sector, 1980–1986
(Figures at June each year)

Sector	1980	1981	1982	1983	1984	1985	1986
UK: Northern	101	99	111	132	135	109	73
Southern	9	11	17	24	41	30	35
	110	110	128	156	176	139	108
Norway	43	52	51	51	62	44	60
Netherlands	19	23	28	27	31	37	29
Denmark	4	4	13	7	5	8	5
West Germany	—	3	7	—	1	1	1
Total	176	192	227	241	275	229	203

Source: Coopers & Lybrand report 1986, p. 19.

Table 5.6: The North Sea OSV Fleet by Location of
Building Yard, January 1986
(Number of vessels)

Area of Build	UK	Nor.	Neth.	Flag Den.	W. Ger.	Other	Total
UK	48	—	—	—	—	1	49
Norway	13	81	—	2	—	3	99
Netherlands	8	13	24	3	—	1	49
Denmark	9	2	—	5	—	—	16
West Germany	9	12	2	—	18	2	43
Other Europe	5	4	3	—	—	—	12
Far East	17	1	—	—	—	2	20
Other	4	—	2	—	—	9	15
Not known	—	1	—	—	—	—	1
Total	113	114	31	10	18	18	304

Source: Coopers & Lybrand Report 1986, p. 95.

151

subsidiaries. Their presence was particularly resented because British OSVs could get little work in the Norwegian sector, but the British sector was open to all. British OSV owners demanded the imposition of protectionist restrictions in the British sector. Indeed they felt so strongly that in 1985 they left the General Council of British Shipping (GCBS) and set up the British Offshore Support Vessels Association (BOSVA) because they felt the GCBS would not depart from its traditional commitment to free trade in shipping services. Together with the government's Offshore Supplies Office (OSO), BOSVA commissioned a report into the state of the British OSV industry in 1986. Just as this was being prepared, the world oil price collapsed and OSV operators faced the worst crisis in the North Sea in their short history.[65]

According to the report, prepared by accountants Coopers & Lybrand, in October 1985 the principal British-owned and British flag OSV operators in the North Sea had been Stirling (fifteen PSV owned or managed) and Seaforth (five AHTSV and eight PSV). The former was jointly owned by Harrisons (Clyde) Ltd. and the major trade and shipping group Swires, while the latter was now jointly owned by the overseas trading company James Findlay and the construction company Taylor Woodrow. OIL had only four AHTS vessels in the North Sea at this time, most of its fleet working in West Africa and South America. Star Offshore Services Marine Ltd. had three AHTS and five PS vessels in the North Sea, and other vessels working in the Far East. Suffolk Marine had three AHTS and one PS in the North Sea, while Wimpey Marine had three AHTS and two PS in that area. Lowline's owned AHTS vessel was working in Tunisia, but the company managed one AHTS and two PS vessels in the North Sea on behalf of 3i. Other British flag OSVs in fact had Norwegian, Swedish, Danish, West German, Australian and American beneficial owners.[66]

The Coopers & Lybrand report saw British-owned OSVs in the North Sea facing three main problems. First, the penetration of the UK market by foreign-owned vessels. In 1985 there were 139 OSVs operating in the UK sector. By flag, thirty were Norwegian, ten West German, nine Dutch, two Danish and three other foreign, while at least 25% of the eighty-five British flag vessels were in fact foreign-owned. Secondly, there was the inability of British owners to get work in the Norwegian sector, for in 1985 of the forty-four OSVs working in that area forty-three were Norwegian and one British. Thirdly, there was the need to improve the long-term profitability of the industry and ensure a British presence in it was maintained. The report accepted that the foreign presence in the British sector was inevitable because of the British free competition policy. The report put the blame for the inability of British operators to get much work in the Norwegian sector on the 'unstated protectionism' operated by the Norwegians. Their government put national interests first and even if laws were relaxed, the high level of interdependence between the various sectors of the Norwegian economy would limit business opportunities for outsiders.[67]

In particular the Norwegians, like other foreign countries, gave their shipowners a supportive fiscal regime. British OSV companies, like most British shipowners, felt their own government did not. Their financial problems were greatly increased by the fall in the world price of oil. Oil companies cut back their operations in the North Sea and by late 1986 over 30% of the British OSV fleet was unemployed. It was suggested that the government could assist the industry in three ways. First, by imposing short-term restrictions on entry to the UK market by foreign-flag vessels, combined with tighter control over the registration of OSVs in the UK when they were in fact under foreign control. Secondly, by giving financial assistance, principally in the form of loan moratoria or rescheduling of debt repayments, plus assistance with redundancy payments. Thirdly, the government could encourage a regrouping of British OSV companies into fewer and larger units.[68]

Perhaps to the surprise of BOSVA the government did take some action in response to its complaints. Under the so-called OSO initiative, the OSO decided to check all the OSV contracts in the British North Sea sector made with parties from outside the EEC (which chiefly meant Norway) to see if their terms amounted to fair competition with British operators. The initiative was agreed with the UK Offshore Operators Association (UKOOA) and it helped to keep Norwegian tonnage out of the British sector for eighteen months, which BOSVA described as 'a vital breathing space'. However, the restriction could not last and, after UKOOA pressure, it was ended early in 1989. A less welcome British government intervention occurred in 1987 when the Office of Fair Trading took action against British OSV companies who co-operated in an attempt to set minimum charter rates for vessels operating out of Aberdeen or Great Yarmouth.[69]

The period 1987–90 was a hard one for the British OSV industry and there was considerable restructuring. Seaforth and Wimpey got out of OSVs altogether. In 1989 the Ocean group reviewed its shipping interests. All deep-sea shipping operations were ended, but it was decided to expand the group's OSV interests, with OIL purchasing the West German OSA fleet. With more than a hundred vessels OIL now had the largest OSV fleet outside the USA, with most of its vessels operating worldwide rather than being concentrated in the North Sea.[70] From small beginnings in the early 1970s one British company had successfully exploited its opportunities in the North Sea (and elsewhere) to build up a world-class OSV operation.

Thus in the area of offshore support vessels the traditional shipping industry could be said to have achieved a large measure of success. The shipowners had done much less well in operating offshore drilling rigs, while the shipbuilders had not much better success in building them, the Clydebank yard's long-running production being balanced by Scott Lithgow's failure to survive in offshore construction. The ports had provided the necessary facilities to keep the offshore oil and gas industry going, and the redundant fishing trawlers had found employment for a time as safety standby vessels. Nevertheless the overall conclusion must be that the British maritime industries largely failed to reap any substantial, long-term benefits from the opportunities offered by Britain's new offshore energy sector. The Norwegians did considerably better and there were no British equivalents to the Aker H-3 drilling rig, the 'condeep' concrete production platform, or the Ulstein UT704 offshore support vessel, designs which set the standard not just in the North Sea but in offshore operations around the world.

6

Conclusion

The 1990 working party on British shipping concluded that it was 'a vital national asset. After its years of contraction, it is lean and fit. The industry is well placed to take advantage of the upturn in world trade, in the right conditions.'[1] World shipping certainly regained some prosperity during the 1990s, but the British shipping industry on the whole did not take a great share in this. The principal exception was P&O under the leadership of Lord Sterling, who as Sir Jeffrey Sterling had been closely involved in the 1990 report as President of the General Council of British Shipping for 1990–91.

With a background of success in finance and property investment rather than the maritime industries, Sterling had become chairman of P&O in 1983. In 1986 he had secured sole ownership of the OCL container consortium for P&O and in 1987 took control of European Ferries.[2] Building on these acquisitions, P&O merged its container operations with those of the Dutch firm Nedlloyd in 1996, creating in P&O Nedlloyd one of the top container shipping operators in the world, and then P&O and the Swedish firm Stena linked their European ferry operations.[3] However, perhaps the most important P&O success was in the world of cruise ships. The firm built up the world's third largest fleet, with all the new vessels constructed outside Britain, and when P&O's *Grand Princess* (109,000 gross tons; built in Italy) appeared in 1998 she was the largest cruise ship in the world.[4] P&O no longer had any significant British rivals in the cruise area, Cunard having been sold to the Norwegian firm Kvaerner in 1996 and then to the American company Carnival, the world's leading cruise line, in 1998.[5] In 1999 Lord Sterling announced that P&O was to return to its roots, restructuring around its maritime operations and selling off non-maritime interests.[6]

155

Yet one company, no matter how successful, is not an industry. If P&O prospered, other British shipping firms gave up the struggle. Ropners, once Britain's largest tramp shipping company, was sold in 1997, albeit to Jacobs Holdings, a British firm with shipping and port interests.[7] The most dynamic British independent tanker owner of the postwar period, London and Overseas Freighters, was merged with John Fredriksen's Frontline shipping group, also in 1997.[8] In the same year a new Labour government came to power and among its commitments was one to revive British shipping. In late 1998 the government published a strategy aimed at enhancing the UK's attractiveness to shipping enterprises.[9] In 1999 the government promised to bring in a tonnage tax, like that in Germany, Norway and the Netherlands, which it was hoped would bring tonnage back under the British flag. In return for this fiscal concession, British shipowners were to expand their training of seafarers.[10] For the first time in years, a British government seemed to be taking active measures to assist British shipping, but the long-term effects are as yet uncertain.

If British shipping did show some glimmers of hope during the 1990s, British shipbuilding largely remained lost in the gloom, and this continued malaise was in a decade when world shipbuilding was enjoying a general recovery. By 1994 shipbuilding had ceased at Cammell Laird (Birkenhead) and Swan Hunter (Newcastle), and in March 1995 Britain had only five merchant shipyards left, of which only Kvaerner-Govan and Harland & Wolff were building vessels of more than 30,000 dwt.[11] Both yards were owned by Norwegian firms. From 1995 there began some revival in the shipyards, but not initially in new building. Cammell Laird, bought from Vickers, began to revive as a ship repairer, then moved into ship conversions. A similar process was taking place at Swan Hunter by 1996.[12] Nevertheless at the start of 1997 the principal British shipyards were still three naval ones—Vickers (VSEL) at Barrow, Yarrows at Glasgow and Vosper Thornycroft at Southampton—and four merchant: Harland & Wolff, Kvaerner-Govan, Ferguson at Glasgow and Appledore in North Devon.[13] The end of the Cold War had reduced naval orders and one of the naval yards, Vickers, was undertaking merchant work as well. The industry remained at a low ebb, although new naval orders were promised at the end of the decade. When in 1999 P&O ordered five new cruise ships at a total cost of £1.25 billion the orders all went abroad, the company claiming that no British shipyard was capable of building them.[14]

If British shipping had only limited success in the 1990s and British shipbuilding did little more than avoid final extinction, the country's ports continued to improve their efficiency. The 1991 Ports Act made possible the compulsory privatisation of all trust ports with an annual turnover of £5 million or more. A private company was set up to run Tilbury, and the Clyde, Forth, Tees, Medway and other port authorities soon followed Tilbury into the private sector. Some municipal ports also followed the trend, with Bristol, for example, passing to a private company on a 150-year lease in 1991. The private company did much to revive the port of Bristol, while another private company took over the old BP refinery site on the Isle of Grain and built a new container facility called Thamesport. By 1993 nine of the ten top British ports were wholly or largely controlled by private interests. The exception was Sullom Voe, which was still run by the Shetland Islands Council. In 1994 it was announced that Felixstowe, the flagship of the privately owned ports, was the leading container port in the UK, the fourth in Europe, and fifteenth in the world, handling almost half of Britain's deep-sea container traffic. Felixstowe was also, after Dover, the second largest ro-ro port in the UK. The triumphs of privatisation seemed complete, and although the dispute from 1995 to 1998 over sacked dockers at Liverpool brought back memories of an embittered past, in general the port companies felt they had made a successful transition to a modern and efficient industry.[15]

In the North Sea oil and gas production kept up better than expected during the 1990s with new peaks in oil and gas production. In 1996 UKOOA suggested that UK North Sea oil production would stay above consumption for at least ten years and reserves would last for at least another twenty years.[16] Nevertheless the North Sea was a 'mature' oil and gas province, and new exploration was pushed into areas in the Atlantic west of the Shetlands. New fields were found, but developments were hampered by various factors, not least the fall in crude oil prices at the end of the 1990s. In 1999 BP and its partners agreed to suspend work on the huge Clair field (with an estimated five billion barrels of oil) west of the Shetlands.[17]

One of the emerging problems in the North Sea during the 1990s was the huge cost of removing redundant structures from the UKCS. The fate of the (floating) Brent Spar caused an outcry from environmentalists in 1995, but at least fifty of the 200 or so structures on the UKCS were noted in 1996 as having to be removed in the next ten years at a cost of £1.4 billion.[18] For this reason oil to be extracted from fields west of the Shetlands would be taken out by floating production platforms.[19] A few of these were built in Britain, but most were not. The share of the British maritime industries in offshore energy suffered a major blow in 1997 when OIL, the second largest OSV operator in the world, was sold by its owner Ocean to the number one operator, the American firm Tidewater. OIL had become a worldwide operator, with the North Sea just one part of its scheme, but its disappearance marked the end of perhaps the main British maritime success story from the North Sea opportunity. Now only Stirling Shipping remained as the principal British OSV operator in the North Sea.[20]

Thus during the 1990s the situation in the British maritime industries remained little changed from that in 1990. Despite the success of P&O, British shipping in general showed no great signs of revival, although the government finally offered some support at the end of the decade. Shipbuilding remained in a poor condition and despite a few hopeful signs, it is clear the remaining shipyards have a hand to mouth existence, with the prospect of total shutdown never far away. The ports alone of the old maritime industries have successfully completed the transition to a modern and efficient operation, although largely concentrated on only a handful of major ports. North Sea oil and gas still remain of vital importance to the British economy and will continue to do so for ten to twenty years. On the whole the British maritime industries failed to take much advantage of the North Sea opportunity and what was achieved, such as OIL, was not sustained in the long term. Compared to the situation in 1914, Britain's maritime industries—other than offshore energy—are now of minor importance in her national economic life. How has this great change come about?

The Course of Decline

'For one half century [1870–1920], British shipping had dominated the world; complacency was one effect of this supremacy. The shipping industry of 1920 was one geared to the maintenance of supremacy, not the meeting of changes.'[21] So wrote one commentator on the history of British shipping. His charge of complacency and reluctance to change might cover British shipbuilding and ports as well as shipping, but it would seem unwise to put all the blame for the decline of the British maritime industries on internal failings, at least in the interwar period.

Whatever action those industries took between 1920 and 1939, one fundamental external factor could not be wished away. During most of the interwar period world trade showed little growth, only exceeding the 1914 level in a few years. The demand for shipping services, new ships and more port facilities was not growing. If demand was less, supply was more, with more countries expanding their maritime industries and steadily reducing Britain's maritime supremacy. Two challenges faced the British maritime industries. First and most immediate was the need to adapt to the negative change of the collapse in demand. Secondly, there was the need to adjust to changes in marine technology and trade patterns. It can be argued that by adapting to the second challenge the British maritime industries might have been better able to deal with the first, and Norway has often been put forward as an example of what an enterprising maritime state could achieve in the interwar period.

However, Norway did not have the array of maritime commitments that burdened Britain in good times and in bad. At this time Norway had little shipbuilding of her own, only a comparatively small national trade needing few major ports, and her national merchant fleet was almost entirely devoted to tramp shipping, which required little infrastructure but did put a premium on rapid response to changes in the world shipping market. In contrast Britain had the world's largest shipbuilding industry, a huge national trade which had led to massive investment in port facilities, and the world's largest merchant fleet, of which the majority was liner shipping, with an expensive worldwide infrastructure which not only bound the British empire together but also provided the basic framework for world seaborne trade through the British-dominated liner conference system.

Norway was comparatively free to seize new opportunities such as motorships and oil tankers to see her through the grim interwar years. Britain also made progress in those areas, but she was also held back by the burden of past maritime assets which had now become liabilities. Shipbuilding was probably the most depressed of all British industries in the interwar period; the ports saw comparatively little new investment while providing a declining service; and in shipping while the liner system had to be maintained for economic and political reasons, the collapse of the Royal Mail shipping group made liner shipping less attractive to investors. British tramp shipping suffered what was almost to be a fatal blow. Damaged by the boom and bust of 1919–20, it was further hit by the steady decline in British coal exports after then. Tramp companies disappeared—as did many of the shipyards that had provided their ships—and few new firms took their place. This was of fundamental importance since tramping was the entry level for the shipping industry. With no new blood coming in, the long-term health of the industry was undermined.

One reaction to the problems of the interwar period was a shift away from free trade and towards economic nationalism in the 1930s. In 1931–32 Britain took this road, ending her commitment to free trade and turning in upon herself. British shipbuilding became more dependent on home orders and British shipping more geared to empire and commonwealth trade. For the first time since the repeal of the Navigation Acts, the British government took measures to aid shipbuilding and shipping, industries which had not received protection when the country turned away from free trade. Still weakened by the effects of the interwar depression, the British maritime industries were thrown into a new world war in 1939, a conflict which would strain their resources much more than the Great War. Yet, when the Second World War was over, the British maritime industries enjoyed in the first ten years after 1945 a return to a prosperity unknown since before 1914. Most of Britain's maritime rivals had been incapacitated by the war and the USA's wartime maritime expansion could not be translated into peacetime dominance in world shipping and shipbuilding. In the immediate postwar years Britain continued to be the top shipping and shipbuilding nation. It was almost a return to the Victorian heyday, but unfortunately with maritime industries still with basically Victorian structures and outlooks.

Between 1945 and 1973 the non-communist world economy enjoyed an unprecedented boom, with world trade increasing almost every year. The demand for shipping services and new ships to provide them was immense. Yet Britain largely failed to seize these opportunities and by the 1960s the decline of her maritime industries was becoming increasingly obvious. With such favourable external conditions, unlike in the interwar period, the British maritime industries could not put all the blame for their failings on external factors (although they tried). Internal obstacles to change and modernisation were the main problem. At first attempts were made to ignore the need for change. Shipyards tried to survive on the basis of the British home market for ships; shipowners stuck to the old empire and commonwealth trades. But soon it was obvious such attitudes could not be sustained. British shipyards just did not produce what the world market required, so even British shipowners came to have most of their ships built abroad; the inefficient performance of British ports led foreign shipowners to base their European operations increasingly in continental ports; and the end of empire and closer links with Europe undermined the basis of the old British liner shipping routes. By the mid-1960s all this was becoming clear and with government support the British shipbuilding, ports and shipping industries sought to modernise in order to obtain a greater share of the still-growing world markets. Another stimulus to change and promise of new opportunities was the growth of the North Sea oil and gas industry from the mid-1960s.

Yet the modernisation and restructuring of British ports, ship-yards and shipping companies that took place in the 1965–73 period was too late, at least ten years too late. What was the use of three British shipyards trying to get into the supertanker market around 1970 when the Japanese had been turning out such vessels quicker and cheaper by production line methods for more than a decade? The modernisation of the port of London was welcome, but its re-export trade to Europe had long since disappeared; now it was ports such as Rotterdam which re-exported cargoes to London. British liner shipping companies certainly adjusted to the challenge of the container revolution with speed, but the Americans led the way and Asian shipping lines were not far behind.

Excessive fragmentation and individualism had been among the legacies of Victorian Britain to the structure of the maritime industries. Internal efforts at co-ordinated responses to change by industry trade organisations, such as the National Shipbuilders Security in the interwar shipyards, did something to overcome this, but not a great deal. The liner shipping companies had perhaps the longest experience of co-operation through the conference system, making the move into container consortia comparatively easy, but competitive rivalry between shipping firms still existed. In Japan the government took an active role in restructuring both the shipping and the shipbuilding industries when required. The British government tried to do something similar in shipbuilding and the ports from the mid-1960s, but with less success. Mergers produced shipbuilding groups and larger, estuarial port authorities, but had only limited impact on the difficult labour relations that were one of the main problems in both industries.

Successive British governments simply did not have a co-ordinated policy for the maritime industries. In Whitehall and Westminster those industries were disappearing off the political radar screen by the 1960s and only fears of large-scale unemployment in certain sectors pushed them back on. Ambitious civil servants in the transport bureaucracy avoided shipping after 1960.[22] Few shipowners sat in the House of Commons after the early 1960s.[23] Only the trade unions of the dockers and the shipyard workers, and their political supporters, kept the maritime industries in the public eye, all too often generating negative images which discouraged both potential customers and investors. Government intervention in those industries was usually aimed at preventing unemployment, or at least easing redundancies, rather than assisting the transition to a new stage in an industry's development. The ultimate measure was nationalisation, as proposed for the ports in the late 1960s and carried out for the shipyards in 1977, but it was too often seen as an end in itself. Without some overall plan for future development, nationalisation was just a pooling of individual inefficiency.

The nationalisation of the shipyards had little hope of reviving British shipbuilding because it was carried out against the background of the worst shipbuilding and shipping depression since the 1930s. Between 1975 and 1990 all the major maritime countries suffered large reductions in their merchant fleets and shipbuilding capacity. The problem was that Britain fell faster and further than the others. The attempted modernisation of her maritime industries from the mid-1960s was beginning to make some progress in the early 1970s just when the world markets for shipping services and new ships collapsed. At a time when British maritime industries seemed to be overcoming internal problems, external difficulties were renewed with immense power. The Conservative governments from 1979 sought to end state assistance to the maritime industries and leave their fate to the free market. Only the ports really prospered as a modern and efficient industry. Offshore energy was of vital importance to the British economy, but the opportunities it offered to the maritime industries were either not taken up or not sustained over time. By 1990, when world shipping and shipbuilding were at last beginning to revive, the British maritime industries were in no condition to derive much benefit from the upturn.

It was inevitable that the great British maritime predominance of 1914 would be undermined as other nations established or expanded their own maritime industries. That competition became significant in the interwar period, but the chief reason for the relative decline of the British maritime industries in those years was the collapse of world trade. After the Second World War world trade grew rapidly and so did foreign competition. The failure of the British maritime industries to adapt to this new reality was due to internal constraints, to industrial structures still little changed from the pre-1914 period. Only in the second half of the 1960s, with government support, did shipping, shipbuilding and the ports begin to modernise, and additional new openings were offered to them by the growing oil and gas industry in the North Sea. The problem was that modernisation was at least ten years too late and did not take place fast enough. Internal constraints had barely been addressed when the world shipping and shipbuilding markets collapsed after 1975. By the 1980s it was clear that the government was no longer willing to pour money into the maritime industries, and they were left to sink or swim in the open market. For 400 years the maritime industries had been considered of vital importance to Britain, but by 1990 this seemed no longer to be the government view. Others viewed the decline of those industries with greater concern.

Does the Decline Matter?

> In short, the moment the British, an island race, who have always earned their living from maritime trade, cease to wish to sail out into distant seas, Britain will wither and decline. The sea is her natural habitat; it surrounds, comforts, guards and beckons her. From it, all through her history, she has drawn her strength.[24]

Fine words indeed. They come from a book that first appeared in 1993. Had the book been published in 1893, 1793, 1693 or perhaps even 1593 the sentiments of the quotation would have seemed unexceptional. In the 1990s they seem old-fashioned, irrelevant in a time of globalisation and a possible United States of Europe. Yet strong arguments are still made that Britain should take action to revive her maritime industries. The reasons given are usually three-fold: financial, commercial and strategic.

Financially the foreign currency earnings of British shipping have been seen as an important part of those invisible earnings of the service industries that do so much to cover the imbalance between Britain's imports and exports. In the age of British maritime dominance between 1870 and 1914 shipping provided major invisible earnings.[25] However, shipping's contribution began to fall thereafter. Between 1952 and 1960 the contribution of British shipping to the balance of payments fell from 12.2% to 6.1% of the import bill.[26] Between 1975 and 1985 shipping's contribution to all invisible services earnings fell from 5.7% to 0.9%.[27] That British shipping can still make a positive contribution to the balance of payments cannot be denied. However, shipping's contribution is not vital and some economists have long argued that the gain may be purchased at a high cost, shipping producing a low return on capital and labour resources that might be better invested elsewhere in the economy.[28]

In addition to the direct foreign currency earnings of shipping are the foreign currency earnings of the related maritime services sector, sometimes called 'Maritime London'. These are the financial, insurance, legal and other services which became established to support British shipping in its heyday and still find a worldwide market for their expertise. In 1998 Maritime London generated £948 million in overseas earnings, with principal contributors being the Baltic Exchange (£297 million), legal services (£190 million), insurance brokers (£160 million) and banks (£100 million).[29] Other centres such as Athens (Piraeus), Singapore and Hong Kong have sought to challenge London's predominance in maritime services, but so far with only limited success. Nor does such business greatly rely on British maritime activities any more. In 1999 the chairman of the Baltic Exchange, whilst supporting an enhanced British merchant fleet, stated that as long as business came to London the flag was immaterial to the Baltic.[30]

The second reason to support the British maritime industries, and particularly shipping, is said to be commercial. Fears are expressed that if all British seaborne trade is carried by foreigners this will lead to exploitation via high freight rates and a possible refusal to provide direct services to the UK, just trans-shipping British cargoes at continental ports, thus raising costs.[31] However, such alarming scenarios are only really possible if one foreign carrier were to dominate the British carrying trade. In a world of numerous competing shipping companies, with few obstacles to market entry, fears of monopoly control seem unrealistic. Cheap ocean transportation is one of the fundamental factors in the globalisation of the 1990s under American leadership just as it was one of the basic characteristics of the free trade system under British leadership in the late nineteenth century. The big difference is that the British dominated world seaborne trade in their time, while the USA allows a wide range of competing shipping companies from many countries to keep world seaborne trade flowing. As long as the present liberal world trading system exists, nations should not be bothered who carries their goods at sea as long as they do it cheaply and efficiently.

The third reason given for supporting British maritime industries is strategic, so that ships will be available to support the navy and other armed forces in time of war or crisis. The end of the Cold War would seem to have reduced this requirement, and anyway in the 1990–91 conflict with Saddam Hussein only five of the 162 ships chartered to support British forces in the Gulf were British vessels.[32] Britain now seems to be following the USA in moving away from reliance on a national flag merchant fleet to supply transport tonnage. Instead the United States Navy has built up a transport fleet under its own direct control, and the Royal Navy seems in the process of doing the same.[33] Defence has always been used by US governments to justify their traditional protectionist maritime policies, but it now seems to have little further relevance. Support may be given to shipbuilding to preserve a basic naval building/repairing capacity, but the subsidising of merchant shipping for supposed defence needs seems to have been a costly failure.[34] A nation which preaches free trade to the world seems strangely blind to the costly folly of its own maritime protectionism.

The American example should do much to discourage those who seem to crave some sort of return to the Navigation Acts to protect British maritime industries. In addition membership of the European Union would seem to rule out any such action. Common European policies towards the maritime industries have been slow to emerge, perhaps because, as one scholar has put it, the 'conceivers of the unification of Europe do not seem to have taken greatly into account its maritime possibilities.'[35] Nevertheless such policies are now being put forward and Britain has a part in their formulation.[36]

Thus there are financial, commercial and strategic arguments for supporting Britain's maritime industries, but they seem less compelling in a world seeking to establish a global system of free trade and free markets. The maritime industries were vital to Britain when she was an offshore nation state battling for survival against European rivals and seeking to extend her commercial and imperial dominance around the world. Once British hegemony was achieved, the maritime industries remained supreme even after Britain espoused a liberal worldwide trading system after 1850. The wars and depression of the 1914–45 period ended British hegemony, which passed to the USA. Under the pax Americana a liberal worldwide trading system has again been created, but, outside the naval sphere, with no one nation achieving overall maritime dominance. In a fiercely competitive world the British maritime industries have largely failed to adapt to the new challenges. Their belated modernisation, barely begun before the world markets collapsed in the mid-1970s, could not prevent them slipping from relative to absolute decline.

The British maritime industries reached their zenith in the 1870–1914 period. Some decline after the First World War was inevitable, but external factors hastened it in the interwar period. The Second World War strained the industries further. The postwar boom brought those industries a short return to prosperity, but on the basis of largely unchanged internal structures. When foreign rivals re-emerged with modernised industries geared to the world market, the British maritime industries failed to adapt fast enough. When they finally made the effort it was too late and decline came dangerously close to complete collapse.

One may view the fall from greatness of the British maritime industries with regret and hope for some revival in the coming years, but it seems certain that never again will it be possible to speak of the British merchant fleet as a government report did in 1959: 'The ubiquity of British shipping is in itself a world wide advertisement for British industry and commerce, and for things British generally.'[37]

Notes

Chapter 1

1. Churchill to the Chancellor of the Exchequer and the President of the Board of Trade, 29 April 1953; British shipping and shipbuilding—joint report to the prime minister by the First Lord of the Admiralty and the Minister of Transport, June 1953 (Public Record Office (PRO), PREM 11/538). See A.G. Jamieson, 'British Government Shipping Policy from 1945 to 1990', in J.R. Bruijn, A.M.C. van Dissel, G. Jackson and P.C. van Royen (eds), *Strategy and Response in the Twentieth Century Maritime World: Papers Presented to the Fourth British-Dutch Maritime History Conference* (Amsterdam, 2001), pp. 51–61.
2. *The Economist*, 27 October 1956.
3. D. Sanders, 'The British Merchant Fleet', in the Navy League, *Maritime Survey 1973*, p. 73.
4. A.G. Jamieson, 'An Inevitable Decline? Britain's Shipping and Shipbuilding Industries since 1930', in D.J. Starkey and A.G. Jamieson (eds), *Exploiting the Sea: Aspects of Britain's Maritime Economy since 1870* (Exeter, 1998), pp. 80, 81, 87–88.
5. G. Jackson, 'Ports, Ships and Government in the Nineteenth and Twentieth Centuries', in P.C. van Royen, L.R. Fischer and D.M. Williams (eds), *Frutta di Mare: Evolution and Revolution in the Maritime World in the 19th and 20th Centuries* (Amsterdam, 1998), p. 173.
6. For the Navigation Acts see C.E. Fayle, *A Short History of the World's Shipping Industry* (London, 1933), pp. 186–192, and R. Davis, *The Rise of the English Shipping Industry in the Seventeenth and Eighteenth Centuries* (2nd impression, Newton Abbot, 1972), pp. 300–310. See also P.K. O'Brien, 'Inseparable Connections: Trade, Economy, Fiscal State, and the Expansion of Empire, 1688–1815', in P.J. Marshall (ed.), *The Oxford History of the British Empire: Volume II—The Eighteenth Century* (Oxford, 1998), pp. 52–77. For the view that the

essentials of British maritime power were established in the sixteenth century rather than later, see D. Loades, *England's Maritime
Empire: Seapower, Commerce and Policy, 1490–1690* (Harlow, 2000).

7. R. Harding, *Seapower and Naval Warfare, 1650–1830* (London,
    1999), p. 48.

8. Figures in P.J. Cain and A.G. Hopkins, *British Imperialism:
    Innovation and Expansion, 1688–1914* (London, 1993), pp. 87–88.

9. Sir Horace Mann, MP, 1779, quoted in J. Black, *War and the World:
    Military Power and the Fate of Continents, 1450–2000* (New Haven,
    CT, and London, 1998), p. 128.

10. B.W. Labaree et al., *America and the Sea: A Maritime History* (Mystic,
    CT, 1998), pp. 101, 103–105, 110.

11. Fayle, *Short History of World's Shipping Industry*, pp. 232–234;
    S. Palmer, *Politics, Shipping and the Repeal of the Navigation Acts*
    (Manchester, 1990), passim.

12. P. Kennedy, *The Rise and Fall of British Naval Mastery* (London,
    1976), p. 152.

13. A. Gibson and A. Donovan, *The Abandoned Ocean: A History of United
    States Maritime Policy* (Columbia, SC, 2000), pp. 64–72.

14. Cain and Hopkins, *British Imperialism: Innovation and Expansion*, pp.
    170–171, 179–180.

15. A.W. Kirkaldy, *British Shipping: Its History, Organisation and
    Importance* (London, 1914), Appendix 17.

16. E.H. Lorenz, *Economic Decline in Britain: The Shipbuilding Industry,
    1890–1970* (Oxford, 1991), p. 137.

17. Census figures in D.J. Starkey, 'Growth and Transition in Britain's
    Maritime Economy, 1870–1914: The Case of South-West England',
    in Starkey and Jamieson (eds), *Exploiting the Sea*, pp. 9–10.

18. A.W. Cafruny, *Ruling the Waves: The Political Economy of International
    Shipping* (Berkeley and Los Angeles, CA, 1987), p. 4.

19. R.H. Thornton, *British Shipping* (2nd edition, Cambridge, 1959), p.
    v.

20. D. Yergin and J. Stanislaw, *The Commanding Heights: The Battle
    between Government and the Marketplace that is Remaking the Modern
    World* (New York, 1998), p. 16.

21. Macmillan to the Minister of Transport, 8 December 1961 (PREM
    11/3991).

22. Minute of the inter-departmental committee on the contraction of
    the shipbuilding industry, 13 November 1962 (PRO, BT 291/141).

23. The General Council of British Shipping in its *Survey of British
    Shipping* (London, 1960) put the blame for most of the industry's
    problems on foreign competition. Stanley Sturmey in his *British
    Shipping and World Competition* (London, 1962) put most of the
    blame on the industry's own internal failings.

24. Paper on the future of international shipping by J. Hughes-Hallett,

10 January 1964 (PRO, MT 73/370); minutes of the Shipping Advisory Panel, June 1964 (BT 291/139).

25. Report of the Committee of Inquiry into the Fishing Industry [Fleck report] (Cmnd. 1266), British Parliamentary Papers (BPP) 1960–61, vol. XV; Report of the Committee of Inquiry into the Major Ports of Great Britain [Rochdale report] (Cmnd. 1824), BPP 1961–62, vol. XX; Final Report of the Committee of Inquiry into Certain Matters concerning the Port Transport Industry [Devlin report] (Cmnd. 2734), BPP 1964–65, vol. XXI; Report of the Shipbuilding Inquiry Committee [Geddes report] (Cmnd. 2937), BPP 1965–66, vol. VII; Final Report of the Committee of Inquiry into Certain Matters concerning the Shipping Industry [Pearson report] (Cmnd. 3211), BPP 1966–67, vol. XXXVI; Report of the Committee of Inquiry into Shipping [Rochdale report] (Cmnd. 4337), BPP 1969–70, vol. XXVII.

26. M. Davies, *Belief in the Sea: State Encouragement of British Merchant Shipping and Shipbuilding* (London, 1992), pp. 203–65.

27. Central Office of Information (COI), *Britain 1988: An Official Handbook* (London, 1988), p. 377.

28. R. Hope, *A New History of British Shipping* (London, 1990), p. 448.

29. P.J. Cain and A.G. Hopkins, *British Imperialism: Crisis and Deconstruction, 1914–1990* (London, 1993), pp. 287, 291–292.

30. D.C. Watt, 'British Sea Policy: Past Achievements and Future Prospects', in the Greenwich Forum IX, *Britain and the Sea: Future Dependence—Future Opportunities* (Edinburgh, 1984), pp. 233–234.

31. C.J. Bartlett, *The Long Retreat: A Short History of British Defence Policy, 1945–1970* (London, 1972), pp. 138–142.

32. For the fishing industry since 1918 see D.J. Starkey, C. Reid and N. Ashcroft (eds), *England's Sea Fisheries: The Commercial Sea Fisheries of England and Wales since 1300* (London, 2000); R. Robinson, *Trawling: The Rise and Fall of the British Trawl Fishery* (Exeter, 1996); J.R. Coull, *The Sea Fisheries of Scotland* (Edinburgh, 1996); J. Dyson, *Business in Great Waters: The Story of British Fishermen* (London, 1977); J.R. Coull, *The Fisheries of Europe* (London, 1972).

33. For the Royal Navy since 1918 see S. Roskill, *Naval Policy between the Wars* (2 vols, London, 1968 and 1976); G. Gordon, *British Seapower and Procurement between the Wars* (London, 1988); C. Barnett, *Engage the Enemy More Closely: The Royal Navy in the Second World War* (London, 1991); D. Wettern, *The Decline of British Seapower* (London, 1982); E.J. Grove, *Vanguard to Trident: British Naval Policy since World War II* (London, 1987); J.R. Hill (ed.), *The Oxford Illustrated History of the Royal Navy* (Oxford, 1995). For naval dockyards see J. Cantlie Stewart, *The Sea Our Heritage: British Maritime Interests Past and Present* (revised edition, Keith, Banffshire, 1995), Chapter XVI; P. MacDougall, *Royal Dockyards* (Newton

Abbot, 1982); R.J. Winklareth, *Naval Shipbuilders of the World: From the Age of Sail to the Present Day* (London, 2000), Chapter 2.

34. For the social history of the shipping industry see A.G. Course, *The Merchant Navy: A Social History* (London, 1963) and the social history sections in each chapter of Hope, *New History of British Shipping*.

35. For the opposing sides in the shipping industry see L. Powell, *The Shipping Federation, 1890–1950* (London, 1950) and A. Marsh and V. Ryan, *The Seamen: A History of the National Union of Seamen* (Oxford, 1989).

36. G. Owen, *From Empire to Europe: The Decline and Revival of British Industry since the Second World War* (London, 1999), p. 446.

Chapter 2

1. Report of the Departmental Committee appointed by the Board of Trade to consider the position of the Shipping and Shipbuilding Industries after the War [Booth committee], British Parliamentary Papers (BPP), 1918, vol. XIII, p. 473.

2. C.E. Fayle, *A Short History of the World's Shipping Industry* (London, 1933), p. 297.

3. C.E. Fayle, *The War and the Shipping Industry* (London, 1927), passim; R. Hope, *A New History of British Shipping* (London, 1990), pp. 349–353; A.J. Arnold, 'The Great War, Government Policy and Financial Returns in the Liner Trade', *Journal of Transport History* (3rd series), vol. 18, no. 1, March 1997, pp. 16–30. See also A.J. Arnold, 'Privacy or Concealment? The Accounting Practices of Liner Shipping Companies, 1914–1924', *International Journal of Maritime History*, vol. VIII, no. 1, 1996, pp. 43–57.

   For examples of high profits made by neutral Spanish and Swedish shipping firms in the First World War see J.M. Valdaliso, 'Management, Profitability and Finance in Twentieth Century Spanish Shipping: the Compania Maritima del Nervion as a Case Study, 1899–1986', in S.P. Ville and D.M. Williams (eds), *Management, Finance and Industrial Relations in Maritime Industries: Essays in International Maritime and Business History* (St. John's, Newfoundland, 1994), pp. 80–81, and M. Fritz and K. Olsson, 'Twentieth Century Shipping Strategies: Brostrom and Transatlantic, Gothenburg's Leading Shipping Companies', in ibid., pp. 94–99.

   The idea that foreign shipowners had derived an 'unfair' postwar advantage from their profits during the Great War was an often repeated view in British shipping circles during the interwar period; see Sir Archibald Hurd, 'The British Maritime Industries: A National Problem', in *Brassey's Naval Annual 1939*, p. 68.

4. Report of the Departmental Committee appointed by the Board of

Trade to consider the position of the Shipping and Shipbuilding Industries after the War [Booth committee] , BPP, 1918, vol. XIII, p. 473. The committee was asked to consider the likely postwar position 'especially in relation to international competition' and to recommend measures to safeguard British interests.

5. P.G. Halpern, *A Naval History of World War I* (London, 1994), pp. 335–344, 351–370.

6. M. Davies, *Belief in the Sea: State Encouragement of British Merchant Shipping and Shipbuilding* (London, 1992), pp. 96–98; J. Salter, *Allied Shipping Control: An Experiment in International Administration* (Oxford, 1921), pp. 102–108.

7. Booth committee, Final Report, pp. 63–65, 122–123. For wartime (and prewar) expansion of liner groups see G.H. Boyce, *Information, Mediation and Institutional Development: The Rise of Large-Scale Enterprise in British Shipping, 1870–1919* (Manchester, 1995), Chapter Six.

8. Booth committee, Final Report, p. 71. For growth of rival foreign fleets in World War I see S.G. Sturmey, *British Shipping and World Competition* (London, 1962), pp. 37–45.

9. D.H. Aldcroft, 'Port Congestion and the Shipping Boom of 1919–20', in D.H Aldcroft, *Studies in British Transport History, 1870–1970* (Newton Abbot, 1974), pp. 169–86; D. Jenkins, *Shipowners of Cardiff: A Class by Themselves. A History of the Cardiff and Bristol Channel Incorporated Shipowners' Association* (Cardiff, 1997), pp. 39–41.

10. In 1935 a commentator observed that 'British shipping has been uniformly depressed since 1920'; see L. Isserlis, 'The World Economic Crisis and British Shipping', in British Association for the Advancement of Science, *Britain in Depression: A Record of British Industries since 1929* (London, 1935), p. 236. See also Sir Archibald Hurd, *The Eclipse of British Sea Power: An Increasing Peril* (London, 1933) and *British Maritime Policy: The Decline of Shipping and Shipbuilding* (London, 1938).

11. S.G. Sturmey, *British Shipping and World Competition*, p. 65. For a detailed examination of world trade in the interwar period see J. Foreman-Peck, *A History of the World Economy: International Economic Relations since 1850* (Brighton, 1983), Chapter Seven.

12. R. Hope, *A New History of British Shipping*, p. 359; Sturmey, *British Shipping and World Competition*, p. 65; H.J. Dyos and D.H. Aldcroft, *British Transport: An Economic Survey from the Seventeenth Century to the Twentieth* (Harmondsworth, 1974), pp. 343–344.

13. G.C. Allen, *British Industries and their Organization* (3rd edition, London, 1951), p. 52.

14. J.A. Todd (ed.), *The Shipping World* (London, 1929), pp. 130–139; R. McAuley, *The Liners* (London, 1997), pp. 62–65.

15. A. Gibson and A. Donovan, *The Abandoned Ocean: A History of United States Maritime Policy* (Columbia, SC, 2000), Chapters Six and Seven; B.W. Labaree et al., *America and the Sea: A Maritime History* (Mystic, CT, 1998), pp. 524, 527–528, 530, 536, 541; G.C. Kennedy, 'Great Britain's Maritime Strength and the British Merchant Marine, 1922–1935', *Mariner's Mirror*, vol. 80 (1994), pp. 66–76. See also G. Kennedy, 'American and British Merchant Shipping: Competition and Preparation, 1933–1939', in G. Kennedy (ed.), *The Merchant Marine in International Affairs, 1850–1950* (London, 2000), pp. 107–154.

16. S.C. Heal, *Conceived in War, Born in Peace: Canada's Deep Sea Merchant Marine* (Vancouver, BC, 1992), pp. 21–24; R.G. Halford, *The Unknown Navy: Canada's World War II Merchant Navy* (St Catharine's, ON, 1995), pp. 15–22; F. Broeze, *Island Nation: A History of Australians and the Sea* (St Leonard's, NSW, 1998), pp. 103–104, 135.

17. Sturmey, *British Shipping and World Competition*, Chapter Five.

18. S. Glynn and A. Booth, *Modern Britain: An Economic and Social History* (London, 1996), pp. 118–124.

19. R.P. de Kerbrech, *Harland & Wolff's Empire Food Ships, 1934–1948: A Link with the Southern Dominions* (Freshwater, IOW, 1998); P.J. Cain and A.G. Hopkins, *British Imperialism: Crisis and Deconstruction, 1914–1990* (London, 1993), pp. 36–38.

20. Chamber of Shipping of the United Kingdom, Report of the Special Committee on Tramp Shipping, 23 November 1933, Chamber of Shipping Archives, Modern History Archive, University of Warwick. The request led to the formation of a Cabinet committee on the British mercantile marine which was active 1933–34 (PRO, Cabinet papers, CAB 27/557).

21. M. Davies, *Belief in the Sea*, pp. 119–136; L. Isserlis, 'British Shipping since 1934', in British Association for the Advancement of Science, *Britain in Recovery* (London, 1938), pp. 328–333.

22. Sturmey, *British Shipping and World Competition*, pp. 73–85. A different view from Sturmey was taken by Peter Davies: 'It is unlikely that British shipowners were any less enterprising after 1920 than they were before, although their performance and achievements were so dramatically different. The difference in results may well lie in the changed circumstances in which they were forced to operate.' (P.N. Davies, 'British Shipping and World Trade: Rise and Decline, 1820–1939', in T. Yui and K. Nakagawa (eds), *Business History of Shipping: Strategy And Structure* (Tokyo, 1985), p. 80).

23. A. Greenway (ed.), *Conway's History of the Ship: The Golden Age of Shipping—The Classic Merchant Ship, 1900–1960* (London, 1994),

pp. 157–160; S. Howarth, *Sea Shell: The Story of Shell's British Tanker Fleet, 1892–1992* (Wadswick, Wiltshire, 1992), pp. 57–60.

24. K. Petersen, *The Saga of Norwegian Shipping: An Outline of the History, Growth and Development of a Modern Merchant Marine* (Oslo, 1955), pp. 84–87.

25. Lloyd's Register of Shipping.

26. E.C. Talbot-Booth, *Ships and the Sea* (5th edition, London, 1940), p. 341.

27. P.N. Davies and A.M. Bourn, 'Lord Kylsant and the Royal Mail', *Business History*, vol. XIV (1972), pp. 103–123.

28. A.J. Robertson, 'Backward British Businessmen and the Motor Ship, 1918–39: The Critique Reviewed', *Journal of Transport History*, 3rd series, vol. IX (1988), pp. 190–197; J. Orbell, *From Cape to Cape: The History of Lyle Shipping* (Edinburgh, 1978), pp. 87–88. See also G. Henning and K. Trace, 'Britain and the Motor Ship: A Case of the Delayed Adoption of a New Technology', *Journal of Economic History*, vol. 35 (1975), pp. 353–385, and M.E. Fletcher, 'From Coal to Oil in British Shipping', *Journal of Transport History*, new series, vol. III (1975), pp. 1–19.

29. G. Boyce, 'Union Steamship Company of New Zealand and the Adoption of Oil Propulsion: Learning-by-Using Effects', *Journal of Transport History*, 3rd series, vol. 18, no. 2, September 1997, pp. 134–155; D. Griffiths, 'British Shipping and the Diesel Engine: The Early Years', *Mariner's Mirror*, vol. 81 (1995), pp. 313–331.

    In 1933 British tramp shipowners denied they had been slow to build diesel tonnage 'for those trades where it is suitable' and stated 'that the relative merits of steam and diesel engined vessels can only be settled in relation to the particular conditions of each owner's business in each trade.' (Government questionnaire to tramp shipowners 1933, Chamber of Shipping archives, University of Warwick).

30. A.G. Jamieson, 'The British Tanker Company and the Marine Diesel Engine, 1929', *Mariner's Mirror*, vol. 83 (1997), pp. 335–336; R.W. Ferrier, *The History of the British Petroleum Company. Volume 1: The Developing Years, 1901–1932* (Cambridge, 1982), pp. 533–534.

31. D. Griffiths, *Steam at Sea: Two Centuries of Steam-Powered Ships* (London, 1997), Chapter 13.

32. K. Petersen, *Saga of Norwegian Shipping*, pp. 86–87.

33. M. Ratcliffe, *Liquid Gold Ships: A History of the Tanker, 1859–1984* (London, 1985), pp. 62–65. See also 'Viator', 'Shipping and the Oil Industry', in *Brassey's Naval & Shipping Annual 1930*, pp. 153–160.

34. W.J. Harvey, *Hadley* (Gravesend, 1997), p. 13; Sturmey, *British Shipping and World Competition*, pp. 75–76.

35. Petersen, *Saga of Norwegian Shipping*, pp. 109–110; L.A. Sawyer and

W.H. Mitchell, *Tankers* (London, 1967), pp. 46–47. Aristotle Onassis had his first three tankers built by Gotaverken in Sweden in the late 1930s. (N. Fraser et al., *Aristotle Onassis* (London, 1977), pp. 46 and 50).

36. M. Ratcliffe, *Liquid Gold Ships*, p. 67.

37. Calculated from figures in E.C. Talbot-Booth, *His Majesty's Merchant Navy* (London, 1941), p. 431.

38. J.H. Bamberg, *The History of the British Petroleum Company. Volume 2: The Anglo-Iranian Years, 1928–1954* (Cambridge, 1993), p. 138.

39. E.C. Talbot-Booth, *His Majesty's Merchant Navy*, p. 497; P. Hunting (ed.), *The Hunting History: Hunting plc since 1874* (London, 1991), pp. 56– 58.

40. Harvey, *Hadley*, p. 23.

41. A.G. Jamieson, 'British Use of Neutral Shipping in Time of War: An Historical Outline', *War Studies Journal*, vol. 4, issue 1, summer 1999, pp. 84–96.

42. Glynn and Booth, *Modern Britain: An Economic and Social History*, pp. 63, 71, 73.

43. Sturmey, pp. 95–96, 397.

44. Hope, *New History of British Shipping*, p. 363. Shipowners were among the richest men in Britain at this time. When Sir John Ellerman died in 1932, leaving £37 million, he was not only the wealthiest British shipowner but also the nation's richest man. Most of the shipowners made their fortunes in the 1870–1914 period of increasing world trade and British maritime predominance. See W.D. Rubinstein, *Men of Property: The Very Wealthy in Britain since the Industrial Revolution* (London, 1981), pp. 97–101.

45. E. Green and M. Moss, *A Business of National Importance: The Royal Mail Shipping Group, 1902–1937* (London, 1982), p. 4.

46. See T. Atkinson and K. O'Donoghue, *Blue Star* (Kendal, 1985) and L. Dunn and P.M. Heaton, *Palm Line* (Abergavenny, 1994).

47. S. Jones, 'The P&O in War and Slump, 1914–1932: The Chairmanship of Lord Inchcape', in S. Fisher (ed.), *Innovation in Shipping and Trade* (Exeter, 1989), pp. 131–143; S. Jones, *Trade and Shipping: Lord Inchcape 1852–1932* (Manchester, 1989), Chapters 6 and 7; C.J. Napier, 'Secret Accounting: The P&O Group in the Inter-War Years', *Accounting, Business and Financial History*, vol. 1, no. 3, 1991, pp. 303–333.

48. E. Green and M. Moss, *A Business of National Importance: The Royal Mail Shipping Group, 1902–1937* (London, 1982); A.J. Arnold, 'No Substitute for Hard Cash?: An Analysis of Returns on Investment in the Royal Mail Steam Packet Company, 1903–1929', *Accounting, Business and Financial History*, vol. 1, no. 3, 1991, pp. 335–353.

49. The financial consequences of the collapse of the postwar shipping boom in 1920 and the fall of the Royal Mail group in 1930 left both

borrowers and lenders wary. Shipowners returned to their traditional reluctance to depend on external finance, while bankers and stockbrokers became reluctant to finance shipping companies. See E. Green, 'Very Private Enterprise: Ownership and Finance in British Shipping, 1825–1940', in T. Yui and K. Nakagawa (eds), *Business History of Shipping: Strategy and Structure* (Tokyo, 1985), pp. 235–244.

50. Booth committee, Final Report (1918), pp. 54, 61, 85. In 1914 Clyde shipowners (mostly Glasgow) owned 422 deep-sea tramps totalling 1,327,609 gross tons divided among sixty-one owners. By 1918 the figures had slumped to 145 deep-sea tramps totalling 424,151 gross tons divided among twenty-three owners. (A.G. Course, *The Deep Sea Tramp* (London, 1960), pp. 104–105.)

51. D. Jenkins, *Shipowners of Cardiff: A Class by Themselves* (Cardiff, 1997), pp. 39–41; D.J. Morgan, 'Boom and Slump—Shipowning in Cardiff, 1919–1921', *Maritime Wales*, no. 12, 1989, pp. 127–132. See also M. Kajimoto, *Cardiff Shipping between the Wars* (Tezukayama University, Nara, Japan, 1996).

52. Report of the Special Committee on Tramp Shipping, 23 November 1933 (Chamber of Shipping Archives, University of Warwick).

53. See P.M. Heaton, *Jack Billmeir: Merchant Shipowner* (Abergavenny, 1989). Cardiff was one of the leading tramp shipping ports and of the thirty-six shipping companies covered in J.G. Jenkins and D. Jenkins, *Cardiff Shipowners* (Cardiff, 1986), only three were set up after 1920.

54. S. Pollard, *The Development of the British Economy, 1914–1980* (3rd edition, London, 1983), pp. 94–95; G. Harlaftis, *A History of Greek-Owned Shipping: The Making of an International Tramp Fleet, 1830 to the Present Day* (London, 1996), pp. 200–201.

55. Statistics can be found in the British official histories of the Second World War relating to British shipping: C.B.A. Behrens, *Merchant Shipping and the Demands of War* (London, 1955) for passenger liners and dry cargo shipping; D.J. Payton-Smith, *Oil: A Study of Wartime Policy and Administration* (London, 1971) for tankers; and C.I. Savage, *Inland Transportation* (London, 1957) for coastal shipping. See also Tony Lane, *The Merchant Seamen's War* (Liverpool, 1990).

56. R. Hope, *New History of British Shipping*, pp. 385–389; P. Duff, *British Ships and Shipping: A Survey of Modern Ship Design and Shipping Practice* (London, 1949), pp. 217–220.

57. Sturmey, *British Shipping and World Competition*, pp. 142–151.

58. Hope, *New History of British Shipping*, p. 389; P. Duff, *British Ships and Shipping*, pp. 220–224.

59. Gibson and Donovan, *Abandoned Ocean*, Chapter 8; Labaree et al., *America and the Sea*, Chapter 15. For Canada see Halford, *Unknown Navy*, Part 1.

60. J.S. Maclay, 'The General Shipping Situation', *International Affairs*, vol. 22 (October 1946), p. 487.

61. Duff, *British Ships and Shipping*, p. 229.

62. Labaree et al., *America and the Sea*, pp. 591–592; Gibson and Donovan, *Abandoned Ocean*, pp. 170–171; Organisation for European Economic Co-operation (OEEC), *Maritime Transport 1954* (Paris, 1954), pp. 19–21; H. Gripaios, *Tramp Shipping* (London, 1959), pp. 124–128.

63. Gibson and Donovan, *Abandoned Ocean*, pp. 171, 174–175.

64. R.P. Carlisle, *Sovereignty for Sale: The Origins and Evolution of the Panamanian and Liberian Flags of Convenience* (Annapolis, MD, 1981), passim; A.W. Cafruny, *Ruling the Waves: The Political Economy of International Shipping* (Berkeley and Los Angeles, CA, 1987), pp. 89–103. The rise of flags of convenience during the 1950s led to much controversy, including labour unrest and legal cases. These peaked in the period 1958–61, but the Norwegian-born, US-based shipowner Erling Naess, then chairman of the American Committee for Flags of Necessity, led those in favour of flags of convenience to victory. See E.D. Naess, *The Great PanLibHon Controversy: The Fight Over the Flags of Shipping* (Epping, Essex, 1972).

65. OEEC, *Maritime Transport 1954*, table XIII; ibid., *Maritime Transport 1959*, table I.

66. In 1948 the UK had a fleet of eighteen million gross tons, 22% of the world fleet. It grew to almost twenty million tons in 1957, but the share of the world fleet dropped to 18%. (Lloyd's Register of Shipping) The competition of subsidised air transport and flag discrimination to aid foreign fleets led some commentators to worry about the future of British shipping as early as the mid-1950s; see Sir Archibald Hurd, 'British Shipping's Fight for Survival', *Brassey's Annual: The Armed Forces Year-Book 1955*, pp. 124–130.

67. S. Howarth, *Sea Shell*, pp. 123–138; J.H. Bamberg, *History of British Petroleum, Volume 2*, pp. 289–292.

68. G. Harlaftis, *A History of Greek-Owned Shipping* (London, 1996), pp. 262–264; G. Harlaftis, *Greek Shipowners and Greece, 1945–1975: From Separate Development to Mutual Interdependence* (London, 1993), pp. 41–45; M. Ratcliffe, *Liquid Gold Ships* (London, 1985), pp. 128–133.

69. S. Sedgwick, M. Kinnaird and K.J. O'Donoghue, *London and Overseas Freighters plc, 1948–1992* (Kendal, 1992), pp. 7–14; Sturmey, *British Shipping and World Competition*, pp. 360–361; P. Hunting (ed.), *The Hunting History: Hunting plc since 1874* (London, 1991), pp. 54–62.

70. I. Dear, *The Ropner Story* (London, 1986), p. 111.

71. W.J Harvey, *Hadley* (Gravesend, 1997), p. 33.

72. D. Haws, *Merchant Fleets 32: Clan, Houston, Turnbull Martin and*

Scottish Tankers (Pembroke, 1997), pp. 132–137; D. Howarth and S. Howarth, *The Story of P&O*, pp. 156–157.

73. J. Lingwood and K. O'Donoghue, *The Trades Increase* [History of Common Brothers/Norex] (Kendal, 1993), pp. 76, 78, 81–83, 86–87.

74. Sturmey, *British Shipping and World Competition*, pp. 359–362; Ratcliffe, *Liquid Gold Ships*, p. 128.

75. G. Harlaftis, *Greek Shipowners and Greece, 1945–1975*, pp. 45–57.

76. General Council of British Shipping, *Survey of British Shipping* (London, 1960). In 1959 only twelve British ocean tramp firms had more than ten ships each. The leading firms, with twenty ships each, were Hogarth of Glasgow and Counties, the British dry cargo arm of LOF. (E.C. Talbot-Booth, *Merchant Ships 1959* (Liverpool and London, 1959).)

77. Report of the Rochdale Committee of Inquiry into Shipping (1970), pp. 140–141.

78. L. Dunn, *British Tramps, Coasters and Colliers* (London, 1962), pp. 34–35, 64–65.

79. R. Munro Smith, *Merchant Ship Types* (London, 1975), pp. 124–136.

80. Lingwood and O'Donoghue, *The Trades Increase*, pp. 83–84; Orbell, *From Cape to Cape*, pp. 122–125. See also *The Economist*, 20 October 1956; A.G. Course, *The Deep Sea Tramp* (London, 1960), pp. 259–263; Iron and Steel Board, *Development in the Iron and Steel Industry: Special Report 1964* (London, 1964), pp. 102–103.

81. R. Hackman, *The Fleet Past and Present of Hunting & Son Ltd.* (Newcastle, 1969), pp. 27–28; Sedgwick, Kinnaird and O'Donoghue, *London and Overseas Freighters*, pp. 68, 70, 72–73. In 1960 LOF also set up a joint venture, Welsh Ore Carriers, with the Gibbs shipping firm of South Wales (ibid., p. 14).

82. Sturmey, *British Shipping and World Competition*, pp. 363–364.

83. Morel sold up in 1956 (J.M. Gibbs, *Morels of Cardiff: The History of a Family Shipping Firm* (Cardiff, 1982), pp. 136–138) and Billmeir in 1963 (P.M. Heaton, *Jack Billmeir, Merchant Shipowner* (Abergavenny, 1989), p. 63).

84. Dear, *Ropner Story*, pp. 103–104; Lingwood and O'Donoghue, *Trades Increase*, pp. 74–75, 77. For the Sugar Line see A. Hugill, *Sugar and All That . . . The History of Tate & Lyle* (London, 1978), pp. 182–187.

85. B.M. Deakin, (with T. Seward.), *Shipping Conferences. A Study of their Origins, Development and Economic Practices* (Cambridge, 1973); Sturmey, *British Shipping and World Competition*, Chapter XIII.

86. Air passengers exceeded sea passengers on the North Atlantic route for the first time in 1957 and were almost double the sea passenger figure in 1959 (OEEC, *Maritime Transport 1959* (Paris, 1960), table VIII).

87. F.E. Hyde, *Cunard and the North Atlantic, 1840–1973* (London, 1973), pp. 296–302.

88. McAulay, *Liners*. For the development of cruise ships see P. Dawson, *Cruise Ships: An Evolution in Design* (London, 2000).

89. R. De La Pedraja, *Latin American Merchant Shipping in the Age of Global Competition* (Westport, CT, 1999), pp. 3–14.

90. A.D. Couper, *The Geography of Sea Transport* (London, 1972), pp. 179–203. The postwar growth of the Soviet merchant fleet caused alarm in some quarters, but while it sought to monopolise trade with the USSR it had little wider impact on world shipping before the 1970s. See D. Fairhall, *Russia Looks to the Sea: A Study of the Expansion of Soviet Maritime Power* (London, 1971).

91. A.G. Jamieson, 'Facing the Rising Tide: British Attitudes to Asian National Shipping Lines, 1958–1964', *International Journal of Maritime History*, vol. VII (1995), pp. 135–148.

92. P.N. Davies, *The Trade Makers: Elder Dempster in West Africa, 1852–1972, 1973–1989* (2nd edition, St John's, Newfoundland, 2000), pp. 299–300.

93. M. Davies, *Belief in the Sea*, pp. 186–189. The shipowner body was the Council of European and Japanese Shipowners Associations (CENSA) and the inter-governmental body the Consultative Shipping Group (CSG). The British view of US shipping policy and anti-trust action about conferences is set out in the letter from British prime minister Harold Macmillan to US President John F. Kennedy, 7 April 1961 (PRO, PREM 11/3530).

94. Howarth and Howarth, *Story of P&O*, pp. 156–157, 170–171. P&O ordered its first bulk carriers in 1962 and in 1964 it agreed to set up a joint bulk carrier venture, Associated Bulk Carriers Ltd., with Erling Naess. By 1970 the firm had twenty-five ships, with another eleven on order. See E.D. Naess, *Autobiography of a Shipping Man* (Colchester, 1977), Chapter 28.

95. D. Burrell, *Furness Withy, 1891–1991* (Kendal, 1992), pp. 132–134, 142–143; R.B. Stoker, *The Saga of Manchester Liners* (Douglas, IOM, 1985), pp. 30–36.

96. Sturmey, *British Shipping and World Competition*, pp. 366–367.

97. Sturmey, *British Shipping and World Competition*, pp. 365–375. See also Political and Economic Planning (PEP), 'The British Shipping Industry', *Planning*, vol. XXV, no. 437, 16 November 1959, pp. 203–208.

98. A. Sampson, *Anatomy of Britain Today* (London, 1965), pp. 533, 535–536.

99. Rochdale Report on Shipping (1970), pp. 333–337.

100. Report on the prospects of the shipping and shipbuilding industries, 30 January 1959 (PRO, CAB 134/1682); Report on the prospects of British shipping to 1965 (PRO, MT 59/3189);

Memorandum on the British shipping industry, 20 July 1962 (CAB 129/110). See also A.G. Jamieson, 'British Government Shipping Policy from 1945 to 1990', in J.R. Bruijn, A.M.C. van Dissel, G. Jackson and P.C. van Royen (eds), *Strategy and Response in the Twentieth Century Maritime World: Papers presented to the Fourth British-Dutch Maritime History Conference* (Amsterdam, 2001), pp. 51–61.

101. Ernest Marples, Minister of Transport, in debate on 15 February 1962, Hansard, House of Commons, 1961–62, vol. 653, column 1555.

102. Prime Minister's meeting with Minister of Transport, 5 December 1961, and PM's letter to Minister of Transport, 8 December 1961 (PREM 11/3991).

103. Prime Minister's meeting with Minister of Transport, 22 October 1962 (PREM 11/3991); Shipping Advisory Panel (SAP) report on foreign shipping protectionism is in SAP minutes and papers, 1962–63 (PRO, BT 291/138).

104. Paper on the future of international shipping by J. Hughes-Hallett, 10 January 1964 (MT 73/370); Minutes of SAP, June 1964 (BT 291/139).

105. Memorandum on the British shipping industry, 20 July 1962 (CAB 129/110); Papers on the one-year shipbuilding subsidy, 1963 (PREM 11/4482); M. Davies, *Belief in the Sea*, pp. 174–175.

106. T. Chida and P.N. Davies, *The Japanese Shipping and Shipbuilding Industries: A History of their Modern Growth* (London, 1990), pp. 139–145.

107. For turn-round problems and docker militancy in the 1950s see below Chapter 4.

108. G. Van Den Burg, *Containerisation and Other Unit Load Transport* (revised edition, London, 1975), Chapters 6 and 10.

109. Rochdale Report on Shipping (1970), p. 106.

110. H. Rees, *British Ports and Shipping* (London, 1958), pp. 254–255; R.C. Sinclair, *Across the Irish Sea: Belfast-Liverpool Shipping since 1819* (London, 1990), pp. 123–126, 136, 148.

111. Van Den Burg, *Containerisation*, pp. 111–121; Gibson and Donovan, *Abandoned Ocean*, pp. 209–214; W.L. Worden, *Cargoes: Matson's First Century in the Pacific* (Honolulu, Hawaii, 1981), pp. 143–148; R. De La Pedraja, *Latin American Merchant Shipping in the Age of Global* Competition, pp. 87–88. See entry on Malcolm McLean in R. De La Pedraja, *A Historical Dictionary of the U.S. Merchant Marine and Shipping Industry since the Introduction of Steam* (Westport, CT, 1994) and his obituary in *The Times*, 30 May 2001.

112. A. Cafruny, *Ruling the Waves*, pp. 184–198.

113. Rochdale Report on Shipping (1970), pp. 108–110.

114. Howarth & Howarth, *Story of P&O*, pp. 172–173; Burrell, *Furness*

Withy 1891–1991, pp. 155–156; Van Den Burg, *Containerisation*, pp. 126–128. For Tilbury strike see below Chapter 4.

For a list prepared for the British government of deep-sea container lines in operation or planned, June 1968, see ministerial committee on industrial policy, sub-committee on containers (CAB 134/2921).

115. For ACT see J. Taylor, *Ellermans. A Wealth of Shipping* (London, 1976), Chapter 21; M. Strachan, *The Ben Line, 1825–1982: An Anecdotal History* (Norwich, 1992), pp. 172–195; Rochdale Report on Shipping (1970), pp. 108–109.

116. Stoker, *Saga of Manchester Liners*, pp. 38–44; Burrell, *Furness Withy*, pp. 151–152.

117. Hyde, *Cunard and the North Atlantic*, p. 314; Rochdale Report on Shipping (1970), p. 109; Obituary of Philip Bates, *The Times*, 23 March 2000.

118. For Dart container line, see D. Haws, *Merchant Fleets—The Burma Boats: Henderson and Bibby* (1996), pp. 79–80.

119. F. Broeze, 'Containerization and the Globalization of Liner Shipping', p. 387, in D.J. Starkey and G. Harlaftis (eds), *Global Markets: The Internationalization of the Sea Transport Industry since 1850* (St John's, Newfoundland, 1998), pp. 385–423.

120. Rochdale Report on Shipping (1970), p. 150; Burrell, *Furness Withy*, pp. 156–157; Hunting, *Hunting History*, pp. 60–61; J. Bes, *Bulk Carriers* (Hilversum, Netherlands, 1972), pp. 72–88. Erling Naess is often credited with being the father of the OBO carrier; see E.D. Naess, *Autobiography of a Shipping Man* (Colchester, 1977), Chapter 21.

121. H. Hodgkinson, 'The Changing Pattern of Oil Supplies', in the Navy League, *Maritime Survey 1973*, pp. 49–50; Hope, *New History of British Shipping*, pp. 418–419. Because of the increasing size of tankers use of the Cape route was increasing even before the closure of the Suez Canal in 1967; see S. Howarth, *A Century in Oil: The 'Shell' Transport and Trading Company, 1897–1997* (London, 1997), p. 290, and J. Bamberg, *British Petroleum and Global Oil, 1950–1975: The Challenge of Nationalism* (Cambridge, 2000), pp. 296–297.

122. A. Couper (ed.), *Conway's History of the Ship—The Shipping Revolution: The Modern Merchant Ship* (London, 1992), pp. 64–70. By the early 1970s plans were being proposed for million ton tankers, but then the tanker market collapsed. See SOCCO, *The Million Ton Carrier: Proceedings of the Super Ocean Carrier Conference (SOCCO), New York 1974* (San Pedro, CA, 1974).

123. The best popular account of the supertanker phenomenon is N. Mostert, *Supership* (London, 1975); for the *Torrey Canyon* disaster see J. Marriott, *Disaster at Sea* (New York, 1987), Chapter 17.

124. Howarth, *Sea Shell*, p. 166.
125. Sedgwick et al., *London and Oversea Freighters*, p. 17.
126. Rochdale Report on Shipping (1970), p. 159; Howarth and Howarth, *Story of P&O*, pp. 156–157, 192.
127. D. Haws, *Merchant Fleets 6: Blue Funnel Line* (Torquay, 1984), pp. 131–132.
128. D. Sanders, 'The British Merchant Fleet', in Navy League, *Maritime Survey 1973*, pp. 85–86.
129. Professor Richard Goss, who was economic adviser to the Rochdale committee, notes that the inquiry into the shipping industry was set up as a concession to the seamen's unions, its purpose being to examine the validity of the employers' arguments about competition, level of profits, and prospects for better wages. See R. Goss, 'Rochdale Remembered: A Personal Memoir', *Maritime Policy and Management*, vol. 25, no. 3, 1998, p. 215. A similar enquiry was made into Dutch shipping in the late 1960s. The resulting Oyevaar report recommended modernisation and merger by Dutch shipping companies in return for government financial aid. See A.H. Flierman, 'Mayday, or How to Attract Attention. The Dutch Merchant Navy and Politics, 1960–1995', in J. Bruijn et al. (eds), *Strategy and Response in the Twentieth Century Maritime World* (Amsterdam, 2001), p. 70.
130. See below Chapter 4.
131. Rochdale Report on Shipping (1970), summary of recommendations, pp. 415–423. For contemporary comment see *The Economist*, 9 May 1970; D. Aldcroft, 'Reflections on the Rochdale Inquiry into Shipping' (1971), reproduced in D. Aldcroft, *Studies in British Transport History, 1870–1970* (Newton Abbot, 1974), pp. 275–295. Professor Goss has criticised the Rochdale report for being uncritical of the conference system and failing to stress the weaknesses that British shipowners shared with other British industries, such as an amateurish, non-scientific approach to management. According to Goss: 'In shipping, as elsewhere, these effects had been exacerbated by nepotism, a reliance on imperial connections, and thus protected markets, leading to complacency and, in due course, decline.' (R. Goss, 'Rochdale Remembered', pp. 227–228)
132. Central Office of Information (COI), *British Industry Today: Shipping* (London, 1974), pp. 1, 3–4; Sanders, 'British Merchant Fleet', in the Navy League, *Maritime Survey 1973*, pp. 73–88. For the British role in the development of the carriage of gas by ship see R. Ffooks, *Natural Gas by Sea: The Development of a New Technology* (London, 1979), pp. 45–55. See also Howarth, *A Century in Oil*, pp. 171, 279–281.
133. Lloyd's Register of Shipping.

134. Rochdale Report on Shipping (1970), p. 59.
135. Ibid., pp. 340–341.
136. F. Hodne, *The Norwegian Economy, 1920–1980* (London, 1983), p. 217.
137. M. Stopford, *Maritime Economics* (2nd edition, London, 1997), pp. 197–199.
138. B.W. Hogwood, *Government and Shipbuilding: The Politics of Industrial Change* (Farnborough, 1979), pp. 126–130; Hope, *New History of British Shipping*, p. 427; Davies, *Belief in the Sea*, pp. 204–212.
139. Ibid.
140. For the Geddes report and shipbuilding reorganisation see below, Chapter 3.
141. Hogwood, *Government and Shipbuilding*, pp. 124–126; Davies, *Belief in the Sea*, pp. 213–217.
142. Glynn and Booth, *Modern Britain*, table 11.3, p. 220.
143. Hope, *New History of British Shipping*, p. 448.
144. F. Broeze, *Island Nation: A History of Australians and the Sea*, p. 67.
145. Stopford, *Maritime Economics*, pp. 366–370.
146. D. Yergin, *The Prize: The Epic Quest for Oil, Money and Power* (London, 1991), Chapters 29 and 30.
147. *The Economist*, 23 March 1974 and 11 January 1975; Chamber of Shipping of the UK, annual reports for 1973 and 1974.
148. Stopford, *Maritime Economics*, pp. 63–66.
149. *The Economist*, 17 and 24 May 1975; Ratcliffe, *Liquid Gold Ships*, pp. 138, 159–160. The Norwegians were very badly hit by the collapse of the tanker market, chiefly because they operated mainly in the spot market, with relatively few long-term charters, and they had ordered many very large tankers in the period 1972–73. See S. Tenold and H.W. Nordvik, 'Coping with the International Shipping Crisis of the 1970s: A Study of Management Responses in Norwegian Oil Tanker Companies', *International Journal of Maritime History*, vol. VIII, no. 2, 1996, pp. 51–54. In 1975 the Norwegian government set up the Guarantee Institute to provide support for Norwegian shipowners and it lasted until 1981, using up large sums of public money. (Tenold and Nordvik, pp. 53–54)
150. For the reaction of Shell tankers to the downturn see Howarth, *Sea Shell*, Chapter 10.
151. *The Economist*, 8 March 1975.
152. Sedgwick et al., *London and Overseas Freighters*, p. 21; Lingwood and O'Donoghue, *Trades Increase*, p. 99.
153. Howarth and Howarth, *Story of P&O*, p. 191; *The Economist*, 18 January 1975.
154. Dear, *Ropner Story*, p. 139; Orbell, *From Cape to Cape*, p. 157.
155. Diversification and other aspects of shipping management in the

post-1945 period are covered in P. Shore, 'Sunset Over the Red Ensign: The Decline of British Deep Sea Shipping, 1945–89' (University of Kent Ph.D thesis, 1990).

156. *The Economist*, 29 June and 24 August 1974.

157. Howarth and Howarth, *Story of P&O*, pp. 186–190.

158. Graig Shipping, annual reports for 1974–75 and 1975–76 (courtesy of Mr. Desmond Williams).

159. See below, Chapter 5.

160. T. Farrington, 'The UK Shipping Industry: A History and Assessment', *The Business Economist*, vol. 27, no. 1, 1996, p. 25; Hope, *New History of British Shipping*, pp. 434, 454–455.

161. B. Pedersen and F.W. Hawks, *A History of Norwegian America Line, 1910–1995* (Kendal, 1995), pp. 11–12.

162. B. Kolltveit and M. Crowdy, *Wilh. Wilhelmsen 1861–1994: A Brief History and Fleet List* (Kendal, 1994), pp. 28–36.

163. M. Fritz and K. Olsson, 'Twentieth Century Shipping Strategies: Brostrom and Transatlantic, Gothenburg's Leading Shipping Companies', in S.P. Ville and D.M. Williams (eds), *Management, Finance and Industrial Relations in Maritime Industries: Essays in International Maritime and Business History* (St John's, Newfoundland, 1994), pp. 101–108.

164. Burrell, *Furness Withy*, pp. 171–173.

165. Hunting, *Hunting History*, p. 61. Hunting left shipping in 1983. Howarth and Howarth, *Story of P&O*, pp. 211–212.

166. For Reardon Smith see *The Times*, 31 May and 1 June 1985; for Lyle Shipping see *The Times*, 16 May 1987.

167. Shipping contributed nearly half of Ocean group's turnover and 85% of its profits in 1973, but only 7% of turnover and barely 10% of trading profits by 1987. Thus Ocean's withdrawal from deep-sea shipping in 1989 was unsurprising. (P.N. Davies, *The Trade Makers: Elder Dempster in West Africa, 1852–1972, 1973–1989* (2nd edition, St John's, Newfoundland, 2000), pp. 379–380.

168. In 1985 Peter Le Cheminant, director-general of the General Council of British Shipping, wanted the government to realise the harm done to shipping companies by the 1984 budget. It had discouraged investment in new ships and put British shipowners at a disadvantage in comparison with foreign competitors (*Financial Times*, 21 May 1985).

169. House of Commons transport committee, Report on the Decline of the UK-Registered Merchant Fleet, May 1988, vol. 1, table 24.

170. Quoted in ibid., vol. 1, p. xxvii.

171. See Section V, 'Does the Decline Matter?', in ibid., vol. 1, pp. xxvii–xxix.

172. *British Shipping: Challenges and Opportunities* (London, 1990). Cecil Parkinson was Minister of Transport and Sir Jeffrey Stirling was

chairman of P&O and President of the General Council of British Shipping 1990–91.

173. Ibid., p. 1.

174. House of Commons public accounts committee, Report on Movement of Personnel, Equipment and Stores to and from the Gulf, June 1993, p. 10, 22–23. During the Falklands conflict in 1982 the British merchant fleet had provided almost all the ships supporting the armed forces, being some fifty-eight in number (J. Moore (ed.), *Jane's Naval Review 1982–83* (London, 1982), pp. 142–143.)

175. T. Farrington, 'The UK Shipping Industry: A History and Assessment', *The Business Economist*, vol. 27, no. 1, 1996, pp. 31–32.

Chapter 3

1. Report of the departmental committee appointed by the Board of Trade to consider the position of the shipping and shipbuilding industries after the war [Booth committee], published 1918, Cmd. 9092, British Parliamentary Papers (BPP) 1918, vol. XIII, p. 473—Second report: shipbuilding and marine engineering, p. 21.

2. Ibid. For British shipbuilding before the First World War see S. Pollard and P. Robertson, *The British Shipbuilding Industry, 1870–1914* (Cambridge, MA, 1979). Despite the capital invested in it, pre-1914 British shipbuilding had a labour-intensive, craft basis that reflected practices in British engineering generally (see J.F. Wilson, *British Business History, 1720–1994* (Manchester, 1995), pp. 94, 161–162).

3. H.M. Hallsworth, 'The Shipbuilding Industry', Table A, in British Association for the Advancement of Science, *Britain in Depression: A Record of British Industries since 1929* (London, 1935), p. 253.

4. Booth, second report—shipbuilding and marine engineering, p. 23.

5. Ibid., p. 31.

6. Ibid., pp. 33, 35.

7. M. Davies, *Belief in the Sea: State Encouragement of British Merchant Shipping and Shipbuilding* (London, 1992), pp. 95–117; B.W. Labaree et al., *America and the Sea: A Maritime History* (Mystic, CT, 1998), pp. 497–499. See also C.H. Whitehurst, *The US Shipbuilding Industry: Past, Present and Future* (Annapolis, MD, 1986).

8. Hallsworth, 'Shipbuilding Industry', Table A. See also A.E. Musson, *The Growth of British Industry* (London, 1978), p. 308.

9. A. Slaven, 'Modern British Shipbuilding, 1800–1990', in L.A. Ritchie (ed.), *The Shipbuilding Industry: A Guide to Historical Records* (Manchester, 1992), pp. 10–11. For the decline in naval shipbuilding on Tyneside in the 1920s see D. Dougan, *The History of North East Shipbuilding* (London, 1968), p. 143.

10. For Trade Facilities Act see L. Johnman and H. Murphy, *British*

Shipbuilding and the State since 1918: A Political Economy of Decline (Exeter, 2002), pp. 21, 23, 28–29. Between 1921 and 1926 the TFA and its Northern Ireland equivalent brought shipping and shipbuilding over £31 million in public money (p. 28).

11. M. Moss and J.R. Hume, *Shipbuilders to the World: 125 Years of Harland and Wolff, Belfast, 1861–1986* (Belfast, 1986), Chapters 8 and 9.

12. D. Burrell, *Furness Withy, 1891–1991* (Kendal, 1992), p. 96.

13. Ibid., pp. 95–96.

14. A. Slaven, 'Self-Liquidation: The National Shipbuilders Security Ltd. and British Shipbuilding in the 1930s', in S. Palmer and G. Williams (eds), *Charted and Uncharted Waters* (London, 1981), p. 128.

15. Ibid., pp. 131, 144–146; L. Jones, *Shipbuilding in Britain: Mainly Between the Wars* (Cardiff, 1957), pp. 134–140. For closure of Beardmore shipyard at Dalmuir, see I. Johnston, *Beardmore Built: The Rise and Fall of a Clydeside Shipyard* (Clydebank, 1993), pp. 132–151. By 1935 some three-fifths of the labour force in private shipbuilding was concentrated in thirty-four large shipyards (Musson, *Growth of British Industry*, p. 311).

16. E.H. Lorenz, *Economic Decline in Britain: The Shipbuilding Industry, 1890–1970* (Oxford, 1991), Chapters 2 and 3.

17. Hallsworth, 'Shipbuilding Industry', Table, p. 256. For interwar labour relations and wage rates see Jones, *Shipbuilding in Britain*, Chapters 7 and 8.

18. A. Greenway (ed.), *Conway's History of the Ship—The Golden Age of Shipping: The Classic Merchant Ship, 1900–1960* (London, 1994), p. 145; K. Warren, *Steel, Ships and Men: Cammell Laird, 1824–1993* (Liverpool, 1998), p. 195. See also E.F. Spanner, 'Welding in Ship Construction', *Brassey's Naval and Shipping Annual 1934*, pp. 161–172.

19. Moss and Hume, *Shipbuilders to the World*, pp. 155–156, 208–244. For favourable comments on the marine diesel engine by Lord Kylsant (and Sir Frederick Lewis of Furness Withy) see (at p. 223) C. Maughan, 'The Balance-Sheet of the Motorship', *Brassey's Naval and Shipping Annual 1926*, pp. 222–230. See also J. Richardson, 'The Marine Oil Engine', *Brassey's Naval and Shipping Annual 1920–21*, pp. 182–193.

20. In 1933 J. Ramsay Gebbie of Doxfords observed: '. . . unless we can build oil engines at a lower cost than the foreigner, we shall not obtain any material share of foreign work, as the foreigner is certainly not showing signs of "going back to coal" . . .' (quoted in J.F.C. Clarke, *A Century of Service to Engineering and Shipbuilding: A Centenary History of the N.E. Coast Institution of Engineers and Shipbuilders, 1884–1984* (Newcastle, 1984), pp. 103–104). See also

D. Griffiths, 'British Shipping and the Diesel Engine: The Early Years', *Mariner's Mirror*, 81 (1995), pp. 313–331.

21. A. Slaven, 'British Shipbuilders: Market Trends and Order Book Patterns between the Wars', *Journal of Transport History*, 3rd series, vol. 3, no. 2, September 1982, pp. 44–45.

22. Ibid., p. 52.

23. Speech by J.R. Robertson at the launch of the tanker *British Diligence* at Swan Hunter shipyard, Tyneside, as reported in *The Petroleum Times*, 27 March 1937.

24. Davies, *Belief in the Sea*, pp. 121–128; Johnman and Murphy, *British Shipbuilding and the State since 1918*, pp. 52–53.

25. Davies, *Belief in the Sea*, pp. 132–136; Johnman and Murphy, *British Shipbuilding and the State since 1918*, pp. 53–55. See also Jones, *Shipbuilding in Britain*, Chapter 6. The government also gave financial aid to Cunard to support the construction of the *Queen Mary* and the *Queen Elizabeth* at John Brown's shipyard on the Clyde during the 1930s (see I. Johnston, *Ships for a Nation: John Brown & Company, 1847–1971* (Dunbartonshire, 2000), pp. 184–192, 195–210).

26. G.H. Parker, *Astern Business: 75 Years of UK Shipbuilding* (Kendal, 1996), pp. 20–25; A. Gordon, 'Naval Procurement and Ship-building Capacity, 1918–1939', in D.J. Starkey and A.G. Jamieson (eds), *Exploiting the Sea: Aspects of Britain's Maritime Economy since 1870* (Exeter, 1998), pp. 104–117; Johnman and Murphy, *British Shipbuilding and the State since 1918*, pp. 55–58. See also H.M. Hallsworth, 'The Shipbuilding Industry', in British Association for the Advancement of Science, *Britain in Recovery* (London, 1938), pp. 339–360, and G.A.H. Gordon, *British Seapower and Procurement Between the Wars* (London, 1988).

27. L. Dunn and P.M. Heaton, *Palm Line* (Abergavenny, 1994), pp. 23–24.

28. P. Hunting (ed.), *The Hunting History: Hunting plc since 1874* (London, 1991), pp. 57–58. The principal foreign builders of new tonnage for UK registration in the period 1920–38 were the Netherlands (203 vessels totalling 233,241 gt, chiefly motor coasters) and Germany (fifty-four vessels totalling 276,080 gt) (see Jones, *Shipbuilding in Britain*, p. 87).

29. Quotation from First Lord of the Admiralty, 16 March 1944, used by Correlli Barnett as the title for his chapter on shipbuilding in C. Barnett, *The Audit of War* (London, 1986), Chapter Six.

30. Figures given by First Lord of the Admiralty in the House of Commons on 1 November 1944 (see Davies, *Belief in the Sea*, p. 151 (and footnote 93)).

31. Barnett, *Audit of War*, pp. 114–120; Johnman and Murphy, *British Shipbuilding and the State since 1918*, pp. 78, 80–83. The only British

shipyard destroyed by enemy action and rebuilt during the war was White's of Cowes, which produced all-welded destroyers (see D.L. Williams, *Maritime Heritage: White's of Cowes* (Peterborough, 1993), Chapter 5).

32. Barnett, *Audit of War*, p. 111. For the Liberty ship programme see F.C. Lane, *Ships for Victory: A History of Shipbuilding under the US Maritime Commission in World War II* (Baltimore, MD, 1951), and L.A. Sawyer and W.H. Mitchell, *The Liberty Ships* (revised edition, Newton Abbot, 1973).

33. Cabinet reconstruction committee, 10 July 1944, quoted in Barnett, *Audit of War*, p. 123.

34. J.R. Parkinson, *The Economics of Shipbuilding in the United Kingdom* (Cambridge, 1960), p. 213.

35. A. Gorst and L. Johnman, 'British Naval Procurement and Ship-building, 1945–1964', in Starkey and Jamieson (eds), *Exploiting the Sea*, pp. 118–119.

36. Shipbuilding returns of Lloyd's Register of Shipping.

37. G.C. Allen, *British Industries and their Organization* (3rd edition, London, 1951), p. 145.

38. Johnman and Murphy, *British Shipbuilding and the State since 1918*, pp. 95–97.

39. Parkinson, *Economics of Shipbuilding in the UK*, Chapter 10.

40. C. Thompson, chairman of J.L. Thompson, shipbuilders, 31 August 1948, quoted in L. Johnman, 'Old Attitudes and New Technology: British Shipbuilding, 1945–1965', in P.C. van Royen, L.R. Fischer and D.M. Williams (eds), *Frutta di Mare: Evolution and Revolution in the Maritime World in the 19th and 20th Centuries* (Amsterdam, 1998), p. 141.

41. *The Economist*, 27 October 1956. British shipbuilding had already received a shock in 1955 when for the first time BP placed some of its tanker orders outside the UK, ordering six tankers from Italian shipyards (see J. Bamberg, *British Petroleum and Global Oil, 1950–1975: The Challenge of Nationalism* (Cambridge, 2000), p. 294).

42. A. Shonfield, *British Economic Policy Since the War* (Harmondsworth, 1958), pp. 41–42.

43. *The Economist*, 27 October 1956. By 1959 shipbuilder Sir William Lithgow was writing of Japanese competition: 'We are presently witnessing the beginning of a fight for survival between a newly developed industry backed by a nation, and an established leader backed by insular complacency' (quoted (at p. 110) in H.E. Horan, 'The British Shipping Industries', *Brassey's Annual: The Armed Forces Year-Book 1959*, pp. 102–110).

44. G.C. Allen, *British Industries and their Organization* (5th edition, London, 1970), p. 34; T. Chida and P.N. Davies, *The Japanese*

Shipping and Shipbuilding Industries: A History of their Modern Growth (London, 1990), pp. 106–108.

45. N. Harris (ed.), *Portrait of a Shipbuilder: Barrow-Built Vessels from 1873* (St. Michael's-on-Wyre, Lancashire, 1989), pp. 40–42.
46. L. Johnman and H. Murphy, 'The Norwegian Market for British Shipbuilding, 1945–1967', *Scandinavian Economic History Review*, vol. 46, no. 2, 1998, pp. 62, 67.
47. A. Slaven, 'Marketing Opportunities and Marketing Practices: The Eclipse of British Shipbuilding, 1957–1976', in L.R. Fischer (ed.), *From Wheel House to Counting House: Essays in Maritime Business History in Honour of Professor Peter N. Davies* (St John's, Newfoundland, 1992), pp. 128–131, 134.
48. Chida and Davies, *Japanese Shipping and Shipbuilding Industries*, pp. 111–114. See also P.N. Davies, 'The Role of National Bulk Carriers in the Advance of Shipbuilding Technology in Post-War Japan', *International Journal of Maritime History*, vol. IV, no. 1, June 1992, pp. 131–142, and the entry on Daniel K. Ludwig (1897–1992) in R. De La Pedraja, *A Historical Dictionary of the U.S. Merchant Marine and Shipping Industry since the Introduction of Steam* (Westport, CT, 1994).
49. K. Olsson, 'Big Business in Sweden: The Golden Age of the Great Swedish Shipyards, 1945–1974', *Scandinavian Economic History Review*, vol. XLIII, no. 3, 1995, pp. 318, 321–322, 326–327.
50. Johnman and Murphy, *British Shipbuilding and the State since 1918*, pp. 116–118.
51. Minutes of the meeting of the economic policy committee of the Cabinet, 4 February 1959 (PRO, CAB 134/1681). For some examples of demarcation disputes and other labour problems in the shipyards in the late 1940s and 1950s see A. Burton, *The Rise and Fall of British Shipbuilding* (London, 1994), pp. 204–208, and C. Barnett, *The Verdict of Peace: Britain Between Her Yesterday and the Future* (London, 2001), pp. 208–217. Between 1949 and 1964 shipyard workers were always near the top of the list of days lost through labour disputes in British industries (see Dougan, *History of North East Shipbuilding*, Table, p. 211).
52. The shipbuilding industry in the United Kingdom, report by officials, July 1959 (CAB 134/1683).
53. Ibid.
54. Ibid.
55. Minutes of the meeting of the economic policy committee of the Cabinet, 8 July 1959 (CAB 134/1681). Between 1960 and 1963 government and industry bodies made some efforts to stimulate improvements in shipbuilding research and development, production methods, marketing, and labour relations (see Shipbuilding

Inquiry Committee 1965–1966: Report [Geddes report] (Cmnd. 2937) (London, 1966), pp. 24–25).

56. Johnman and Murphy, *British Shipbuilding and the State since 1918*, pp. 124–125, 133–134.

57. Ibid., pp. 134–135, 140; Geddes report, pp. 24–25.

58. Johnman and Murphy, *British Shipbuilding and the State*, pp. 128, 155; Parker, *Astern Business*, pp. 41–42; Geddes Report, Appendices E and M, pp. 172 and 186.

59. For details of the scheme and government discussions about it, January to November 1963, see PRO, PREM 11/4482. For details of credit problems of British shipbuilding see Johnman and Murphy, *British Shipbuilding and the State since 1918*, pp. 135–141. The Ship Mortgage Finance Company had been set up in 1951 to finance orders for British shipyards, but had only limited success (p. 136).

60. Johnman and Murphy, *British Shipbuilding and the State*, Table, p. 142.

61. Organisation for Economic Co-operation and Development (OECD), *The Situation of the Shipbuilding Industry* (Paris, 1965), pp. 21, 23, 30.

62. The Shipbuilding Conference et al., *British Shipbuilding Facilities and Services* (London, 1962), p. vi.

63. Parkinson, *Economics of Shipbuilding in the UK*, p. 216.

64. Johnman and Murphy, *British Shipbuilding and the State since 1918*, pp. 159–161, 163. For the history of Fairfields see M. Moss and J. Hume, *Workshop of the British Empire: Engineering and Shipbuilding in the West of Scotland* (London, 1977), pp. 111, 113–144.

65. For the Fairfields 'experiment' see S. Paulden and B. Hawkins, *Whatever Happened to Fairfields?* (London, 1969).

66. Shipbuilding Inquiry Committee 1965–1966: Report [Geddes report] (Cmnd. 2937) (London, 1966), especially Preamble, Parts III, VI and VII, and Appendix A; G.C. Allen, *British Industries and their Organization* (5th edition, London, 1970), pp. 145–146; 'The Shipbuilders—A Special Survey', *The Economist*, 2 March 1968. At almost the same time Geddes was at work in Britain, an inquiry was taking place into the state of Dutch shipbuilding. The Keyzer report appeared in 1966 and recommended the modernisation and merger of Dutch shipyards in return for state financial aid. See C. de Voogd, 'Dutch Government Policy and the Decline of Shipbuilding in the Netherlands', in J. Bruijn et al. (eds), *Strategy and Response in the Twentieth Century Maritime World* (Amsterdam, 2001), p. 104.

67. Johnman and Murphy, *British Shipbuilding and the State*, pp. 166–167; Slaven, 'Modern British Shipbuilding, 1800–1990', in Ritchie, (ed.), *The Shipbuilding Industry: A Guide to Historical Records*, pp. 18–19; Allen (1970), pp. 146–147; *Economist* shipbuilding survey.

68. Johnman and Murphy, *British Shipbuilding and the State*, pp. 167–182, 198.

69. G. Owen, *From Empire to Europe: The Decline and Revival of British Industry since the Second World War* (London, 1999), p. 113.

70. Parker, *Astern Business*, pp. 53–55.

71. S. Sedgwick, M. Kinnaird and K.J. O'Donoghue, *London and Overseas Freighters plc: History and Fleet List, 1948–1992* (Kendal, 1992), pp. 13, 17–18. See also J. Lingwood, *SD14—The Great British Shipbuilding Success Story* (London, 1976). Austin and Pickersgill was said to have secured about half of all new tonnage orders placed in British yards in 1976 (see M. Dintenfass, *The Decline of Industrial Britain, 1870–1980* (London, 1992), p. 54). See also J.F. Clarke, *Building Ships on the North East Coast* (2 vols, Whitley Bay, 1997), vol. 2, pp. 378–380, 449–451.

72. Lloyds Register, annual reports for 1968 and 1969.

73. For a discussion of the success of Austin and Pickersgill and of a smaller British shipyard, Appledore, owned by Court Line, see P. Hilditch, 'The Decline of British Shipbuilding since the Second World War', in S. Fisher (ed.), *Lisbon as a Port Town, the British Seaman, and other Maritime Themes* (Exeter, 1988), pp. 137–138.

74. Parker, *Astern Business*, p. 64.

75. Owen, *From Empire to Europe*, p. 114.

76. Lloyd's Register, annual reports for 1969 and 1970. The *Esso Northumbria* was part of one of the few big VLCC orders placed by a major oil company with British shipyards. Esso ordered four 250,000 dwt tankers: two from Swan Hunter's Wallsend yard and two from Harland & Wolff, Belfast. All were delivered in 1970–1971. (L.A. Sawyer and W.H. Mitchell *Sailing Ship to Supertanker: The Hundred-Year Story of British Esso and its Ships* (Lavenham, 1987), pp. 184–185.)

77. Chamber of Shipping of the UK, *British Shipping Statistics 1974*, pp. 53, 55.

78. Johnman and Murphy, *British Shipbuilding and the State since 1918*, pp. 186–189; Johnston, *Ships for a Nation*, pp. 281–288.

79. Johnman and Murphy, *British Shipbuilding and the State*, pp. 197–200, 202–203; Davies, *Belief in the Sea*, pp. 232–233, 235–236. The collapse of Court Line in 1974 brought shipyards at Appledore and Sunderland under government control as well (see *The Economist*, 29 June and 24 August 1974).

80. M. Stopford, *Maritime Economics* (2nd edition, London, 1997), pp. 466–467.

81. Chida and Davies, *Japanese Shipping and Shipbuilding Industries*, pp. 181–182.

82. B. Strath, *The Politics of De-Industrialisation: The Contraction of the West European Shipbuilding Industry* (London, 1987), Chapter 4; D.

Todd, *Industrial Dislocation: The Case of Global Shipbuilding* (London, 1991), pp. 76–78; B. Fullerton and R. Knowles, *Scandinavia* (London, 1991), pp. 100–101.

83. Johnman and Murphy, *British Shipbuilding and the State since 1918*, pp. 204, 209. Government action was made more urgent by the collapse of the Israeli-American consortium Maritime Fruit Carriers in 1975–76. It had formed a number of subsidiary companies with British shipyards, e.g. Swan Maritime with Swan Hunter, and at the end of 1975 accounted for 35% of the UK order book (Johnman and Murphy, p. 208).

84. Parker, *Astern Business*, pp. 72–74, 77, 78, 82; Todd, *Industrial Dislocation*, pp. 78–81; Strath, *Politics of De-Industrialisation*, Chapter 5. The Blackpool agreement of 1979 was to replace 168 separate agreements between shipyard workers and management with a single agreement, with the aim of achieving contraction without compulsory redundancies. However, it was short-lived and British Shipbuilders was soon compelled to reduce its workforce (Strath, p. 153).

85. Lloyd's Register, annual report for 1977. Although these three shipyards were invited to tender for BP's VLCC building programme in the late 1960s and early 1970s, their bids could not match those of foreign competitors. Most of BP's VLCC orders went to Japan; the rest to Dutch and French shipyards (Bamberg, *British Petroleum and Global Oil, 1950–1975*, p. 297).

86. Parker, *Astern Business*, p. 75.

87. Johnman and Murphy, *British Shipbuilding and the State since 1918*, pp. 211–213. See also below Chapter 5.

88. Lloyd's Register, annual report for 1980; Parker, *Astern Business*, p. 78.

89. Davies, *Belief in the Sea*, p. 294.

90. Johnman and Murphy, *British Shipbuilding and the State*, p. 212.

91. K. Pottinger, 'The British Shipbuilding Industry', in the Greenwich Forum IX, *Britain and the Sea: Future Dependence, Future Opportunities* (Edinburgh, 1984), p. 288.

92. For the rise of South Korean shipbuilding see D. Todd, *The World Shipbuilding Industry* (London, 1985), pp. 340–345; Stopford, *Maritime Economics*, pp. 456–458, 464.

93. Johnman and Murphy, *British Shipbuilding and the State since 1918*, pp. 214–215.

94. Ibid., pp. 217–223; Parker, *Astern Business*, pp. 80, 82.

95. Parker, p. 82.

96. Davies, *Belief in the Sea*, pp. 310–317; Parker, p. 84; L. Johnman, 'The Privatisation of British Shipbuilders', *International Journal of Maritime History*, vol. VIII, no. 2, 1996, pp. 1–31.

97. Stopford, *Maritime Economics*, p. 467.

98. For a general view of British economic decline and its possible causes, with the obligatory mention of the shipbuilding industry (footnote, p. 456), see D. Landes, *The Wealth and Poverty of Nations: Why Some are so Rich and some so Poor* (London, 1998), pp. 450–458.

99. The 'institutional' approach is best represented by E.H. Lorenz and F. Wilkinson, 'The Shipbuilding Industry, 1880–1965', in B. Elbaum and W. Lazonick (eds), *The Decline of the British Economy* (Oxford, 1986), pp. 109–134, and E.H. Lorenz, *Economic Decline in Britain: The Shipbuilding Industry, 1890–1970* (Oxford, 1991).

100. The 'entrepreneurial failure' approach is seen in D. Thomas, 'Shipbuilding—Demand Linkage and Industrial Decline', in K. Williams, J. Williams and D. Thomas, *Why are the British Bad at Manufacturing?* (London, 1983), pp. 179–216; P. Hilditch, 'The Decline of British Shipbuilding since the Second World War', in S. Fisher (ed.), *Lisbon as a Port Town, the British Seaman and Other Maritime Themes* (Exeter, 1988), pp. 129–142; A. Slaven, 'Marketing Opportunities and Marketing Practices: The Eclipse of British Shipbuilding, 1957–1976', in L.R. Fischer (ed.), *From Wheel House to Counting House: Essays in Maritime Business History in Honour of Professor Peter N. Davies* (St John's, Newfoundland, 1992), pp. 125–151; and L. Johnman, 'Internationalization and the Collapse of British Shipbuilding, 1945–1973', in D.J. Starkey and G. Harlaftis (eds), *Global Markets: The Internationalization of the Sea Transport Industry since 1850* (St John's, Newfoundland, 1998), pp. 319–353.

101. L. Johnman and H. Murphy, *British Shipbuilding and the State since 1918: A Political Economy of Decline* (Exeter, 2002), passim; G. Owen, *From Empire to Europe: The Decline and Revival of British Industry since the Second World War* (London, 1999), pp. 113–114. See also B.W. Hogwood, *Government and Shipbuilding: The Politics of Industrial Change* (Farnborough, 1979); and R.M. Stopford and J.R. Barton, 'The Economic Problems of Shipbuilding and the State', in *Maritime Policy and Management*, vol. 13 (1986), no. 1, pp. 27–44.

Chapter 4

1. Sir Arthur Kirby, *The Effect of Port Re-Organisation in Great Britain* (London, 1965), p. 9. (Kirby was chairman of the British Transport Docks Board 1963–67 and of the National Ports Council 1967–71.) Parts of this chapter have appeared in D.J. Starkey and A.G. Jamieson, ' "Change on a Scale Unequalled": The Transformation of Britain's Port Industry in the Twentieth Century', in J.R. Bruijn et al. (eds), *Strategy and Response in the Twentieth Century Maritime World* (Amsterdam, 2001), pp. 131–146.

2. Report on the efficiency of British ports, 15 December 1960 (PRO, Cabinet papers, CAB 134/1688).

3. Report on the British shipping industry, 20 July 1962 (CAB 129/110).

4. Port authorities alleged the degree of congestion was exaggerated by the media, see Port of London Authority (PLA) annual report 1965, pp. 7–8.

5. Meeting of the Cabinet docks committee, 5 January 1965 (CAB 130/220).

6. Memorandum from the Minister of Transport, 1 February 1965 (CAB 130/220).

7. See A.G. Jamieson, 'Not More Ports, but Better Ports: The Development of British Ports since 1945', *The Northern Mariner*, vol. VI, no. 1, 1996, pp. 29–34.

8. R.B. Oram, *Cargo Handling and the Modern Port* (Oxford, 1965), Chapters 4, 5, 6.

9. G. Van Den Burg, *Containerisation: A Modern Transport System* (London, 1969), Chapters 6–9.

10. Report of the Committee of Inquiry into the Major Ports of Great Britain [Rochdale report] (Cmnd. 1824), British Parliamentary Papers (BPP) 1961–62, vol. XX.

11. Final Report of the Committee of Inquiry into Certain Matters concerning the Port Transport Industry [Devlin report] (Cmnd. 2734), BPP 1964–65, vol. XXI.

12. See G. Jackson, *The History and Archaeology of Ports* (Tadworth, 1983), pp. 72–139, and G. Jackson, 'The Ports', in M.J. Freeman and D.H. Aldcroft (eds), *Transport in Victorian Britain* (Manchester, 1988), pp. 218–252. British port expansion at this time was not controlled by any government plan or policy. See L.R. Fischer, 'Port Policies: Seaport Planning around the North Atlantic, 1850–1939', in L.R. Fischer and A. Jarvis (eds), *Harbours and Havens: Essays in Port History in Honour of Gordon Jackson* (St John's, Newfoundland, 1999), pp. 229–244.

13. See I.S. Greeves, *London Docks 1800–1980: A Civil Engineering History* (London, 1980); A. Jarvis, *The Liverpool Dock Engineers* (Stroud, 1996); L.F.V. Harcourt, *Harbours and Docks* (2 vols, London, 1885).

14. D.A. Farnie, *The Manchester Ship Canal and the Rise of the Port of Manchester, 1894–1975* (Manchester, 1980); G. Jackson, 'Do Docks Make Trade?: The Case of the Port of Great Grimsby', in L.R. Fischer (ed.), *From Wheel House to Counting House: Essays in Maritime Business History in Honour of Professor Peter Neville Davies* (St John's, Newfoundland, 1992), pp. 17–41.

15. F.E. Hyde, *Liverpool and the Mersey: The Development of a Port, 1700–1970* (Newton Abbot, 1971), pp. 72–94, 115–141; Mersey Docks and Harbour Board, *Business in Great Waters: An Account of*

the Activities of the Mersey Docks & Harbour Board, 1858–1958 (Liverpool, 1958), pp. 7–12.

16. For Bristol see Sir David Owen, *Ports of the United Kingdom* (revised edition, London, 1948), pp. 129–140, and J. Bird, *The Major Seaports of the United Kingdom* (London, 1963), Chapter 7; for London see A. Bryant, *Liquid History: Fifty Years of the Port of London Authority* (London, 1960), pp. 39–49; R.D. Brown, *The Port of London* (Lavenham, 1978), pp. 85–93; and Bird, *Major Seaports of the UK*, Chapters 14 to 17.

17. A.R. Henderson and S. Palmer, 'The Early Nineteenth Century Port of London: Management and Labour in Three London Dock Companies, 1800–1825', in S. Ville and D.M. Williams (eds), *Management, Finance and Industrial Relations in Maritime Industries: Essays in International Maritime and Business History* (St John's, Newfoundland, 1994), pp. 31–50.

18. D.F. Wilson, *Dockers: The Impact of Industrial Change* (London, 1972), pp. 23–25.

19. Ibid., p. 42. See also G. Phillips and N. Whiteside, *Casual Labour: The Unemployment Question in the Port Transport Industry, 1880–1970* (Oxford, 1985).

20. T. McCarthy, *The Great Dock Strike 1889* (London, 1988); J. Lovell, *Stevedores and Dockers: A Study of Trade Unionism in the Port of London, 1870–1914* (London, 1969), pp. 92–120; K. Coates and T. Topham, *The History of the Transport and General Workers Union: Volume I—The Making of the TGWU: The Emergence of the Labour Movement 1870–1922: Part I, 1870–1911: From Forerunners to Federation* (Oxford, 1991), pp. 51–77.

21. See L.H. Powell, *The Shipping Federation: A History of the First Sixty Years, 1890–1950* (London, 1950).

22. K. Coates and T. Topham, *History of the TGWU, Volume I, Part II, 1912–1922: From Federation to Amalgamation* (Oxford, 1991), pp. 449–467.

23. A. Bullock, *The Life and Times of Ernest Bevin: Volume 1—Trade Union Leader, 1881–1940* (London, 1960), pp. 116–142; Coates and Topham, *History of TGWU, Vol. I, Part II*, pp. 727–771.

24. Report of the Enquiry into the Wages and Conditions of Employment of Dock and Waterside Labourers [Shaw report] (Cmnd. 936 and 937), BPP 1920, vol. XXIV.

25. For details of national wage agreements from 1920 to the 1960s see Box 295, archives of the British Ports Association, Docklands Library and Archive, London.

26. *Report of the Enquiry into Port Labour* [Maclean Report] (London, 1931); F.G. Hanham, *Report of the Enquiry into Casual Labour in the Merseyside Area* (Liverpool, 1930), especially Sections 3 and 4; W. Hamilton Whyte, *Decasualisation of Dock Labour, with Special*

Reference to the Port of Bristol (Bristol, 1934); Wilson, *Dockers*, pp. 82–85. For an example of dock labour relations in a French port in this period see J. Barzman, 'Port Labour Relations in Le Havre, 1928–47', *International Journal of Maritime History*, 9 (2), 1997, pp. 83–106.

27. Jackson, *History and Archaeology of Ports*, pp. 145–147; Brown, *Port of London*, pp. 104–108; Owen, *Ports of the UK*, pp. 84–85; Bird, *Major Seaports of the UK*, Chapter 6 (Southampton), Chapters 11–13 (Liverpool), and Chapters 14–17 (London).

28. S. Palmer, 'Ports', in M. Daunton (ed.), *Cambridge Urban History of Britain: Volume III, 1840–1950* (Cambridge, 2000), p. 145.

29. Final Report of the Royal Commission on Transport (Cmnd. 3751), BPP 1930–31, vol. XVII. Although £27 million had been spent between 1918 and 1930 on improving port facilities at London, Liverpool, Manchester, Clyde, Belfast and Bristol, shipowners felt that loading and unloading of cargoes had not been greatly improved (Shipowners Parliamentary Committee, Minute Book no. 5 (1930– 34), meeting of 5 March 1930, in Chamber of Shipping Archives, Modern Records Centre, University of Warwick).

30. Jackson, *History and Archaeology of Ports*, pp. 144–145; B. Lenman, *From Esk to Tweed: Harbours, Ships and Men of the East Coast of Scotland* (Glasgow, 1975), pp. 171–172; R.W. Ferrier, *The History of the British Petroleum Company. Volume 1: The Developing Years, 1901–1932* (Cambridge, 1982); S. Howarth, *A Century in Oil: The 'Shell' Transport and Trading Company, 1897–1997* (London, 1997), p. 164; D.J. Payton-Smith, *Oil: A Study of Wartime Policy and Administration* (London, 1971), pp. 65–67. For foreign ports in the interwar period, especially Antwerp, Rotterdam and Hamburg, see A.J. Sargent, *Seaports and Hinterlands* (London, 1938).

31. C.B.A. Behrens, *Merchant Shipping and the Demands of War* (London, 1955); M. Doughty, *Merchant Shipping and War: A Study of Defence Planning in Twentieth Century Britain* (London, 1982); L.M. Bates, *The Thames on Fire: The Battle of the London River, 1939–45* (Lavenham, 1985); 'The Battle of the UK Ports' [1939–41], typed internal history, Ministry of Transport, c.1946, in the Chamber of Shipping Archives, Modern Records Centre, University of Warwick.

32. A. Bullock, *The Life and Times of Ernest Bevin. Volume II: Minister of Labour, 1940–45* (London, 1967), pp. 30–31, 58–59; H.M.D. Parker, *Manpower: A Study of Wartime Policy and Administration* (London, 1957), pp. 129–130, 140.

33. Dock and Harbour Authorities Association, 'Postwar Organisation of Docks and Harbours', report adopted by the association on 14 February 1945 (Box 166, British Ports Association Archives, Docklands Library and Archive, London); Sir Gilmour Jenkins,

The Ministry of Transport and Civil Aviation (London, 1959), pp. 87–88.

34. P.S. Bagwell, *The Transport Revolution* (revised edition, London, 1988), pp. 293–295; Jenkins, *Ministry of Transport*, pp. 87–89. Perhaps surprisingly the nationalised ports receive no mention in A.W.J. Thomson and L.C. Hunter, *The Nationalized Transport Industries* (London, 1973).

35. C. Barnett, *The Lost Victory: British Dreams, British Realities, 1945–1950* (London, 1995), pp. 267–271.

36. Docks and Inland Waterways Executive, British Transport Commission, *Review of Trade Harbours, 1948–50* (London, 1951); Jenkins, *Ministry of Transport*, p. 89.

37. Ministry of Transport, *Report of the Working Party on the Turn-Round of Shipping in UK Ports* (London, 1948); A.H.J. Brown, 'Ports and Shipping Turn-Round: Causes of Delay and Suggested Remedies', reprinted from *The Dock and Harbour Authority*, January 1953 (Box 166, British Ports Association Archives, Docklands Library and Archive, London); Jenkins, *Ministry of Transport*, pp. 89–90; R.B. Oram, *Cargo Handling and the Modern Port*, p. 4.

38. Ministry of Transport, *Report by the Working Party on Increased Mechanisation in the UK Ports* (London, 1950); Anglo-American Council on Productivity, *Productivity Team—Freight Handling —Report on Visit to the USA in 1950* (1951); *First and Second Reports of the Ports Efficiency Committee to the Secretary of State* (London, 1952); Oram, *Cargo Handling and the Modern Port*, pp. 66–76.

39. Bagwell, *Transport Revolution*, p. 326.

40. National Dock Labour Board, *An Introduction to Port Working* (London, 1955); Oram, *Cargo Handling and the Modern Port*, pp. 53–55; P. Turnbull, C. Woolfson and J. Kelly, *Dock Strike: Conflict and Restructuring in Britain's Ports* (Aldershot, 1992), pp. 14–15.

41. Wilson, *Dockers*, p. 294. See also C. Barnett, *The Verdict of Peace: Britain between her Yesterday and the Future* (London, 2001), pp. 239–256.

42. Report of the Committee of Inquiry into Unofficial Stoppages in the London Docks [Leggett report] (Cmnd. 8236), BPP 1950–51, vol. XVI.

43. Report of the Committee to Inquire into the Operation of the Dock Workers (Regulation of Employment) Scheme 1947 [Devlin report] (Cmnd. 9813), BPP 1955–56, vol. XXVI.

44. H. Rees, *British Ports and Shipping* (London, 1958), pp. 281–282, 284, 288; Bird, *Major Seaports of the UK*, pp. 92, 211–213.

45. Wilson, *Dockers*, p. 308.

46. Oram, *Cargo Handling and the Modern Port*, pp. 51–53; for US West Coast and New York labour agreements relating to containerisation

see G. Van Den Burg, *Containerisation: A Modern Transport System* (London, 1969), pp. 76–78.

47. Minutes of meetings of the economic policy committee of the Cabinet, 15 December 1960 and 9 and 15 February 1961 (CAB 134/1688, 1689). As late as 1967 the National Ports Council still found it necessary to reject the idea that British ports should just run a feeder service to a 'mainport' on the continent, see National Ports Council—Port Planning—A Note by the Director General, 17 January 1967 (PRO, National Ports Council papers, DK 1/108).

48. Report of the Committee of Inquiry into the Major Ports of Great Britain [Rochdale report] (Cmnd. 1824), BPP 1961–62, vol. XX, paragraph 9. Lord Rochdale (John Durivale Kemp) produced his report on the ports in 1962. He was chairman of the National Ports Council 1964–67 and prepared his report on the British shipping industry 1967–70.

49. Rochdale report, paragraph 140; Rochdale committee on ports, policy questions, 1961–62 (PRO, MT 81/482); Cabinet conclusions, 27 July 1962 (CAB 129/110).

50. Rochdale Report, paragraph 47. For development of iron ore terminals see National Port Development Plan—Ore Importing Facilities, 1964 (DK 1/116) and Iron and Steel Board, *Development in the Iron and Steel Industry: Special Report 1964* (London, 1964), Chapter 12.

51. Rochdale report, paragraphs 47–49 and 63. For the development of Rotterdam see P.T. van de Laar, 'The Port of Rotterdam in a Changing Environment. From Rhine Port to Mainport, 1870–1970', in Bruijn et al. (eds), *Strategy and Response in the Twentieth Century Maritime World*, pp. 147–161. See also M.E. Tonizzi, 'Economy, Traffic and Infrastructure in the Port of Genoa, 1861–1970', in G. Boyce and R. Gorski (eds), *Resources and Infrastructures in the Maritime Economy, 1500–2000* (St John's, Newfoundland, 2002), pp. 119–140.

52. Rochdale report, paragraphs 64–66. See W.J. Wren, *Ports of the Eastern Counties* (Lavenham, 1976), Chapters 7–9, for the Haven Ports. One should beware of exaggerating the awareness of the committee (and later of the National Ports Council) in the first half of the 1960s of a need to concentrate development on the ports of the south and east coasts of Britain. In its 1965 interim plan for port development the NPC still saw the position of Liverpool as 'even more impregnable than that of London'. (National Ports Council, *Port Development: An Interim Plan* (2 vols, London, 1965), vol. 1, p. 70.)

53. Rochdale report, Section III; Lord Rochdale, 'The Re-Organisation of British Ports', *Journal of the Royal Society of Arts*, November 1964, pp. 901–915.

54. Rochdale report, paragraphs 330–331. According to *The Economist* (29 September 1962) 'preparing for the wider use of containers is where the committee feels that the docks have fallen down worst'. For ro-ro and container services on Irish Sea routes see R.C. Sinclair, *Across the Irish Sea: Belfast–Liverpool Shipping since 1819* (London, 1990), pp. 140–159. See also J. Pudney, *London's Docks* (London, 1975), p. 173.

55. Rochdale report, Section IX.

56. Cabinet conclusions, 27 July 1962 (CAB 129/110); Central Office of Information (COI), *British Industry Today: Ports* (London, 1974); National Ports Council (NPC), annual report 1974.

57. Brown, *Port of London*, pp. 128–129, 131.

58. Ibid., pp. 134–136, 138.

59. Ibid., pp. 138, 140–141; PLA annual reports 1965 and 1966. For an overview of containerisation in the 1960s see J. Bird, *Seaports and Seaport Terminals* (London, 1971), Chapter 4.

60. Cabinet sub-committee on containers, letters and reports, June 1968 (CAB 134/2921). For the problems in trying to make Newport, South Wales, a container port see correspondence between PM and Minister of Transport, 1968 (PREM 13/2011). For a collection of reports on containerisation, 1966–67, see DK 1/157.

61. Brown, *Port of London*, pp. 132, 142; W. Paul Clegg, *Docks and Ports: 2. London* (Shepperton, 1987), pp. 56–57. The first British oceanic container service began in November 1968 between Manchester and Montreal (see above Chapter 2).

62. Brown, *Port of London*, pp. 143–144; Wilson, *Dockers*, p. 239. For a management view of events in the London docks 1967–70 and at Southampton docks from 1970 see J. Hovey, *A Tale of Two Ports: London and Southampton* (London, 1990).

63. Wilson, *Dockers*, p. 12.

64. Final Report of the Committee of Inquiry into Certain Matters concerning the Port Transport Industry [Devlin report] (Cmnd. 2734), BPP 1964–65, vol. XXI; COI, *Ports* (1974).

65. Wilson, *Dockers*, pp. 122, 186–189, 316–317.

66. *Report of the Labour Party Study Group on the Port Transport Industry* (Labour Party, June 1966).

67. The Reorganisation of the Ports, BPP 1968–69, vol. LIII.

68. Ibid. For National Ports Council and nationalisation proposals see DK 1/159–172.

69. Brown, *Port of London*, p. 167.

70. Wilson, *Dockers*, pp. 273–277, 285–286. For financial troubles at the Mersey Docks & Harbour Board see A. Lynch, *Weathering the Storm: The Mersey Docks Financial Crisis, 1970–74* (Liverpool, 1994).

71. Brown, *Port of London*, pp. 167, 169.

72. Turnbull, Woolfson and Kelly, *Dock Strike*, pp. 27–28.

73. National Ports Council, *Survey of Non-Scheme Ports and Wharves* (London, 1973); COI, *Ports* (1974); G. Adams, *The Organisation of the British Port Transport Industry* (London, 1973).
74. Turnbull, Woolfson and Kelly, *Dock Strike*, p. 28.
75. Brown, *Port of London*, pp. 166–170; National Ports Council (NPC), annual report for 1979.
76. NPC annual reports for 1965 (BPP 1966–67, vol. XXXV), 1966 (BPP 1966–67, vol. XXXV) and 1969 (BPP 1970–71, vol. XLIX). Up to and including 1971 the annual reports of the NPC were published as parliamentary papers. From 1972 they were published separately by HMSO.
77. NPC annual reports for 1965 (BPP 1966–67, vol. XXXV), 1967 (BPP 167–68, vol. XXIII) and 1969 (BPP 1970–71, vol. XLIX).
78. NPC annual reports for 1968 (BPP 1968–69, vol. XXXII) and 1969 (BPP 1970–71, vol. XLIX).
79. NPC annual report for 1971 (BPP 1971–72, vol. XXXVIII).
80. Ibid.
81. Ibid.
82. NPC annual report for 1979; COI, *Ports* (1974).
83. NPC annual reports for 1972 and 1973. For North Sea oil and gas industry see below Chapter 5.
84. NPC annual report 1973; Shetland Islands Council (SIC), *Shetland's Oil Era* (Shetland, 1977), pp. 19–29.
85. NPC annual report for 1974. For an example of changes in a continental port system in this period see M. Hahn-Pedersen, 'Changing Structures: Developments in Danish Commercial Ports since 1960', *International Journal of Maritime History*, 8 (1), 1996, pp. 59–86.
86. NPC annual reports for 1974 and 1975.
87. NPC annual report for 1975; SIC, *Shetland's Oil Era*, pp. 40–57.
88. NPC annual report for 1976. For a comparison of British ports with those of other EEC countries in the mid-1970s see Commission of the European Communities, *Report of an Enquiry into the Current Situation in the Major Community Sea-Ports drawn up by the Port Working Group* (Brussels, 1977).
89. NPC annual report for 1976.
90. NPC annual reports for 1976, 1977 and 1978; SIC, *Shetland's Oil Era*, pp. 40–57. Sullom Voe quickly became the largest oil and liquefied gas terminal in both Britain and Europe. Its peak throughput of crude oil was in 1984 when a figure of over 58 million tonnes was achieved. By the early 1990s throughput had declined to around 40 million tonnes of crude oil per annum. (SIC, *Shetland in Statistics*, no. 23, 1994, pp. 31–35).
91. NPC annual report for 1979.
92. Ibid.

93. J. Reveley and M. Tull, 'Centralised Port Planning: An Evaluation of the British and New Zealand Experience', in G. Boyce and R. Gorski (eds), *Resources and Infrastructures in the Maritime Economy, 1500–2000* (St. John's, Newfoundland, 2002), pp. 141–161.
94. NPC annual report for 1979. The NPC was not formally abolished until the passage of the Transport Act 1981. An internal history of the NPC formed the basis for G.K. Wilson, 'Planning: Lessons from the Ports', *Public Administration*, vol. 61 (1983), pp. 265–281. See also P. Oxley, 'The British Ports Industry, 1965–1980', in Greenwich Forum, *Britain and the Sea* (Edinburgh, 1984), pp. 309–318.
95. Turnbull, Woolfson and Kelly, *Dock Strike*, pp. 47, 85.
96. Ibid., pp. 61–62.
97. Ibid., pp. 63–72.
98. Ibid., pp. 85–92.
99. Ibid., pp. 94–97.
100. Ibid., p. 113.
101. Ibid., pp. 129–138.
102. Ibid., pp. 141, 159, 170; *The Economist*, 5 August 1989.
103. For contrasting views of government ports policy see P. Turnbull and S. Weston, 'Employment Regulation, State Intervention, and the Economic Performance of European Ports', *Cambridge Journal of Economics*, vol. 16, no. 4, 1992, pp. 385–404, and R. Goss, 'British Port Policies since 1945', *Journal of Transport Economics and Policy*, vol. 32, no. 1, 1998, pp. 51–71.

Chapter 5

1. G. Arnold, *Britain's Oil* (London, 1978), p. 333.
2. The Challenge of North Sea Oil (Cmnd. 7143), BPP 1977–78, vol. XXV.
3. C. Harvie, *Fool's Gold: The Story of North Sea Oil* (London, 1994), p. 286.
4. Harvie, *Fool's Gold*, p. 3; Arnold, *Britain's Oil*, p. 8.
5. C. Robinson and D. Hann, 'North Sea Oil and Gas', in P. Johnson (ed.), *The Structure of British Industry* (2nd edition, London, 1988), pp. 30–31.
6. United Kingdom Offshore Operators Association (UKOOA), *The North Sea Achievement: The First 25 Years* (London, 1989), p. 35. Outside the North Sea Britain's only other offshore energy project was the gas field in Morecambe Bay on the Irish Sea. Drilling in the so-called Celtic Sea, to the south-west of the British Isles, failed to find any significant oil or gas deposits.
7. Harvie, *Fool's Gold*, pp. 223–227, 324–329 and 355; 'Survey of North Sea Oil', *The Economist*, 26 July 1975. See also T. Lind and

G.A. Mackay, *Norwegian Oil Policies* (London, 1979) and S.S. Andersen, *The Struggle over North Sea Oil and Gas: Government Strategies in Denmark, Britain and Norway* (Oslo, 1993).

8. J.S. Jennings, 'Opportunities Arising from North Sea Development', in the Greenwich Forum IX, *Britain and the Sea: Future Dependence—Future Opportunities* (Edinburgh, 1984), p. 43. As early as 1978 some commentators were condemning British industry for being slow to seize the North Sea opportunity; see A. Hamilton, *North Sea Impact: Off-Shore Oil and the British Economy* (London, 1978), particularly Chapter 7.

9. For ports and the development of the North Sea oil and gas industry see above, Chapter 4.

10. B. Cooper and T.F. Gaskell, *North Sea Oil: The Great Gamble* (London, 1966), p. 47; R. Robinson, *Trawling: The Rise and Fall of the British Trawl Industry* (Exeter, 1996), p. 225.

11. P. Hinde, *Fortune in the North Sea* (London, 1966), pp. 66–83; Cooper and Gaskell, *North Sea Oil*, pp. 46–61.

12. Hinde, pp. 84–87; Cooper and Gaskell, pp. 46–61; Robinson and Hann, 'North Sea Oil and Gas', pp. 39–40; UKOOA, *North Sea Achievement*, p. 5.

13. Hinde, Appendix I, pp. 191–220; T.A.B. Corley, *A History of the Burmah Oil Company: Volume II, 1924–1966* (London, 1988), pp. 376–378. BP was already offshore—an offshore drilling rig appeared on the front cover of H. Longhurst, *Adventures in Oil: The Story of British Petroleum* (London, 1959) and two chapters covered offshore drilling in the Persian Gulf and off Trinidad. For Shell's first offshore activities, see S. Howarth, *A Century in Oil: The 'Shell' Transport and Trading Company, 1897–1997* (London, 1997), pp. 218, 244–245. For the general history of the international oil industry see A. Sampson, *The Seven Sisters* (revised edition, London, 1988) and D. Yergin, *The Prize: The Epic Quest for Oil, Money and Power* (London, 1991).

14. J. Bamberg, *British Petroleum and Global Oil, 1950–1975: The Challenge of Nationalism* (Cambridge, 2000), pp. 195–199.

15. Cooper and Gaskell, pp. 1–18; Report of the inquiry into the loss of the drilling rig *Sea Gem* (Cmnd. 3409), BPP 1966–67, vol. XXI.

16. T.I. Williams, *A History of the British Gas Industry* (Oxford, 1981), Chapters 15–18; Second report of the House of Commons select committee on nationalised industries: Exploitation of North Sea Gas, BPP 1967–68, vol. XIV; Robinson and Hann, pp. 30, 40–41; Bamberg, *British Petroleum and Global Oil*, pp. 200–202.

17. Department of Energy, *The Development of the Oil and Gas Resources of the United Kingdom* (London, 1988). This annual government publication is known as the Brown Book. Appendix 3 of the Brown Book 1988 gives details of all major hydrocarbon (gas and oil)

discoveries on the UKCS since 1965. See also Bamberg, pp. 202–203, and Howarth, *A Century in Oil*, pp. 278–279, 305, 316–319.

18. The Department of Trade and Industry published the IMEG report as *Study of the Potential Benefits to British Industry from Offshore Oil and Gas Development* (London, 1972). See also R.E.D. Bishop and W. Elkan, 'Offshore Oil : Responses to Employment Opportunities', in Greenwich Forum, *Britain and the Sea*, pp. 64–66.

19. IMEG report; House of Commons public accounts committee, First Report: North Sea Oil and Gas, 14 February 1973; M. Jenkin, *British Industry and the North Sea: State Intervention in a Developing Industrial Sector* (London, 1981), pp. 51–53, 63–68.

20. Jenkin, *British Industry and the North Sea*, pp. 78–81.

21. UK Offshore Oil and Gas Policy (Cmnd. 5696), BPP 1974, vol. XII; First report of the House of Commons select committee on the nationalised industries: The Nationalised Industries and the Exploitation of North Sea Oil and Gas, BPP 1974– 75, vol. XXVI; The Challenge of North Sea Oil (Cmnd. 7143), BPP 1977–78, vol. XXV; Central Office of Information (COI), *British Industry Today: Energy* (London, 1979), offshore oil and gas sections; Jenkin, pp. 82–90; Robinson and Hann, pp. 41–44.

22. For OSO claims see COI, *Britain's Offshore Equipment and Services Industry* (London, 1982), pp. 1, 20, 26, and the Brown Book 1988, pp. 75–76, 80. For criticisms of OSO figures see Robinson and Hann, p. 32; Harvie, pp. 146–147; Bishop and Elkan, pp. 67–68.

23. *Offshore Oil and Gas Yearbook 1981–82: UK and Continental Europe*, pp. 113– 114; The Brown Book 1988, Appendix 6; Robinson and Hann, pp. 41, 43–44; Jennings, 'Opportunities Arising from North Sea Developers', in Greenwich Forum, *Britain and the Sea*, p. 40; COI, *Britain 1988: An Official Handbook* (London, 1988), pp. 273–279; S.M. Hoopes, *Oil Privatization, Public Choice and International Forces* (London, 1997), especially Chapter 3.

24. Third report of the House of Commons select committee on energy: The Effect of Oil and Gas Prices on Activity in the North Sea, May 1987, HC 175; Offshore Supplies Office (OSO), *Global Horizons: Oil and Gas Technology for World Markets* (London, 1989); Foreign and Commonwealth Office (FCO), *British Offshore Industry* (London, 1992); Harvie, *Fool's Gold*, p. 363.

25. Bush quotation in H. Benford and W.A. Fox (eds), *A Half Century of Marine Technology, 1943–1993* (Jersey City, NJ, 1993), p. 593.

26. Benford and Fox, *Half Century of Marine Technology*, Part XI—The Offshore Industry, pp. 561–616; UKOOA, *Britain's Offshore Oil and Gas Industry: Harnessing a Vital Resource* (London, 1992), p. 10; M. Lovegrove, *Our Islands Oil* (London, 1975), pp. 23–24.

27. Cooper and Gaskell, *North Sea Oil*, p. 75; Hinde, *Fortune in the North*

Sea, Appendix II, pp. 221–238; J.F. Clarke, *Building Ships on the North East Coast* (2 vols, Whitley Bay, 1997), vol. 2, p. 363.

28. M. Moss and J.R. Hume, *Shipbuilders to the World: 125 Years of Harland & Wolff, Belfast, 1861–1986* (Belfast, 1986), pp. 422–423, 481, 562, 565. In the late 1980s Harland & Wolff built a SWOPS (Single Well Oil Production System) ship, the *Seillean*, for BP. This floating oil production facility was completed in 1990 (see Lloyd's Register annual reports for 1988–90).

29. F.M. Walker, *Song of the Clyde: A History of Clyde Shipbuilding* (Cambridge, 1984), p. 206; G.H. Parker, *Astern Business: 75 Years of UK Shipbuilding* (Kendal, 1996), pp. 42–43, 69; Jenkin, *British Industry and the North Sea*, p. 53; Harvie, *Fool's Gold*, p. 73; S. McKinstry, 'Transforming John Brown's Shipyard: The Drilling Rig and Offshore Fabrication Businesses of Marathon and UIE, 1972–1997', *Scottish Economic and Social History*, vol. 18 (1998), part 1, pp. 33–60. Between 1961 and 1971 John Brown built half (six) of all drilling rigs built by British shipyards. From 1973 to 1980, under Marathon, the yard built ten jack-up rigs, and between 1981 and 1986 five jack-up rigs for UIE. It was basically a construction yard, with most research and development done abroad (McKinstry, pp. 58–59).

30. Walker, *Song of the Clyde*, pp. 206, 209; Parker, *Astern Business*, pp. 53, 76–78; Third report of the Commons energy committee 1987 (HC 175), Memorandum 27, submission of the Scottish TUC, January 1987; COI, *Britain's Offshore Equipment and Services Industry* (1982), pp. 3–4, 11; L. Johnman and H. Murphy, 'A Triumph of Failure: The British Shipbuilding Industry and the Offshore Structures Market, 1960–1990: A Case Study of Scott Lithgow Ltd.', *International Journal of Maritime History*, forthcoming. The only British shipyard other than John Brown and Scott Lithgow to build a drilling rig after 1967 was Cammell Laird at Birkenhead, which completed the semi-submersible rig *Sovereign Explorer* for Dome Petroleum of Canada in 1984. For a wider view of the offshore option for shipbuilders see D. Todd, *Industrial Dislocation: The Case of Global Shipbuilding* (London, 1991), pp. 150–154.

31. Arnold, *Britain's Oil*, p. 93.

32. P. Hunting (ed.), *The Hunting History: Hunting plc since 1874* (London, 1991), pp. 84–90.

33. G. Somner, *Ben Line: Fleet List and Short History* (Kendal, 1980), pp. 14–15, 105–109.

34. Ibid.; *Sea Breezes*, June 1980, pp. 352–355; M. Strachan, *The Ben Line, 1825–1982: An Anecdotal History* (Norwich, 1992), pp. 214–218.

35. See N. Watson, *The Story of Christian Salvesen, 1846–1996* (London,

1996). Also G. Somner, *From 70 North to 70 South: A History of the Christian Salvesen Fleet* (Edinburgh, 1984).

36. Watson, p. 20; Somner, pp. 120–126; Christian Salvesen annual reports 1976– 1986.

37. Watson, p. 20; Somner, pp. 117–119; Christian Salvesen annual reports 1976–79.

38. D. Burrell, *Furness Withy: The Centenary History, 1891–1991* (Kendal, 1992), pp. 167–168, 172, 174–177.

39. Ibid., pp. 174–177; Third report of the Commons energy committee 1987 (HC 175), Memorandum 23, submission of the British Rig Owners' Association, December 1986. KCA was a subsidiary of a London-based oil finance company.

40. B. Kolltveit and M. Crowdy, *Wilh. Wilhelmsen, History and Fleet List, 1861–1994* (Kendal, 1994), pp. 33–36, and offshore entries in fleet list.

41. For an analysis of the workforce at Nigg, see Harvie, *Fool's Gold*, p. 159.

42. Harvie, p. 79; Shell UK Exploration and Production, *North Sea Fields: Facts and Figures* (4th edition, 1991).

43. Harvie, p. 80.

44. Ibid., pp. 79–80, 158–160; Arnold, *Britain's Oil*, pp. 98–100; Jenkin, *British Industry and the North Sea*, pp. 28, 84–85, 114, 127, 157–159; The Brown Book 1988, Appendix 10: Oil Production Platforms; 'Meeting the Offshore Challenge', in Lloyd's Register annual report for 1974. A complete and detailed guide to all North Sea installations is given in *The North Sea Platform Guide* (Ledbury, 1985).

45. Harvie, *Fool's Gold*, pp. 158–160; Ultramar, *A Golden Adventure: The First Fifty Years of Ultramar* (London, 1985), pp. 217–222; Third report of the Commons energy committee 1987 (HC 175), Memorandum 5, submission from the Highland Regional Council, January 1987.

46. The Brown Book 1988, Appendix 10; FCO, *British Offshore Industry* (1992), p. 9.

47. The Brown Book 1988, Appendix 11: Major Offshore Pipelines; Harvie, *Fool's Gold*, pp. 81, 145.

48. Quoted in Harvie, p. 222.

49. COI, *Britain's Offshore Equipment and Services Industry* (1982), pp. 14–16.

50. Much of this section is taken from A.G. Jamieson, 'British OSV Companies in the North Sea, 1964–1997', *Maritime Policy and Management*, vol. 25, 1998, no. 4, pp. 305–312. (Journal published by Francis and Taylor.)

51. V. Gibson, 'Support to the Offshore Industry' in A. Couper (ed.), *Conway's History of the Ship: The Shipping Revolution—The Modern*

Merchant Ship (London, 1992), pp. 140–146; Coopers & Lybrand, 'UK Offshore Support Vessel Industry: Final Report, November 1986' (for the Offshore Supplies Office (OSO) and the British Offshore Support Vessels Association (BOSVA)), p. 19. (Copy of report courtesy of H.G. Davy.)

52. Hinde, *Fortune in the North Sea*, Appendix I, pp. 191–220; D. Howarth and S. Howarth, *The Story of P&O* (revised edition, London, 1994), p. 180; S. Rabson and K. O'Donoghue, *P&O: A Fleet History* (Kendal, 1988), p. 221; Coopers and Lybrand report 1986; information from Suffolk Marine; W.P. Clegg, *British Shipping* (Shepperton, 1988), pp. 114, 126. Also information from Mr H.G. Davy, CBE, of Lowline Ltd. Mr Davy was kind enough to provide documents and share his extensive knowledge of Lowline, BOSVA and the British OSV industry in general with the author.

53. IMEG report 1972, p. 33.

54. Outline of OIL's twenty-five-year history in the company's *Global Review*, May 1996; M. Falkus, *The Blue Funnel Legend* (London, 1990), p. 339; S. Jones, *Two Centuries of Overseas Trading: The Origins and Growth of the Inchcape Group* (London, 1986), pp. 266, 282.

55. J. Orbell, *From Cape to Cape: The History of Lyle Shipping* (Edinburgh, 1978), pp. 164–166. See also *Sea Breezes*, October 1982, pp. 728–729.

56. Publicity material of Stirling Shipping and Harrisons (Clyde) Ltd.; various issues of *Clanger*, the house magazine of Harrisons (Clyde) Ltd. Also in 1974 Star Offshore Services was set up by United Towing of Hull and became an important OSV operator (*Sea Breezes*, May 1976, p. 268, and November 1984, pp. 768–769).

57. 'Maritime Logistic Support for Offshore Oil and Gas Industry' (report, c.1975), Section 3—Supply of Offshore Support Craft, Tables 3.6, 3.9, 3.22. (Courtesy of H.G. Davy.)

58. Ibid., Tables 3.22, 3.25, 3.26, 3.27. For Ulstein's UT704 see Gibson in Couper, *Shipping Revolution*, p. 143.

59. *Clanger 28*, December 1994; Orbell, *From Cape to Cape*, p. 166.

60. F. Hodne, *The Norwegian Economy, 1920–1980* (London, 1983), p. 255. A.P. Möller's monopoly included oil and gas production as well as shipping services.

61. S. Rabson and K. O'Donoghue, *P&O: A Fleet History* (Kendal, 1988), p. 361. For Australia's offshore energy industry see F. Broeze, *Island Nation: A History of Australians and the Sea* (St Leonards, NSW, 1998), pp. 194–195.

62. Third report of the House of Commons select committee on energy: The Effect of Oil and Gas Prices on Activity in the North Sea, May 1987 (HC 175), Memorandum 22, submission of BOSVA, January 1987; Coopers & Lybrand report 1986, p. 2; information from H.G. Davy, Lowline Ltd.

63. OIL history in *Global Review*, May 1996; H. Clarkson and Co. Ltd., *The Offshore Service Vessel Register 1983* (London, 1983).
64. *Clanger* 23, June 1990.
65. Coopers and Lybrand report 1986, p. 24; Third report of Commons energy committee 1987 (HC 175), submission of BOSVA.
66. Coopers and Lybrand report 1986, Tables 2.11, 2.13.
67. Ibid., pp. 6–7.
68. Ibid., pp. 1 and 8.
69. BOSVA note on the offshore support vessel sector, January 1989, pp. 5–6, 7–8. (Courtesy of H.G. Davy.)
70. OIL history in *Global Review*, May 1996; List of BOSVA members, April 1990; BOSVA list of supply vessels operating in the North Sea, April 1990. (Courtesy of H.G. Davy.)

Chapter 6

1. Joint Working Party chaired by the Secretary of State for Transport and the President of the General Council of British Shipping: Department of Transport and the GCBS, *British Shipping: Challenges and Opportunities* (London, 1990), p. 1.
2. D. Howarth and S. Howarth, *The Story of P&O* (revised edition, London, 1994), pp. 200, 204, 211–213.
3. F. Broeze, 'Containerization and the Globalization of Liner Shipping', in D.J. Starkey and G. Harlaftis (eds), *Global Markets: The Internationalization of the Sea Transport Industry since 1850* (St John's, Newfoundland, 1998), pp. 398–399; *Marine News*, November 1996 and May 1998. By 1999 P&O Nedlloyd, with 108 ships and a total capacity of 252,638 teu, was the world's second largest container fleet (*Lloyd's List*, 23 July 1999) (In 2002 P&O demerged its ferry operations from Stena.)
4. Howarth and Howarth, *P&O*, p. 232; R. McAuley, *The Liners* (London, 1997), pp. 140–141; *The Guardian*, 27 May 1998.(In 2002 P&O was attempting to sell its cruise ship operations to Royal Caribbean in face of a counterbid by Carnival.)
5. *The Observer*, 10 March 1996; *The Guardian*, 4 April 1998.
6. *The Guardian*, 24 March 1999.
7. *Marine News*, April 1997.
8. Ibid., November 1997.
9. Department of the Environment, Transport and the Regions (DETR), *British Shipping: Charting a New Course* (London, 1998).
10. *Marine News*, October 1999. (That some revival of British shipping has taken place is seen in UNCTAD figures which show that at the start of 2000 Britain was tenth in the world table of merchant fleets by ownership—but less than 40% of British-owned shipping was under the British flag (*The Economist*, 10 February 2001).)

11. Clarkson Research Studies Ltd., *World Shipyard Monitor*, vol. 2, no. 3, March 1995.

12. *The Observer*, 10 March 1996; *The Guardian*, 21 June 1997; K. Warren, *Steel, Ships and Men: Cammell Laird, 1824–1993* (Liverpool, 1998), pp. 299–300. (After considerable expansion Cammell Laird went into receivership in April 2001.)

13. *The Observer*, 26 January 1997.

14. *Daily Mail*, 23 June 1999. The orders went to Japanese, French and Italian shipyards. German shipyards have also built a number of P&O cruise ships.

15. P. Turnbull, C. Woolfson and J. Kelly, *Dock Strike: Conflict and Restructuring in Britain's Ports* (Aldershot, 1992), pp. 200–201; Bristol Port Company brochure 1995; information from R. McLeod, managing director of Thamesport (London) Ltd., April 1995; Central Office of Information, *Britain 1995: An Official Handbook* (London, 1995); Shetland Islands Council ports handbook 1995–96; Port of Felixstowe brochure 1995. For the Liverpool dockers' dispute 1995–98 see *The Guardian*, 4 December 1995; 23 November 1996; 14 December 1996; 27 September 1997; 27 January 1998.

16. *The Guardian*, 12 March 1996.

17. Ibid., 6 April 1999. In 1999 North Sea oil output was 124 million tonnes, the highest since 1986 and not far short of the 1980s peak of 127 million tonnes (Office of National Statistics, *Britain 2001: The Official Handbook of the United Kingdom* (London, 2000).

18. [London] *Evening Standard*, 15 May 1996; *The Guardian*, 14 January 1997; S. Howarth, *A Century in Oil: The 'Shell' Transport and Trading Company, 1897–1997* (London, 1997), pp. 381–383.

19. *The Independent*, 2 December 1996.

20. A.G. Jamieson, 'British OSV Companies in the North Sea, 1964–1997', *Maritime Policy and Management*, vol. 25, no. 4, September 1998, p. 310. (Stirling Shipping was acquired by the American company SEACOR Smit in May 2001.) Nevertheless British oil services groups such as John Wood and Balmoral continued to enjoy international success based on expertise acquired in the North Sea. See Balmoral Group, *Black Gold and the Silver City: The Oil Revolution in Aberdeen and the North of Scotland, 1965–2000* (Aberdeen, 2000).

21. S.G. Sturmey, ' "British Shipping and World Competition" Revisited', *Maritime Policy and Management*, vol. 18, 1991, no. 4, p. 277. Sturmey remains true to the argument of his 1962 book that the decline of British shipping was due to internal constraints rather than external factors.

22. See the obituary of Sir Colin Goad, *The Times*, 6 April 1998. In 1963 Goad was an under-secretary in the Ministry of Transport. 'He had

spent much of his career on the maritime side, which had been the most prestigious branch after the war. By the early 1960s, however, the emphasis had changed . . . As interest suddenly shifted to internal transport, [he] was wrongly placed to take advantage.' Goad moved to the UN's Inter-governmental Maritime Consultative Organisation (IMCO—now IMO) and was its Secretary-General from 1968 to 1973.

23. In a House of Commons debate on 15 July 1964, Colonel Sir Leonard Ropner MP, who was to retire at the next election, said 'for many years I have been the only shipowner in this House' and he had tried to the best of his ability to be the voice of the British merchant navy (Hansard, Commons debates, vol. 698, 1963–64, col. 1229).

24. J. Cantlie Stewart, *The Sea Our Heritage: British Maritime Interests Past and Present* (revised edition, Keith, Banffshire, 1995), p. vi.

25. P.J. Cain and A.G. Hopkins, *British Imperialism: Innovation and Expansion, 1688–1914* (London, 1993), p. 170.

26. S.G. Sturmey, *British Shipping and World Competition* (London, 1962), pp. 185–187, 406–408, 415–418.

27. House of Commons, session 1987–88, transport committee, 1st report: Decline in the UK-Registered Merchant Fleet, vol. 1, report and minutes of proceedings (1988), p. xxix.

28. Rochdale report on the shipping industry (1970), p. 360.

29. Details of report by British Invisibles on maritime services given in press release by the Maritime London group, 15 June 2000. See also the Department of Transport and the General Council of British Shipping, *British Shipping: Challenges and Opportunities* (1990), pp. 47–48, and J. Cantlie Stewart, *The Sea Our Heritage*, pp. 264–274.

30. Hugh McCoy, chairman of the Baltic Exchange, to House of Commons transport committee, reported in *Marine News*, April 1999. The Baltic Exchange is one of the main centres in the world for shipbroking and related activities.

31. House of Commons transport committee: Report on Decline of UK-Registered Merchant Fleet (1988), p. xxviii.

32. House of Commons public accounts committee: Report on Movements of Personnel, Equipment and Stores to and from the Gulf, June 1993, pp. 10, 22–23.

33. The 'in-house strategic lift capabilities' of the Ministry of Defence are to be strengthened with additional ships. If further ships are needed they are to be chartered in the open market, with no special preference for British vessels (DETR, *British Shipping: Charting a New Course* (1998), p. 11). For US policy see A. Gibson and A. Donovan, *The* Abandoned Ocean: A History of United States Maritime Policy (Columbia, SC, 2000), p. 253.

34. Gibson and Donovan, *The Abandoned Ocean*, Chapter 15.

35. M. Mollat du Jourdin, *Europe and the Sea* (Oxford, 1993), p. 236.
36. For EU policy see A. Bredima-Savopoulou and J. Tzoannos, *The Common Shipping Policy of the EC* (Amsterdam, 1990); Commission of the European Communities, *Towards a New Maritime Strategy* (Brussels, 1996).
37. Report on the prospects of British shipping to 1965 (PRO, MT 59/3189).

Bibliography

Primary Sources

(1) Unpublished

Public Record Office, Kew, London
Board of Trade papers (BT)
BT 291/138—Shipping Advisory Committee, reports, 1962–63.
BT 291/139—Hughes-Hallett proposal on shipping protectionism, 1964.
BT 291/141—Contraction of shipbuilding committee, 1962.

Cabinet papers (CAB)
CAB 27/557—Committee on the British Mercantile Marine, 1933–34.
CAB 129/110—Memorandum on British shipping industry and Cabinet conclusions, 27 July 1962.
CAB 130/220—Minutes of Cabinet docks committee, 5 January 1965; memorandum of Minister of Transport, 1 February 1965.
CAB 134/1681—Minutes of Cabinet economic policy committee, 4 February & 8 July 1959.
CAB 134/1682—Report on the prospects of British shipping and shipbuilding, 1959.
CAB 134/1683—UK shipbuilding industry, report by officials, July 1959.
CAB 134/1688—Report on efficiency of British ports, 15 December 1960.
CAB 134/1689—Report on efficiency of British ports, 15 February 1961.
CAB 134/2921—Papers of Cabinet sub-committee on containers, 1968.

Ministry of Transport papers (MT)
MT 59/3189—Prospects of British shipping to 1965.
MT 81/482—Rochdale committee on ports, policy questions 1961–62.

National Ports Council papers (DK)

DK 1/108—Port planning—A note by the Director General, 17 January 1967.

DK 1/116—National port development plan—Ore importing facilities, 1964.

DK 1/157—Reports, etc. on containerisation, 1966–67.

DK 1/159–172—Papers relating to proposed nationalisation of the ports.

Prime Minister's papers (PREM)

PREM 11/538—Churchill and shipping, 1953.

PREM 11/3530—Macmillan to President Kennedy about shipping, 1961.

PREM 11/3991—Macmillan and shipping, 1961–62.

PREM 11/4482—Government shipbuilding subsidy, 1963–64.

PREM 13/2011—Wilson and container berths at Newport, South Wales, 1968.

Docklands Library and Museum, London
British Ports Association archives.

Modern Archives Centre, University of Warwick
Chamber of Shipping archives.

(2) Published

British Parliamentary Papers (BPP)

Report of the departmental committee appointed by the Board of Trade to consider the position of the shipping and shipbuilding industries after the war [Booth committee] (Cmnd. 9092), BPP 1918, vol. XIII.

Report of the enquiry into the wages and conditions of employment of dock and waterside labourers [Shaw report] (Cmnd. 936 & 937), BPP 1920, vol. XXIV.

Final report of the Royal Commission on Transport (Cmnd. 3751), BPP 1930–31, vol. XVII.

Report of the committee of inquiry into unofficial stoppages in the London docks [Leggett report] (Cmnd. 8236), BPP 1950–51, vol. XVI.

Report of the committee to inquire into the operation of the Dock Workers (Regulation of Employment) Scheme 1947 [Devlin report] (Cmnd. 9813), BPP 1955– 56, vol. XXVI.

Report of the committee of inquiry into the fishing industry [Fleck report] (Cmnd. 1266), BPP 1960–61, vol. XV.

Report of the committee of inquiry into the major ports of Great Britain [Rochdale report] (Cmnd. 1824), BPP 1961–62, vol. XX.

Final report of the committee of inquiry into certain matters concerning the port transport industry [Devlin report] (Cmnd. 2734), BPP 1964–65, vol. XXI.

Report of the shipbuilding inquiry committee [Geddes report] (Cmnd. 2937), BPP 1965–66, vol. VII.

NPC annual reports for 1965, BPP 1966–67, vol. XXXV; 1966, BPP 1966–67, vol. XXXV; and 1969, BPP 1970–71, vol. XLIX.

Final report of the committee of inquiry into certain matters concerning the shipping industry [Pearson report] (Cmnd. 3211), BPP 1966–67, vol. XXXVI.

Report of the inquiry into the loss of the drilling rig *Sea Gem* (Cmnd. 3409), BPP 1966–67, vol. XXI.

Second report of the House of Commons select committee on nationalised industries, Exploitation of North Sea Gas, BPP 1967–68, vol. XIV.

The Reorganisation of the Ports, BPP 1968–69, vol. LIII.

Report of the committee of inquiry into shipping [Rochdale report] (Cmnd. 4337), BPP 1969–70, vol. XXVII.

House of Commons public accounts committee, first report, North Sea Oil and Gas, 14 February 1973, BPP 1974, vol. XXII.

UK Offshore Oil and Gas Policy (Cmnd. 5696), BPP 1974, vol. XII.

First report of the House of Commons select committee on the nationalised industries, The Nationalised Industries and the Exploitation of North Sea Oil and Gas, BPP 1974–75, vol. XXVI.

The Challenge of North Sea Oil (Cmnd. 7143), BPP 1977–78, vol. XXV.

Third report of the House of Commons select committee on energy, The Effect of Oil and Gas Prices on Activity in the North Sea, May 1987, HC 175.

House of Commons transport committee, Report on the Decline in the UK-Registered Merchant Fleet, May 1988, HC 3031–11.

House of Commons public accounts committee, Report on the Movement of Personnel, Equipment and Stores to and from the Gulf, June 1993.

Secondary Sources

Place of publication London unless otherwise stated.

Abell, W., *The Shipwright's Trade* (1948).

Adams, G., *The Organisation of the British Port Transport Industry* (1973).

Aldcroft, D.H., 'Port Congestion and the Shipping Boom of 1919–20', in Aldcroft, *Studies in British Transport History*, pp. 169–186.

Aldcroft, D.H., 'Reflections on the Rochdale Inquiry into Shipping', in Aldcroft, *Studies in British Transport History*, pp. 275–295.

Aldcroft, D.H., *Studies in British Transport History, 1870–1970* (Newton Abbot, 1974).

Allen, G.C., *British Industries and their Organization* (3rd edition 1951, 5th edition 1970).

Ambrose, A.J. (ed.), *Jane's Merchant Shipping Review* (1983).

Andersen, S.S., *The Struggle over North Sea Oil and Gas: Government Strategies in Denmark, Britain and Norway* (Oslo, 1993).

Anglo-American Council on Productivity, *Productivity Team—Freight Handling—Report on Visit to the USA in 1950* (1951).

Arnold, A.J., 'No Substitute for Hard Cash?: An Analysis of Returns on Investment in the Royal Mail Steam Packet Company, 1903–1929', *Accounting, Business and Financial History*, vol. 1, no. 3, 1991, pp. 335–353.

Arnold, A.J., 'Privacy or Concealment? The Accounting Practices of Liner Shipping Companies, 1914–1924', *International Journal of Maritime History*, vol. VIII, no. 1, 1996, pp. 43–57.

Arnold, A.J., 'The Great War, Government Policy and Financial Returns in the Liner Trade', *Journal of Transport History*, 3rd series, vol. 18, no. 1, 1997, pp. 16–30.

Arnold, G., *Britain's Oil* (1978).

Ashworth, W., *A Short History of the International Economy since 1850* (3rd edition, 1975).

Atkinson, T., and O'Donoghue, K., *Blue Star* (Kendal, 1985).

Bagwell, P.S., *The Transport Revolution* (revised edition, 1988).

Balmoral Group, *Black Gold and the Silver City: The Oil Revolution in Aberdeen and the North of Scotland, 1965–2000* (Aberdeen, 2000).

Bamberg, J., *The History of the British Petroleum Company. Volume 2: The Anglo-Iranian Years, 1928–1954* (Cambridge, 1993).

Bamberg, J., *British Petroleum and Global Oil, 1950–1975: The Challenge of Nationalism* (Cambridge, 2000).

Barnett, C., *The Audit of War* (1986).

Barnett, C., *Engage the Enemy More Closely: The Royal Navy in the Second World War* (1991).

Barnett, C., *The Lost Victory: British Dreams, British Realities, 1945–1950* (1995).

Barnett, C., *The Verdict of Peace: Britain between her Yesterday and the Future* (2001).

Bartlett, C.J., *The Long Retreat: A Short History of British Defence Policy, 1945–1970* (1972).

Barzman, J., 'Port Labour Relations in Le Havre, 1928–47', *International Journal of Maritime History*, 9 (2), 1997, pp. 83–106.

Bates, L.M., *The Thames on Fire: The Battle of the London River, 1939–45* (Lavenham, 1985).

214

Behrens, C.B.A., *Merchant Shipping and the Demands of War* (1955).

Benford, H., and Fox, W.A. (eds), *A Half Century of Marine Technology, 1943–1993* (Jersey City, NJ, 1993).

Bes, J., *Bulk Carriers* (Hilversum, Netherlands, 1972).

Bird, J., *The Major Seaports of the United Kingdom* (1963).

Bird, J., *Seaports and Seaport Terminals* (1971).

Bishop, R.E.D., and Elkan, W., 'Offshore Oil: Responses to Employment Opportunities', in Greenwich Forum, *Britain and the Sea*, pp. 61–71.

Black, J., *War and the World: Military Power and the Fate of Continents, 1450– 2000* (1998).

Bowen, F.C., *Ships for All* (1952).

Boyce, G.H., *Information, Mediation and Institutional Development: The Rise of Large-Scale Enterprise in British Shipping, 1870–1919* (Manchester, 1995).

Boyce, G.H., 'Union Steamship Company of New Zealand and the Adoption of Oil Propulsion: Learning-by-Using Effects', *Journal of Transport History*, 3rd series, vol. 18, no. 2, 1997, pp. 134–155.

Boyce, G., and Gorski, R. (eds), *Resources and Infrastructures in the Maritime Economy, 1500–2000* (St John's, Newfoundland, 2002).

Branch, A.E., *Elements of Shipping* (5th edition, 1981).

Bredima-Savopoulou, A., and Tzoannos, J., *The Common Shipping Policy of the EC* (Amsterdam, 1990).

British Association for the Advancement of Science, *Britain in Depression: A Record of British Industries since 1929* (1935).

British Association for the Advancement of Science, *Britain in Recovery* (1938).

Broeze, F., *Island Nation: A History of Australians and the Sea* (St Leonard's, New South Wales, 1998).

Broeze, F., 'Containerization and the Globalization of Liner Shipping', in Starkey and Harlaftis (eds), *Global Markets*, pp. 385–423.

Brown, A.H.J., 'Ports and Shipping Turn-Round: Causes of Delay and Suggested Remedies', *The Dock and Harbour Authority*, January 1953.

Brown, R.D., *The Port of London* (Lavenham, 1978).

Bruijn, J., van Dissel, M., Jackson, G., and van Royen, P. (eds), *Strategy and Response in the Twentieth Century Maritime World: Papers Presented to the Fourth British-Dutch Maritime History Conference* (Amsterdam, 2001).

Bryant, A., *Liquid History: Fifty Years of the Port of London Authority* (1960).

Bullock, A., *The Life and Times of Ernest Bevin*, Volumes 1 and 2 (1960 and 1967).

Burrell, D., *Furness Withy: The Centenary History of Furness, Withy & Company Ltd., 1891–1991* (Kendal, 1992).

Burton, A., *The Rise and Fall of British Shipbuilding* (1994).

Buxton, I.L., 'The Development of the Merchant Ship, 1880–1990', *Mariner's Mirror*, vol. 79, no. 1, 1993, pp. 71–82.

Cafruny, A.W., *Ruling the Waves: The Political Economy of International Shipping* (Berkeley and Los Angeles, CA, 1987).

Cain, P.J., and Hopkins, A.G., *British Imperialism: Innovation and Expansion, 1688–1914* (1993).

Cain, P.J., and Hopkins, A.G., *British Imperialism: Crisis and Deconstruction, 1914–1990* (1993).

Cantlie Stewart, J., *The Sea Our Heritage: British Maritime Interests Past and Present* (revised edition, Keith, Banffshire, 1995).

Carlisle, R.P., *Sovereignty for Sale: The Origins and Evolution of the Panamanian and Liberian Flags of Convenience* (Annapolis, MD, 1981).

Central Office of Information (COI), *British Industry Today: Shipping* (1974).

COI, *British Industry Today: Ports* (1974).

COI, *British Industry Today: Energy* (1979).

COI, *Britain's Offshore Equipment and Services Industry* (1982).

COI, *Britain 1988: An Official Handbook* (1988).

COI, *Britain 1995: An Official Handbook* (1995).

Chamber of Shipping of the UK, *British Shipping Statistics 1974*.

Chandler, G., *Liverpool Shipping: A Short History* (1960).

Chida, T., and Davies, P.N., *The Japanese Shipping and Shipbuilding Industries: A History of their Modern Growth* (1990).

Clarke, J.F., *A Century of Service to Engineering and Shipbuilding: A Centenary History of the North East Coast Institution of Engineers and Shipbuilders, 1884–1984* (Newcastle, 1984).

Clarke, J.F., *Building Ships on the North East Coast* (2 vols, Whitley Bay, 1997).

Clarkson, H., and Co. Ltd., *The Offshore Service Vessel Register 1983*.

Clarkson Research Studies Ltd., *World Shipyard Monitor*, vol. 2, no. 3, March 1995.

Clegg, W.P., *Docks and Ports: 2. London* (Shepperton, 1987).

Clegg, W.P., *British Shipping* (Shepperton, 1988).

Coates, K., and Topham, T., *The History of the Transport and General Workers Union: Volume I—The Making of the TGWU: The Emergence of the Labour Movement, 1870–1922* (Oxford, 1991).

Commission of the European Communities, *Report of an Enquiry into the Current Situation in the Major Community Sea-Ports drawn up by the Port Working Group* (Brussels, 1977).

Commission of the European Communities, *Towards a New Maritime Strategy* (Brussels, 1996).

Cooper, B., and Gaskell, T.F., *North Sea Oil: The Great Gamble* (1966).

Coopers & Lybrand, 'UK Offshore Support Vessel Industry: Final Report, November 1986'.

216

Corlett, E., *The Revolution in Merchant Shipping, 1950–1980* (1981).

Corley, T.A.B., *A History of the Burmah Oil Company: Volume II, 1924–1966* (1988).

Coull, J.R., *The Fisheries of Europe* (1972).

Coull, J.R., *The Sea Fisheries of Scotland* (Edinburgh, 1996).

Couper, A.D., *The Geography of Sea Transport* (1972).

Couper, A.D. (ed.), *The Times Atlas of the Oceans* (1983).

Couper, A.D. (ed.), *Conway's History of the Ship: The Shipping Revolution —The Modern Merchant Ship* (1992).

Course, A.G., *The Merchant Navy To-day* (Oxford, 1956).

Course, A.G., *The Deep Sea Tramp* (1960).

Course, A.G., *The Merchant Navy: A Social History* (1963).

Course, A.G., *Docks and Harbours of Britain* (1964).

Craig, R., *Steam Tramps and Cargo Liners, 1850–1950* (1980).

Daunton, M. (ed.), *Cambridge Urban History of Britain: Volume III, 1840–1950* (Cambridge, 2000).

Davies, M., *Belief in the Sea: State Encouragement of British Merchant Shipping and Shipbuilding* (1992).

Davies, P.N., 'British Shipping and World Trade: Rise and Decline, 1820–1939', in Yui and Nakagawa (eds), *Business History of Shipping*, pp. 39–85.

Davies, P.N., 'The Role of National Bulk Carriers in the Advance of Shipbuilding Technology in Post-War Japan', *International Journal of Maritime History*, vol. IV, no. 1, 1992, pp. 131–142.

Davies, P.N., *The Trade Makers: Elder Dempster in West Africa, 1852–1972, 1973– 1989* (2nd edition, St John's, Newfoundland, 2000).

Davies, P.N., and Bourn, A.M., 'Lord Kylsant and the Royal Mail', *Business History*, XIV (1972), pp. 103–123.

Davis, R., *The Rise of the English Shipping Industry in the Seventeenth and Eighteenth Centuries* (2nd impression, Newton Abbot, 1972).

Dawson, P., *Cruise Ships: An Evolution in Design* (2000).

De La Pedraja, R., *The Rise and Decline of U.S. Merchant Shipping in the Twentieth Century* (New York, NY, 1992).

De La Pedraja, R., *A Historical Dictionary of the U.S. Merchant Marine and Shipping Industry since the Introduction of Steam* (Westport, CT, 1994).

De La Pedraja, R., *Latin American Merchant Shipping in the Age of Global Competition* (Westport, CT, 1999).

Deakin, B.M. (with Seward, T.), *Shipping Conferences. A Study of their Origins, Development and Economic Practices* (Cambridge, 1973).

Dear, I., *The Ropner Story* (1986).

Department of Energy, *The Development of the Oil and Gas Resources of the United Kingdom* (1988).

Department of Environment, Transport and the Regions, *British Shipping: Charting a New Course* (1998).

Department of Trade and Industry, *Study of the Potential Benefits to British Industry from Offshore Oil and Gas Development* (1972).

Department of Transport and the General Council of British Shipping, *British Shipping: Challenges and Opportunities* (1990).

Dintenfass, M., *The Decline of Industrial Britain, 1870–1980* (1992).

Docks and Inland Waterways Executive, British Transport Commission, *Review of Trade Harbours, 1948–50* (1951).

Dougan, D., *The History of North East Shipbuilding* (1968).

Doughty, M., *Merchant Shipping and War: A Study of Defence Planning in Twentieth Century Britain* (1982).

Duff, P., *British Ships and Shipping: A Survey of Modern Ship Design and Shipping Practice* (1949).

Dunn, L., *British Tramps, Coasters and Colliers* (1962).

Dunn, L., and Heaton, P.M., *Palm Line* (Abergavenny, 1994).

Dyos, H.J., and Aldcroft, D.H., *British Transport: An Economic Survey from the Seventeenth Century to the Twentieth* (Harmondsworth, 1974).

Dyson, J., *Business in Great Waters: The Story of British Fishermen* (1977).

Elbaum, B., and Lazonick, W. (eds), *The Decline of the British Economy* (Oxford, 1986).

Fairhall, D., *Russia Looks to the Sea: A Study of the Expansion of Soviet Maritime Power* (1971).

Falkus, M., *The Blue Funnel Legend* (1990).

Farnie, D.A., *The Manchester Ship Canal and the Rise of the Port of Manchester, 1894–1975* (Manchester, 1980).

Farrington, T., 'The UK Shipping Industry: A History and Assessment', *The Business Economist*, vol. 27, no. 1, 1996, pp. 25–37.

Fayle, C.E., *The War and the Shipping Industry* (1927).

Fayle, C.E., *A Short History of the World's Shipping Industry* (1933).

Ferrier, R.W., *The History of the British Petroleum Company. Volume 1: The Developing Years, 1901–1932* (Cambridge, 1982).

Ffooks, R., *Natural Gas by Sea: The Development of a New Technology* (1979).

First and Second Reports of the Ports Efficiency Committee to the Secretary of State (1952).

Fischer, L.R. (ed.), *From Wheel House to Counting House: Essays in Maritime Business History in Honour of Professor Peter Neville Davies* (St John's, Newfoundland, 1992).

Fischer, L.R., 'Port Policies: Seaport Planning around the North Atlantic, 1850–1939', in Fischer and Jarvis (eds), *Harbours and Havens*, pp. 229–244.

Fischer, L.R., and Jarvis, A. (eds), *Harbours and Havens: Essays in Port History in Honour of Gordon Jackson* (St John's, Newfoundland, 1999).

Fisher, S. (ed.), *Lisbon as a Port Town, the British Seaman, and Other Maritime Themes* (Exeter, 1988).

Fisher, S. (ed.), *Innovation in Shipping and Trade* (Exeter, 1989).

Fletcher, M.E., 'From Coal to Oil in British Shipping', *Journal of Transport History*, new series, III (1975), pp. 1–19.

Flierman, A.H., 'Mayday, or How to Attract Attention. The Dutch Merchant Navy and Politics, 1960–1995', in Bruijn et al. (eds), *Strategy and Response in the Twentieth Century Maritime World*, pp. 62–76.

Floud, R., and McCloskey, D. (eds), *The Economic History of Britain since 1700. Volume 2, 1860 to the 1970s* (Cambridge, 1981).

Foreign and Commonwealth Office, *British Offshore Industry* (1992).

Foreman-Peck, J., *A History of the World Economy: International Economic Relations since 1850* (Brighton, 1983).

Fraser, N., Jacobson, P., Ottaway, M., and Chester, L., *Aristotle Onassis* (1977).

Freeman, M.J., and Aldcroft, D.H. (eds), *Transport in Victorian Britain* (Manchester, 1988).

Fritz, M., and Olsson, K., 'Twentieth Century Shipping Strategies: Brostrom and Transatlantic, Gothenburg's Leading Shipping Companies', in Ville and Williams (eds), *Management, Finance and Industrial Relations in Maritime Industries*, pp. 91–109.

Frost, J.F.A., 'Away From It All: The Growth of Holiday Cruising', in Navy League, *Maritime Survey 1973*, pp. 89–97.

Fullerton, B., and Knowles, R., *Scandinavia* (1991).

General Council of British Shipping, *Survey of British Shipping* (1960).

Gibbs, J.M., *Morels of Cardiff: The History of a Family Shipping Firm* (Cardiff, 1982).

Gibson, A., and Donovan, A., *The Abandoned Ocean: A History of United States Maritime Policy* (Columbia, SC, 2000).

Gibson, V., 'Support to the Offshore Industry', in A. Couper (ed.), Conway's History of the Ship: The Shipping Revolution—The Modern Merchant Ship (London, 1992), pp. 104–146.

Glynn, S., and Booth, A., *Modern Britain: An Economic and Social History* (1996).

Gordon, A., 'Naval Procurement and Shipbuilding Capacity, 1918–1939', in Starkey and Jamieson (eds), *Exploiting the Sea*, pp. 104–117.

Gordon, G.A.H., *British Seapower and Procurement between the Wars* (1988).

Gorst, A., and Johnman, L., 'British Naval Procurement and Shipbuilding, 1945–1964', in Starkey and Jamieson (eds), *Exploiting the Sea*, pp. 118–147.

Goss, R., 'British Ports Policies since 1945', *Journal of Transport Economics and Policy*, vol. 32, 1998, part 1, pp. 51–71.

Goss, R., 'Rochdale Remembered: A Personal Memoir', *Maritime Policy and Management*, vol. 25, 1998, no. 3, pp. 213–233.

Green, E., 'Very Private Enterprise: Ownership and Finance in British Shipping, 1825–1940', in Yui and Nakagawa (eds), *Business History of Shipping*, pp. 219–248.

Green, E., and Moss, M., *A Business of National Importance: The Royal Mail Shipping Group, 1902–1937* (1982).

Greenway, A. (ed.), *Conway's History of the Ship: The Golden Age of Shipping—The Classic Merchant Ship, 1900–1960* (1994).

Greenwich Forum IX, The, *Britain and the Sea: Future Dependence, Future Opportunities* (Edinburgh, 1984).

Greeves, I.S., *London Docks 1800–1900: A Civil Engineering History* (1980).

Griffiths, D., 'British Shipping and the Diesel Engine: The Early Years', *Mariner's Mirror*, 81 (1995), pp. 313–331.

Griffiths, D., *Steam at Sea: Two Centuries of Steam-Powered Ships* (1997).

Gripaios, H., *Tramp Shipping* (1959).

Grove, E.J., *Vanguard to Trident: British Naval Policy since World War II* (1987).

Hackman, R., *The Fleet Past and Present of Hunting & Son Ltd.* (Newcastle, 1969).

Hahn-Pedersen, M., 'Changing Structures: Developments in Danish Commercial Ports since 1960', *International Journal of Maritime History*, 8 (1), 1996, pp. 59– 86.

Halford, R.G., *The Unknown Navy: Canada's World War II Merchant Navy* (St Catharine's, Ontario, 1995).

Hallsworth, H.M., 'The Shipbuilding Industry', in British Association, *Britain in Depression*, pp. 247–258.

Hallsworth, H.M., 'The Shipbuilding Industry', in British Association, *Britain in Recovery*, pp. 339–360.

Halpern, P.G., *A Naval History of World War I* (1994).

Hamilton, A., *North Sea Impact: Off-Shore Oil and the British Economy* (1978).

Hamilton Whyte, W., *Decasualisation of Dock Labour, with Special Reference to the Port of Bristol* (Bristol, 1934).

Hanham, F.G., *Report of the Enquiry into Casual Labour in the Merseyside Area* (Liverpool, 1930).

Harcourt, L.F.V., *Harbours and Docks* (2 vols, 1885).

Harding, R., *Seapower and Naval Warfare, 1650–1830* (1999).

Hardy, A.C., *World Shipping* (Harmondsworth, 1941).

Hardy, A.C., *History of Motorshipping: The Story of Fifty Years of Progress which have had a Profound Influence upon the Development of Sea Transport during the Twentieth Century* (1955).

Harlaftis, G., *Greek Shipowners and Greece, 1945–1975: From Separate Development to Mutual Interdependence* (1993).

Harlaftis, G., *A History of Greek-Owned Shipping: The Making of an International Tramp Fleet, 1830 to the Present Day* (1996).

Harris, N. (ed.), *Portrait of a Shipbuilder: Barrow-Built Vessels from 1873* (St Michael's-on-Wyre, Lancashire, 1989).

Harvey, W.J., *Hadley* (Gravesend, 1997).

Harvie, C., *Fool's Gold: The Story of North Sea Oil* (1994).

Haws, D., *Merchant Fleets 6: Blue Funnel Line* (Torquay, 1984).

Haws, D., *Merchant Fleets—The Burma Boats: Henderson and Bibby* (1996).

Haws, D., *Merchant Fleets 32: Clan, Houston, Turnbull Martin, and Scottish Tankers* (Pembroke, 1997).

Heal, S.C., *Conceived in War, Born in Peace: Canada's Deep Sea Merchant Marine* (Vancouver, British Columbia, 1992).

Heal, S.C., *A Great Fleet of Ships: The Canadian Forts and Parks* (St Catharine's, Ontario, 1999).

Heaton, P.M., *Reardon Smith Line: The History of a South Wales Shipping Venture* (Newport, Gwent, 1984).

Heaton, P.M., *Jack Billmeir: Merchant Shipowner* (Abergavenny, 1989).

Henderson, A.R., and Palmer, S., 'The Early Nineteenth Century Port of London: Management and Labour in Three London Dock Companies, 1800–1825', in Ville and Williams (eds), *Management, Finance and Industrial Relations in Maritime Industries*, pp. 31–50.

Henning, G., and Trace, K., 'Britain and the Motor Ship: A Case of the Delayed Adoption of a New Technology', *Journal of Economic History*, 35 (1975), pp. 353–385.

Hilditch, P., 'The Decline of British Shipbuilding since the Second World War', in Fisher (ed.), *Lisbon as a Port Town, etc.*, pp. 129–142.

Hill, J.R. (ed.), *The Oxford Illustrated History of the Royal Navy* (Oxford, 1995).

Hinde, P., *Fortune in the North Sea* (1966).

Hodgkinson, H., 'The Changing Pattern of Oil Supplies', in Navy League, *Maritime Survey 1973*, pp. 39–51.

Hodne, F., *The Norwegian Economy, 1920–1980* (1983).

Hogwood, B.W., *Government and Shipbuilding: The Politics of Industrial Change* (Farnborough, 1979).

Hoopes, S., *Oil Privatization, Public Choice and International Forces* (1997).

Hope, R., *The Merchant Navy* (1980).

Hope, R., *A New History of British Shipping* (1990).

Horan, H.E., 'The British Shipping Industries', *Brassey's Annual: The Armed Forces Year-Book 1959*, pp. 102–110.

Hornby, O., 'The Danish Shipping Industry, 1866–1939: Structure and Strategy', in Yui and Nakagawa (eds), *Business History of Shipping*, pp. 157–181.

Hosking, R.O., *A Source Book of Tankers and Supertankers* (1973).

Hovey, J., *A Tale of Two Ports: London and Southampton* (1990).

Howarth, D., and Howarth, S., *The Story of P&O* (revised edition, 1994).

Howarth, S., *Sea Shell: The Story of Shell's British Tanker Fleet, 1892–1992* (Wadswick, Wiltshire, 1992).

Howarth, S., *A Century in Oil: The 'Shell' Transport and Trading Company, 1897– 1997* (1997).

Hugill, A., *Sugar and All That . . . A History of Tate & Lyle* (1978).

Hunting, P. (ed.), *The Hunting History: Hunting plc since 1874* (1991).

Hurd, A., *The Eclipse of British Sea Power: An Increasing Peril* (1933).

Hurd, A., *British Maritime Policy: The Decline of Shipping and Shipbuilding* (1938).

Hurd, A., 'The British Maritime Industries: A National Problem', *Brassey's Naval Annual 1939*, pp. 63–73.

Hurd, A. (ed.), *Britain's Merchant Navy* (1943).

Hurd, A., 'British Shipping's Fight for Survival', *Brassey's Annual: The Armed Forces Year-Book 1955*, pp. 124–130.

Hyde, F.E., *Liverpool and the Mersey: The Development of a Port, 1700–1970* (Newton Abbot, 1971).

Hyde, F.E., *Cunard and the North Atlantic, 1840–1973* (1973).

International Management and Engineering Group, *Study of Potential Benefits to British Industry from Offshore Oil and Gas Developments* (1972).

Iron and Steel Board, *Development in the Iron and Steel Industry: Special Report 1964* (1964).

Isserlis, L., 'The World Economic Crisis and British Shipping', in British Association, *Britain in Depression*, pp. 235–243.

Isserlis, L., 'British Shipping since 1934', in British Association, *Britain in Recovery*, pp. 323–338.

Jackson, G., *The History and Archaeology of Ports* (Tadworth, 1983).

Jackson, G., 'The Ports', in Freeman and Aldcroft (eds), *Transport in Victorian Britain*, pp. 218–252.

Jackson, G., 'Do Docks Make Trade?: The Case of the Port of Great Grimsby', in Fischer (ed.), *Wheel House to Counting House*, pp. 17–41.

Jackson, G., 'Ports, Ships and Government in the Nineteenth and Twentieth Centuries', in van Royen, Fischer and Williams (eds), *Frutta di Mare*, pp. 161– 175.

Jamieson, A.G., 'Facing the Rising Tide: British Attitudes to Asian National Shipping Lines, 1958–1964', *International Journal of Maritime History*, VII (1995), pp. 135–148.

Jamieson, A.G., 'Not More Ports, but Better Ports: The Development of British Ports since 1945', *The Northern Mariner*, vol. VI, no. 1, 1996, pp. 29–34.

Jamieson, A.G., 'The British Tanker Company and the Marine Diesel Engine, 1929', *Mariner's Mirror*, 83 (1997), pp. 335–336.

Jamieson, A.G., 'An Inevitable Decline? Britain's Shipping and Ship-building Industries since 1930', in Starkey and Jamieson (eds), *Exploiting the Sea*, pp. 79–92.

Jamieson, A.G., 'British OSV Companies in the North Sea, 1964–1997', *Maritime Policy and Management*, vol. 25 (1998), no. 4, pp. 305–312.

Jamieson, A.G., 'British Use of Neutral Shipping in Time of War: An Historical Outline', *War Studies Journal*, vol. 4, issue 1, 1999, pp. 84–96.

Jamieson, A.G., 'British Government Shipping Policy from 1945 to

1990', in Bruijn et al. (eds), *Strategy and Response in the Twentieth Century Maritime World*, pp. 51–61.

Jarvis, A., *The Liverpool Dock Engineers* (Stroud, 1996).

Jenkin, M., *British Industry and the North Sea: State Intervention in a Developing Industrial Sector* (1981).

Jenkins, D., *Shipowners of Cardiff: A Class by Themselves. A History of the Cardiff and Bristol Channel Incorporated Shipowners' Association* (Cardiff, 1997).

Jenkins, G., *The Ministry of Transport and Civil Aviation* (1959).

Jenkins, J.G., and Jenkins, D., *Cardiff Shipowners* (Cardiff, 1986).

Jennings, J.S., 'Opportunities Arising from North Sea Development', in Greenwich Forum, *Britain and the Sea*, pp. 40–47.

Johnman, L., 'The Privatisation of British Shipbuilders', *International Journal of Maritime History*, vol. VIII, no. 2, 1996, pp. 1–31.

Johnman, L., 'Old Attitudes and New Technology: British Shipbuilding, 1945–65', in van Royen, Fischer and Williams (eds), *Frutta di Mare*, pp. 133–152.

Johnman, L., 'Internationalization and the Collapse of British Ship-building, 1945–1973', in Starkey and Harlaftis (eds), *Global Markets*, pp. 319–353.

Johnman, L., 'Strategy and Response in British Shipbuilding, 1945–72', in Bruijn et al. (eds), *Strategy and Response in the Twentieth Century Maritime World*, pp. 77–99.

Johnman, L., and Murphy, H., 'The Norwegian Market for British Shipbuilding, 1945– 1967', *Scandinavian Economic History Review*, vol. 46, no. 2, 1998, pp. 55–78.

Johnman, L., and Murphy, H., 'A Triumph of Failure: The British Shipbuilding Industry and the Offshore Structures Market, 1960–1990: A Case Study of Scott Lithgow Ltd.', *International Journal of Maritime History*, forthcoming.

Johnman, L., and Murphy, H., *British Shipbuilding and the State since 1918: A Political Economy of Decline* (Exeter, 2002).

Johnson, P. (ed.), *The Structure of British Industry* (2nd edition, 1988).

Johnston, I., *Beardmore Built: The Rise and Fall of a Clydeside Shipyard* (Clydebank, 1993).

Johnston, I., *Ships for a Nation, 1847–1971: John Brown and Company, Clydebank* (West Dunbartonshire, 2000).

Joint Working Party, *British Shipping Challenges and Opportunities* (1990) [Parkinson/Sterling report].

Jones, L., *Shipbuilding in Britain: Mainly Between the Wars* (Cardiff, 1957).

Jones, S., *Two Centuries of Overseas Trading: The Origins and Growth of the Inchcape Group* (1986).

Jones, S., 'The P&O in War and Slump, 1914–1932: The Chairmanship of Lord Inchcape', in Fisher (ed.), *Innovation in Shipping and Trade*, pp. 131–143.

Jones, S., *Trade and Shipping: Lord Inchcape 1852–1932* (Manchester, 1989).

Kajimoto, M., *Cardiff Shipping Between the Wara* (Nara, Japan, 1996).

Kennedy, G.C., 'Great Britain's Maritime Strength and the British Merchant Marine, 1922–1935', *Mariner's Mirror*, 80 (1994), pp. 66–76.

Kennedy, G.C., 'American and British Merchant Shipping: Competition and Preparation, 1933–1939', in Kennedy (ed.), *The Merchant Marine in International Affairs*, pp. 107–154.

Kennedy, G.C. (ed.), *The Merchant Marine in International Affairs, 1850–1950* (2000).

Kennedy, P., *The Rise and Fall of British Naval Mastery* (1976).

Kerbrech, R.P. de, *Harland & Wolff's Empire Food Ships, 1934–1948: A Link with the Southern Dominions* (Freshwater, Isle of Wight, 1998).

Kirby, A., *The Effect of Port Re-Organisation in Great Britain* (1965).

Kirkaldy, A., *British Shipping: Its History, Organisation and Importance* (1914).

Kolltveit, B., and Crowdy, M., *Wilh. Wilhelmsen, 1861–1994: A Brief History and Fleet List* (Kendal, 1994).

Laar, P.T. van de, 'The Port of Rotterdam in a Changing Environment. From Rhine Port to Mainport, 1870–1970', in Bruijn et al. (eds), *Strategy and Response in the Twentieth Century Maritime World*, pp. 147–161.

Labaree, B.W., Fowler, W.M., Hattendorf, J.B., Safford, J.J., Sloan, E.W., and German, A.W., *America and the Sea: A Maritime History* (Mystic, CT, 1998).

Labour Party, *Report of the Labour Party Study Group on the Port Transport Industry* (June 1966).

Landes, D., *The Wealth and Poverty of Nations: Why Some are so Rich and Some so Poor* (1998).

Lane, F.C., *Ships for Victory: A History of Shipbuilding under the US Maritime Commission in World War II* (Baltimore, MD, 1951).

Lane, T., *The Merchant Seamen's War* (Liverpool, 1990).

Lemos, A.G., *The Greeks and the Sea* (1976).

Lenman, B., *From Esk to Tweed: Harbours, Ships and Men of the East Coast of Scotland* (Glasgow, 1975).

Lind, T., and Mackay, G.A., *Norwegian Oil Policies* (1979).

Lingwood, J., *SD14—The Great British Shipbuilding Success Story* (1976).

Lingwood, J., and O'Donoghue, K., *The Trades Increase* (Kendal, 1993).

Loades, D., *England's Maritime Empire: Seapower, Commerce and Policy, 1490– 1690* (Harlow, 2000).

Longhurst, H., *Adventures in Oil: The Story of British Petroleum* (1959).

Lorenz, E.H., *Economic Decline in Britain: The Shipbuilding Industry, 1890–1970* (Oxford, 1991).

Lorenz, E.H., and Wilkinson, F., 'The Shipbuilding Industry, 1880–

1965', in Elbaum and Lazonick (eds), *Decline of the British Economy*, pp. 109–134.

Lovegrove, M., *Our Islands Oil* (1975).

Lovell, J., *Stevedores and Dockers: A Study of Trade Unionism in the Port of London, 1870–1914* (1969).

Lynch, A., *Weathering the Storm: The Mersey Docks Financial Crisis, 1970–74* (Liverpool, 1994).

Maber, J.M., *Channel Packets and Ocean Liners, 1850–1970* (1980).

McAuley, R., *The Liners* (1997).

McCarthy, T., *The Great Dock Strike 1889* (1988).

MacDougall, P., *Royal Dockyards* (Newton Abbot, 1982).

McKinstry, S., 'Transforming John Brown's Shipyard: The Drilling Rig and Offshore Fabrication Businesses of Marathon and UIE, 1972–1997', *Scottish Economic and Social History*, vol. 18 (1998), part 1, pp. 33–60.

Maclay, J.S., 'The General Shipping Situation', *International Affairs*, 22 (1946).

Marriott, J., *Disaster at Sea* (New York, NY, 1987).

Marsh, A., and Ryan, V., *The Seamen: A History of the National Union of Seamen* (Oxford, 1989).

Marshall, P.J. (ed.), *Oxford History of the British Empire: Volume II—The Eighteenth Century* (Oxford, 1998).

Mathias, P., and Pearsall, A.W.H. (eds), *Shipping: A Survey of Historical Records* (Newton Abbot, 1971).

Maughan, C., 'The Balance-Sheet of the Motorship', *Brassey's Naval and Shipping Annual 1926*, pp. 222–230.

Mersey Docks and Harbour Board, *Business in Great Waters: An Account of the Activities of the Mersey Docks and Harbour Board, 1858–1958* (Liverpool, 1958).

Michie, R.C., *The City of London: Continuity and Change, 1850–1990* (1992).

Middlemiss, N.L., *The British Tankers* (Newcastle, 1989).

Ministry of Transport, *Report of the Working Party on the Turn-Round of Shipping in UK Ports* (1948).

Ministry of Transport, *Report of the Working Party on Increased Mechanisation in the UK Ports* (1950).

Mollat du Jourdin, M., *Europe and the Sea* (Oxford, 1993).

Moore, J. (ed.), *Jane's Naval Review 1982–3* (1982).

Morgan, D.J., 'Boom and Slump—Shipowning in Cardiff, 1919–1921', *Maritime Wales*, no. 12, 1989, pp. 127–132.

Morgan, F.W., and Bird, J., *Ports and Harbours* (1958).

Moss, M., and Hume, J.R., *Workshop of the British Empire: Engineering and Shipbuilding in the West of Scotland* (1977).

Moss, M., and Hume, J.R., *Shipbuilders to the World: 125 Years of Harland and Wolff, Belfast, 1861–1986* (Belfast, 1986).

Mostert, N., *Supership* (1975).

Munro Smith, R., *Merchant Ship Types* (1975).

Murphy, H., 'Scott's of Greenock and Naval Procurement, 1960–77', *Mariner's Mirror*, vol. 87 (2001), pp. 196–211.

Musson, A.E., *The Growth of British Industry* (1978).

Naess, E.D., *The Great PanLibHon Controversy: The Fight Over the Flags of Shipping* (Epping, Essex, 1972).

Naess, E.D., *Autobiography of a Shipping Man* (Colchester, 1977).

Napier, C.J., 'Secret Accounting: The P&O Group in the Inter-War Years', *Accounting, Business and Financial History*, vol. 1, no. 3, 1991, pp. 303–333.

National Dock Labour Board, *An Introduction to Port Working* (1955).

National Ports Council, *Annual Reports*.

National Ports Council, *Port Development: An Interim Plan* (2 vols, 1965).

National Ports Council, *Survey of Non-Scheme Ports and Wharves* (1973).

Navy League, The, *Maritime Survey 1973*.

North Sea Platform Guide (Ledbury, 1985).

O'Brien, P.K., 'Inseparable Connections: Trade, Economy, Fiscal State, and the Expansion of Empire, 1688–1815', in Marshall (ed.), *Oxford History of British Empire: Volume II—The Eighteenth Century*, pp. 52–77.

Office of National Statistics, *Britain 2001: The Official Handbook of the United Kingdom* (2000).

Offshore Oil and Gas Yearbook 1981–82: UK and Continental Europe.

Offshore Supplies Office, *Global Horizons: Oil and Gas Technology for World Markets* (1989).

Olsson, K., 'Big Business in Sweden: The Golden Age of the Great Swedish Shipyards, 1945–1974', *Scandinavian Economic History Review*, vol. XLIII, no. 3, 1995, pp. 310–338.

Oram, R.B., *Cargo Handling and the Modern Port* (Oxford, 1965).

Orbell, J., *From Cape to Cape: The History of Lyle Shipping* (Edinburgh, 1978).

Organisation for Economic Co-operation and Development, *The Situation of the Shipbuilding Industry* (Paris, 1965).

Organisation for European Economic Co-operation, *Maritime Transport 1954, 1959* (Paris, 1954, 1959).

Owen, D., *Ports of the United Kingdom* (revised edition, 1948).

Owen, G., *From Empire to Europe: The Decline and Revival of British Industry since the Second World War* (1999).

Oxley, P., 'The British Ports Industry, 1965–1980', in Greenwich Forum, *Britain and the Sea*, pp. 309–318.

Palmer, S., *Politics, Shipping and the Repeal of the Navigation Acts* (Manchester, 1990).

Palmer, S., 'Ports', in Daunton (ed.), *Cambridge Urban History of Britain: Volume III, 1840–1950*, pp. 133–150.

Palmer, S., and Williams, G. (eds), *Charted and Uncharted Waters* (1981).

Parker, G.H., *Astern Business: 75 Years of UK Shipbuilding* (Kendal, 1996).

Parker, H.M.D., *Manpower: A Study of Wartime Policy and Administration* (1957).

Parkinson, J.R., *The Economics of Shipbuilding in the United Kingdom* (Cambridge, 1960).

Paulden, S., and Hawkins, B., *Whatever Happened to Fairfields?* (1969).

Payton-Smith, D.J., *Oil: A Study of Wartime Policy and Administration* (1971).

Pedersen, K., and Hawks, F.W., *A History of the Norwegian America Line, 1910– 1995* (Kendal, 1995).

Petersen, K., *The Saga of Norwegian Shipping: An Outline of the History, Growth and Development of a Modern Merchant Marine* (Oslo, 1955).

Phillips, G., and Whiteside, N., *Casual Labour: The Unemployment Question in the Port Transport Industry, 1880–1970* (Oxford, 1985).

Political and Economic Planning, 'The British Shipping Industry', *Planning*, vol. XXV, no. 437, 1959.

Pollard, S., *The Development of the British Economy, 1914–1980* (3rd edition, 1983).

Pollard, S., 'Shipping and the British Economy since 1870: A Retrospective View', in Starkey and Jamieson (eds), *Exploiting the Sea*, pp. 93–103.

Pollard, S., and Robertson, P., *The British Shipbuilding Industry, 1870– 1914* (Cambridge, MA, 1979).

Port of London Authority, *Annual Reports*.

Pottinger, K., 'The British Shipbuilding Industry', in Greenwich Forum, *Britain and the Sea*, pp. 287–290.

Powell, L., *The Shipping Federation: A History of the First Sixty Years, 1890– 1950* (1950).

Pudney, J., *London's Docks* (1975).

Rabson, S., and O'Donoghue, K., *P&O: A Fleet History* (Kendal, 1988).

Ratcliffe, M., *Liquid Gold Ships: A History of the Tanker, 1859–1984* (1985).

Rees, H., *British Ports and Shipping* (1958).

Report of the Enquiry into Port Labour [Maclean Report] (1931).

Reveley, J., and Tull, M., 'Centralised Port Planning: An Evaluation of the British and New Zealand Experience', in Boyce and Gorski (eds), *Resources and Infrastructures in the Maritime Economy*, pp. 141– 161.

Richardson, J., 'The Marine Oil Engine', *Brassey's Naval and Shipping Annual 1920–21*, pp. 182–193.

Ritchie, L.A. (ed.), *The Shipbuilding Industry: A Guide to Historical Records* (Manchester, 1992).

Robertson, A.J., 'Backward British Businessmen and the Motor Ship,

1918–39: The Critique Reviewed', *Journal of Transport History*, 3rd series, IX (1988), pp. 190–197.

Robinson, C., and Hann, D., 'North Sea Oil and Gas', in Johnson (ed.), *Structure of British Industry*.

Robinson, R., *Trawling: The Rise and Fall of the British Trawl Fishery* (Exeter, 1996).

Rochdale, Lord, 'The Re-organisation of British Ports', *Journal of the Royal Society of Arts*, November 1964, pp. 901–915.

Roskill, S., *Naval Policy between the Wars* (2 vols, 1968 and 1976).

Royen, P.C. van, Fischer, L.R., and Williams, D.M. (eds), *Frutta di Mare: Evolution and Revolution in the Maritime World in the 19th and 20th Centuries* (Amsterdam, 1998).

Rubinstein, W.D., *Men of Property: The Very Wealthy in Britain since the Industrial Revolution* (1981).

Salter, J., *Allied Shipping Control: An Experiment in International Administration* (Oxford, 1921).

Sampson, A., *Anatomy of Britain Today* (1965).

Sampson, A., *The Seven Sisters* (revised edition, 1988).

Sanders, D., 'The British Merchant Fleet', in Navy League, *Maritime Survey 1973*, pp. 73–88.

Sargent, A.J., *Seaports and Hinterlands* (1938).

Savage, C.I., *Inland Transportation* (1957).

Sawyer, L.A., and Mitchell, W.H., *Tankers* (1967).

Sawyer, L.A., and Mitchell, W.H., *The Liberty Ships* (revised edition, Newton Abbot, 1973).

Sawyer, L.A., and Mitchell, W.H., *Sailing Ship to Supertanker: The Hundred-Year Story of British Esso and its Ships* (Lavenham, 1987).

Scholl, L.U., 'Shipping Business in Germany in the Nineteenth and Twentieth Centuries', in Yui and Nakagawa (eds), *Business History of Shipping*, pp. 185– 213.

Schulze, M.S. (ed.), *Western Europe: Economic and Social Change since 1945* (1999).

Sedgwick, S., Kinnaird, M., and O'Donoghue, K.J., *London and Overseas Freighters plc, 1948–1992* (Kendal, 1992).

Shell UK Exploration and Production, *North Sea Fields: Facts and Figures* (4th edition, 1991).

Shetland Islands Council, *Shetland's Oil Era* (Shetland, 1977).

Shetland Islands Council, *Shetland in Statistics*, no. 23, 1994.

Shipbuilding Conference, The, et al., *British Shipbuilding Facilities and Services* (1962).

Shonfield, A., *British Economic Policy since the War* (Harmondsworth, 1958).

Shore, P., 'Sunset over the Red Ensign: The Decline of British Deep Sea Shipping, 1945–89', University of Kent Ph.D thesis, 1990.

Sinclair, R.C., *Across the Irish Sea: Belfast-Liverpool Shipping since 1819* (1990).

Slaven, A., 'Self-Liquidation: The National Shipbuilders Security Ltd. and British Shipbuilding in the 1930s', in Palmer and Williams (eds), *Charted and Uncharted Waters*, pp. 125–147.

Slaven, A., 'British Shipbuilders: Market Trends and Order Book Patterns between the Wars', *Journal of Transport History*, 3rd series, vol. 3, no. 2, 1982, pp. 37–61.

Slaven, A., 'Marketing Opportunities and Marketing Practices: The Eclipse of British Shipbuilding, 1957–1976', in Fischer (ed.), *From Wheel House to Counting House*, pp. 125–151.

Slaven, A., 'Modern British Shipbuilding, 1800–1990', in Ritchie (ed.), *The Shipbuilding Industry: A Guide to Historical Records*, pp. 1–24.

SOCCO, *The Million Ton Carrier: Proceedings of the Super Ocean Carrier Conference (SOCCO), New York, 1974* (San Pedro, CA, 1974).

Somner, G., *Ben Line: Fleet List and Short History* (Kendal, 1980).

Somner, G., *From 70 North to 70 South: A History of the Christian Salvesen Fleet* (Edinburgh, 1984).

Spanner, E.F., 'Welding in Ship Construction', *Brassey's Naval and Shipping Annual 1934*, pp. 161–172.

Starkey, D.J., 'Growth and Transition in Britain's Maritime Economy, 1870–1914: The Case of South-West England', in Starkey and Jamieson (eds), *Exploiting the Sea*, pp. 7–36.

Starkey, D.J., and Harlaftis, G. (eds), *Global Markets: The Internationalization of the Sea Transport Industry since 1850* (St John's, Newfoundland, 1998).

Starkey, D.J., and Jamieson, A.G. (eds), *Exploiting the Sea: Aspects of Britain's Maritime Economy since 1870* (Exeter, 1998).

Starkey, D.J., and Jamieson, A.G., '"Change on a Scale Unequalled": The Transformation of Britain's Port Industry in the Twentieth Century', in Bruijn et al. (eds), *Strategy and Response in the Twentieth Century Maritime World*, pp. 131–146.

Starkey, D.J., Reid, C., and Ashcroft, N. (eds), *England's Sea Fisheries: The Commercial Sea Fisheries of England and Wales since 1300* (2000).

Stoker, R.B., *The Saga of Manchester Liners* (Douglas, Isle of Man, 1985).

Stopford, M., *Maritime Economics* (2nd edition, 1997).

Stopford, R.M., and Barton, J.R., 'The Economic Problems of Shipbuilding and the State', *Maritime Policy and Management*, vol. 13, 1986, no. 1, pp. 27–44.

Strachan, M., *The Ben Line, 1825–1982: An Anecdotal History* (Norwich, 1992).

Strath, B., *The Politics of De-Industrialisation: The Contraction of the West European Shipbuilding Industry* (1987).

Sturmey, S.G., *British Shipping and World Competition* (1962).

Sturmey, S.G., ' "British Shipping and World Competition" Revisited', *Maritime Policy and Management*, vol. 18, 1991, no. 4, pp. 277–280.

Talbot-Booth, E.C., *Ships and the Sea* (5th edition, 1940).

Talbot-Booth, E.C., *His Majesty's Merchant Navy* (1941).

Talbot-Booth, E.C., *Merchant Ships 1959* (1959).

Taylor, J., *Ellermans. A Wealth of Shipping* (1976).

Tenold, S., and Nordvik, H.W., 'Coping with the International Shipping Crisis of the 1970s: A Study of Management Responses in Norwegian Oil Tanker Companies', *International Journal of Maritime History*, vol. VIII, no. 2, 1996, pp. 33–69.

Thomas, D., 'Shipbuilding—Demand Linkage and Industrial Decline', in Williams, Williams and Thomas, *Why are the British Bad at Manufacturing?*

Thomson, A.W.J., and Hunter, L.C., *The Nationalized Transport Industries* (1973).

Thornton, R.H., *British Shipping* (2nd edition, Cambridge, 1959).

Todd, D., *The World Shipbuilding Industry* (1985).

Todd, D., *Industrial Dislocation: The Case of Global Shipbuilding* (1991).

Todd, J.A. (ed.), *The Shipping World* (1929).

Tonizzi, M.E., 'Economy, Traffic and Infrastructure in the Port of Genoa, 1861–1970', in Boyce and Gorski (eds), *Resources and Infrastructures in the Maritime Economy*, pp. 119–140.

Turnbull, P., and Weston, S., 'Employment Regulation, State Intervention, and the Economic Performance of European Ports', *Cambridge Journal of Economics*, vol. 16, no. 4, 1992, pp. 385–404.

Turnbull, P., Woolfson, C., and Kelly, J., *Dock Strike: Conflict and Restructuring in Britain's Ports* (Aldershot, 1992).

[Ultramar], *A Golden Adventure: The First Fifty Years of Ultramar* (1985).

United Kingdom Offshore Operators Association (UKOOA), *The North Sea Achievement: The First 25 Years* (1989).

UKOOA, *Britain's Offshore Oil and Gas Industry: Harnessing a Vital Resource* (1992).

Valdaliso, J.M., 'Management, Profitability and Finance in Twentieth Century Spanish Shipping: The Compania Maritima del Nervion as a Case Study, 1899–1986', in Ville and Williams (eds), *Management, Finance and Industrial Relations in Maritime Industries*.

Van Den Burg, G., *Containerisation: A Modern Transport System* (1969); revised edition, 1975, with title *Containerisation and Other Unit Load Transport*.

'Viator', 'Shipping and the Oil Industry', *Brassey's Naval and Shipping Annual 1930*, pp. 153–160.

Ville, S.P., and Williams, D.M. (eds), *Management, Finance and Industrial Relations in Maritime Industries: Essays in International Maritime and Business History* (St John's, Newfoundland, 1994).

Voogd, C. de, 'Dutch Government Policy and the Decline of Shipbuilding in the Netherlands', in Bruijn et al. (eds), *Strategy and Response in the Twentieth Century Maritime World*, pp. 100–119.

Walker, F.M., *Song of the Clyde: A History of Clyde Shipbuilding* (Cambridge, 1984).

Warren, K., *Steel, Ships and Men: Cammell Laird, 1824–1993* (Liverpool, 1998).

Watson, N., *The Story of Christian Salvesen, 1846–1996* (1996).

Watt, D.C., 'British Sea Policy: Past Achievements and Future Prospects', in Greenwich Forum, *Britain and the Sea*, pp. 217–234.

Wettern, D., *The Decline of British Seapower* (1982).

Whitehurst, C.H., *The US Merchant Marine: In Search of an Enduring Maritime Policy* (Annapolis, MD, 1983).

Whitehurst, C.H., *The US Shipbuilding Industry: Past, Present and Future* (Annapolis, MD, 1986).

Williams, D.L., *Maritime Heritage: White's of Cowes* (Peterborough, 1993).

Williams, K., Williams, J., and Thomas, D., *Why are the British Bad at Manufacturing?* (1983).

Williams, L.J., *Britain and the World Economy, 1919–1970* (1971).

Williams, T.I., *A History of the British Gas Industry* (Oxford, 1981).

Wilson, D.F., *Dockers: The Impact of Industrial Change* (1972).

Wilson, G.K., 'Planning: Lessons from the Ports', *Public Administration*, vol. 61 (1983), pp. 265–281.

Wilson, J.F., *British Business History, 1720–1994* (Manchester, 1995).

Winklareth, R.J., *Naval Shipbuilders of the World: From the Age of Sail to the Present Day* (2000).

Worden, W.L., *Cargoes: Matson's First Century in the Pacific* (Honolulu, HI, 1981).

Wren, W.J., *Ports of the Eastern Counties* (Lavenham, 1976).

Yamashita, Y., 'Responding to the Global Market in Boom and Recession: Japanese Shipping and Shipbuilding Industries, 1945–1980', in Ville and Williams (eds), *Management, Finance and Industrial Relations in Maritime Industries*.

Yergin, D., *The Prize: The Epic Quest for Oil, Money and Power* (1991).

Yergin, D., and Stanislaw, J., *The Commanding Heights: The Battle between Government and the Marketplace that is Remaking the Modern World* (New York, NY, 1998).

Yui, T., and Nakagawa, K. (eds), *Business History of Shipping: Strategy and Structure* (Tokyo, 1985).

Index

232

Printed and bound by CPI Group (UK) Ltd, Croydon, CR0 4YY

23/04/2025

14660991-0002